WITH FIRE
AND SWORD

By Quentin Reynolds

By Robert Leckie

WITH FIRE
AND SWORD

GREAT WAR ADVENTURES

Edited and with an Introduction by
Quentin Reynolds and Robert Leckie

With Woodcuts by James Grashow

THE DIAL PRESS NEW YORK 1963

Werner E. Keller
To Hal Boyle, the best of us all

ACKNOWLEDGMENTS

Douglas, Henry Kyd: "Stonewall Jackson's Last Days" reprinted from *I Rode with Stonewall* by Henry Kyd Douglas. Copyright 1940 by the University of North Carolina Press. Used with the permission of the publishers.

Churchill, Winston: "The Sensations of a Cavalry Charge" is reprinted with the permission of Charles Scribner's Sons from *A Roving Commission* by Winston Churchill. Copyright 1930 Charles Scribner's Sons; renewal copyright © 1958 Winston Churchill. Reprinted from *My Early Life by Winston Churchill,* copyright Odhams Press Ltd. by permission of Odhams Press Ltd.

Lawrence, T. E.: "Blowing Up a Train" reprinted from *Seven Pillers of Wisdom* by T. E. Lawrence. Copyright 1925, 1935 by Doubleday & Company, Inc. and reprinted by permission. Reprinted by permission of the Executors of the T. E. Lawrence Estate and the publishers, Jonathan Cape Limited.

Empey, Arthur Guy: "Over the Top" reprinted by permission of G. P. Putnam's Sons. From *Over the Top* by Arthur Guy Empey. Copyright 1917, 1945 by Arthur Guy Empey.

Archibald, Norman: "Shot Down" reprinted from *Heaven High, Hell Deep* copyright 1935 by Norman Archibald by permission of the author.

Reed, John: "I Saw the Communist Revolution" reprinted from *Ten Days That Shook the World* by John Reed by permission of Random House, Inc. and International Publishers.

Orwell, George: "A Million-in-One Wound" reprinted from *Homage to Catalonia* by George Orwell, copyright 1952 by Sonia Brownell Orwell. Reprinted by permission of Harcourt, Brace & World, Inc. and Martin Secker & Warburg Limited.

7

de Chambrun, Rene: "Somehow, You Must Get to Paris . . ." from *I Saw France Fall* by Rene de Chambrun, copyright 1940 by Rene de Chambrun, by permission of William Morrow and Company, Inc.

Behan, Brendan: "Up the Republic!" reprinted from *Borstal Boy* by Brendan Behan, copyright 1958, 1959 by Brendan Behan by permission of Alfred A. Knopf, Inc. and Hutchinson and Co. (Publishers) Ltd.

Pyle, Ernie: "The Death of Captain Waskow" from *Brave Men* by Ernie Pyle. Copyright 1943, 1944 by Scripps-Howard Newspaper Alliance. Copyright 1944 by Holt, Rinehart and Winston, Inc. Reprinted by permission of Holt, Rinehart and Winston, Inc.

Leckie, Robert: "Brig-Rat" from *Helmet for My Pillow* by Robert Leckie. © 1957 by Robert Hugh Leckie. Reprinted by permission of Random House, Inc.

Davis, Russell: "The Bloody Ridges" copyright © 1961 by Russell Davis and Brent K. Ashabrannar. Reprinted from *Marine at War* by Russell Davis by permission of Little, Brown and Co.

Hachiya, Michichiko: "The Day the Bomb Fell on Hiroshima" reprinted from *Hiroshima Diary*, copyright 1955 by the University of North Carolina Press. Used by permission of the publishers.

Dean, William: "The Ordeal of General Dean" from *General Dean's Story* by William F. Dean as told to William L. Worden. Copyright 1954 by William F. Dean. Copyright 1954 by The Curtis Publishing Company. Reprinted by permission of The Viking Press, Inc. Reprinted by special permission of The Saturday Evening Post.

8

TABLE OF CONTENTS

9

TABLE OF CONTENTS

WITH FIRE
AND SWORD

Introduction

This is a collection of war adventures gathered according to a simple rule laid down long ago by the Roman poet Vergil: "Most of which I saw, part of which I was." In other words, our authors—some of whom would probably blush to be so labeled—had to be present at the battle, to see it, if not necessarily to take part in it. No exceptions; not so much as a bent rule, let alone a broken one. Because of this—and with great regret—we have had to exclude the Battle of Thermopylae as given to the world by Herodotus. Although Herodotus was a contemporary of Leonidas and the Greeks who held the pass, he was not there, even as a witness. He probably reconstructed his account from the reports of survivors, but this is not enough; and so, the very father of history had to be left out.

An apparent exception is the selection from the Irish writer Brendan Behan. But if Behan did not go to war, he did, at least, attempt to blow up a British warship, for which "peaceful" act he was packed off to prison. Furthermore, to collect a book about war without a piece in it by an Irishman would be the sort of sin that gives story-stealing—anthologizing, as it is called—a very bad name.

Otherwise the ground rules have remained firm. Because of them, such champions of individual combat as Achilles and Hector have had to be kept out. No one has yet claimed that Homer, blind or not, was actually on the plain before Troy when Achilles and Hector had the final go at each other. On the same basis, the wonderful war wanderings of Ulysses are not here, nor is the great tale of the Horse of Troy. The last temptation—also resisted—was to include fictional pieces by some of the great writers who had themselves been in battle—among them Cervantes, Hemingway and Stendhal. Unfortunately, there is generally nothing so misleading about war as war fiction, good literature though it may be. It is too ordered and logical, too swift in action and too sure in result, and it rarely gives a sense of that crushing boredom

13

which so often precedes the queer and ugly sound of a bullet striking. War fiction also takes war for granted, which is a great mistake. Even *The Red Badge of Courage* does this, although Stephen Crane himself does not. When Crane reports of his own experience in the Spanish-American War, combat is not a fictional monster, but the strange compound of the incredible and the commonplace battle actually is.

Another rule has been to include narratives which, though not exclusively about battle, tell of the adventures resulting from it—for example Major General William Dean's gripping story of the ordeal through which he passed following the fall of Taejon in South Korea in late July, 1950. The ordeal of wartime imprisonment also falls into this category, and surely there is no better account of the misery of prisoner-of-war camps than Private John McElroy's description of the Confederate prison at Andersonville.

The narratives appear in chronological order, providing a notion of the development of war from the early accounts in the Bible to those of World War II and Korea. The Spartans of Leonidas were hoplites, or heavily armed and armored footsoldiers, who controlled the outcome of battle in the days before massed maneuver, though, by the Fifth Century B.C., armies were already professional with such divisions of arms as light infantry, cavalry, and artillery, i.e. bowmen. Only a few years after Thermopylae, in the Peloponnesian War described by the great Athenian admiral, Thucydides, part of whose story is here included, there are trained navies battling each other. (In this story, *The Campaign that Crushed the Athenians*, mark in Thucydides such a detachment that one might think, in the end, that it was the enemy, not the Athenians, who were defeated.) Mercenaries are on the scene by the Fourth Century B.C. in one of the greatest war narratives of all time, the *Anabasis of Xenophon*, the splendid tale of how 10,000 Greek professionals fought their way out of a military trap 1,500 miles inside Persia, a selection from which is carried here under the title, *The Death of Cyrus*. By the Jewish-Roman War of 70 A.D., the high organization of the Roman maniples and the complications of siege warfare are already apparent. The collapse of Rome, incidentally, seems to have been followed by a withering of the military art, at least in the west, a fact which may be grasped while reading the Sieur de Joinville's account of the Crusade of

14

King Louis of France, in some passages of which it is almost possible to feel the scimitars of Islam biting Christian flesh.

The Wars of Religion are barren of personal accounts, probably because, unlike classical times, the man of Mars of those days was rarely well educated. St. Ignatius Loyola, founder of one of the world's most learned societies, the Jesuits, did not begin his education until a wound received at the siege of Pamplona in 1521 led him to renounce his military career. Of course, the men who commanded at the top were literate, but their accounts, when they can be believed, are usually so deadly dull as to make a daily cattle market report seem exciting reading. One exception carried here is Oliver Cromwell's report of the bloodletting at Drogheda in 1649.

Even Napoleon, with Julius Caesar the most articulate of generals, did not consider personal experiences worthy of description. Students of warfare still study his maxims, but our purposes would have been better served if the great Corsican had set down how it felt to grab the flag and lead the charge over the bridge at Lodi. Nevertheless, the Napoleonic Wars are represented by General Marbot's story, *Napoleon's Greatest Victory*. The age which produced Napoleon also produced the literate soldier, and from the late 18th Century onward there have been so many of those marching off to war with pencil and notebook in their packs that the editors, so far from hunting for material, have had to hide from it.

From our own Colonial America comes Alexander Henry's hair-raising narrative of his escape from a painful death during an Indian massacre along the Canadian border, while the Revolutionary War gives us Rev. Jonas Clark's eyewitness account of that momentous skirmish "by the rude bridge that arched the flood."

Those who dote on stories of Indian Wars are due for a feast. The *Battle of White Bird Canyon* is told from the Indian side by the movingly eloquent Chief Joseph.

Another general tells us of the fighting on the Mexican Border before World War I. In *The Private War of Captain Douglas MacArthur* you will actually feel what it was like to duel armed bandits on horseback from the swaying steel deck of a railway hand-car. And, of course, representative of World War I that followed, Arthur Guy Empey writes vividly of what happened after the order, "Over the top!"

There is rich material from World War II in this book, but it could not be otherwise when dealing with the greatest of wars; one, incidentally, fought by the most literate soldiers. Here are men adventuring and fighting in the air, on the sea, in jungles, cities and deserts—and here, too, are eyewitness accounts written by the war correspondent, who is himself a characteristic of modern war. Among the latter is that beloved little man, Ernie Pyle and his moving story, *The Death of Captain Waskow.*

Back-pedalling a half-century, to the very beginning of the war correspondent game, the reader will find some of the most illustrious exponents of the I-Was-There experience: Winston Churchill and Richard Harding Davis. From the future Prime Minister and wartime leader of the United Kingdom comes *The Cavalry Charge at Omdurman*, written while Churchill was a newsman covering the Sudanese War of the Anglo-Egyptian forces against the Mahdi. That battle was fought in 1898, which should suggest just how truly impressive and varied the Churchill career has been. Richard Harding Davis also led a thrilling life, and is represented here by his *Execution of Rodriguez.*

If there is a world fifty years from now, and if there are people who can read, they will, of course, be puzzled by the war adventures chronicled in this anthology. To them, such weapons as tanks, manned bombers, aircraft carriers, and even small atom bombs will undoubtedly be considered long obsolete, as we now think of the bow and arrow or the broadsword.

Until now wars have been fought by men with their flesh and blood and courage. To the people of the twenty-first century this will be anachronistic. The war they will know (if it has not by that time erupted) will be a matter of pressing a few buttons and all will be over within an hour. Physicists, mathematicians, chemists, manufacturers of rockets, missiles, capsules equipped with hydrogen war heads, will replace the man with the gun, or the man who flies a plane, or the man who skippers a battlewagon or submarine. This book may well be a farewell to those who, from biblical times, have fought in the old-fashioned way, with old-fashioned weapons, and a brave heart.

QUENTIN REYNOLDS & ROBERT LECKIE

Josue Fights the Battle of Jericho

from the Bible

After Moses had successfully led the Children of Israel out of Egypt, he died and was succeeded by his lieutenant, Josue (Joshua), the son of Nun. It was now up to Josue to lead his people into the Promised Land, then occupied by those Semitic tribes loosely called the Canaanites. One of the Canaanites strongholds was Jericho, a walled city north of Jerusalem which commanded the valley of the lower Jordan. In Josue's own account of this memorable battle, fought about 1400 B.C., we have the first of all eyewitness accounts of battle.

17

And Josue the son of Nun sent from Setim two men to spy secretly: and said to them: Go and view the land and the city of Jericho. They went and entered into the house of a woman that was a harlot named Rahab, and lodged with her.

And it was told the king of Jericho, and was said: Behold there are men come in hither, by night, of the children of Israel, to spy the land.

And the king of Jericho sent to Rahab, saying: Bring forth the men that came to thee, and are entered into thy house: for they are spies, and are come to view all the land. And the woman taking the men, hid them, and said:

I confess they came to me, but I knew not whence they were: And at the time of shutting the gate in the dark, they also went out together. I know not whither they are gone: pursue after them quickly, and you will overtake them.

But she made the men go up to the top of her house, and covered them with the stalks of flax, which was there.

Now they that were sent, pursued after them, by the way that leadeth to the fords of Jordan: and as soon as they were gone out, the gate was presently shut.

The men that were hidden were not yet asleep, when behold the woman went up to them, and said:

I know that the Lord hath given this land to you: for the dread of you is fallen upon us, and all the inhabitants of the land have lost all strength. We have heard that the Lord dried up the water of the Red Sea at your going in, when you came out of Egypt: and what things you did to the two kinds of the Amorrhites, that were beyond the Jordan: Sehon and Og whom you slew.

And hearing these things we were affrighted, and our heart fainted away, neither did there remain any spirit in us at your coming in: for the Lord your God he is God in heaven above, and in the earth beneath.

18

Now therefore swear ye to me by the Lord, that as I have shewn mercy to you, so you also will shew mercy to my father's house: and give me a true token, that you will save my father and mother, my brethren and sisters, and all things that are theirs, and deliver our souls from death.

They answered her: Be our lives for you unto death, only if thou betray us not. And when the Lord shall have delivered us the Land, we will shew thee mercy and truth.

Then she let them down with a cord out of a window; for her house joined close to the wall. And she said to them: Get ye up to the mountains, lest perhaps they meet you as they return: and there lie ye hid three days, till they come back, and so you shall go on your way.

And they said to her: We shall be blameless of this oath, which thou hast made us swear: If when we come into the land, this scarlet cord be a sign, and thou tie it in the window, by which thou hast let us down: and gather together thy father and mother, and brethren and all they kindred into thy house.

Whosoever shall go out of the door of thy house, his blood shall be upon his own head, and we shall be quit. But the blood of all that shall be with thee in the house, shall light upon our head, if any man touch them. But if thou wilt betray us, and utter this word abroad, we shall be quit of this oath which thou hast made us swear.

And she answered: As you have spoken, so be it done. And sending them on their way, she hung the scarlet cord in the window.

But they went and came to the mountains, and stayed there three days till they that pursued them were returned. For having sought them through all the way, they found them not.

And when they were gone back into the city, the spies returned, and came down from the mountain: and passing over the Jordan, they came to Josue the son of Nun, and told him all that befell them, and said: The Lord hath delivered all this land into our hands, and all the inhabitants thereof are overthrown with fear.

AND JOSUE ROSE BEFORE DAYLIGHT, and removed the camp: and they departed from Setim, and came to the Jordan, he, and all the children of Israel, and they abode there for three days.

After which the heralds went through the midst of the camp. And began to proclaim:

When you shall see the ark of the covenant of the Lord your God, and the priests of the race of Levi carrying it, rise you up also, and follow them as they go before: and let there be between you and the ark the space of two thousand cubits: that you may see it afar off, and know which way you must go: for you have not gone this way before: and take care you come not near the ark.

And Josue said to the people: Be ye sanctified: for tomorrow the Lord will do wonders among you.

And he said to the priests: Take up the ark of the covenant, and go before the people. And they obeyed his commands, and took it up and walked before them.

And the Lord said to Josue: This day will I begin to exalt thee before Israel: that they may know that, as I was with Moses, so I am with thee also. And do thou command the priests that carry the ark of the covenant, and say to them: When you shall have entered into part of the water of the Jordan, stand in it.

And Josue said to the children of Israel: Come hither and hear the word of the Lord your God.

And again he said: By this you shall know that the Lord the living God is in the midst of you, and that he shall destroy before your sight the Canaanite and the Hethite, the Hevite and the Pherezite, the Gergesite also and the Jebusite, and the Amorrhite. Behold the ark of the covenant of the Lord of all the earth shall go before you into Jordan. Prepare ye twelve men of the tribes of Israel, one of every tribe.

And when the priests, that carry the ark of the Lord the God of the whole earth, shall set the soles of their feet in the waters of the Jordan, the waters that are beneath shall run down and go off: and those that come from above, shall stand together upon a heap.

So the people went out of their tents, to pass over the Jordan: and the priests that carried the ark of the covenant, went on before them. And as soon as they came into the Jordan, and their feet were dipped in part of the water (now the Jordan, it being harvest time, had filled the banks of its

20

channel) the waters that came down from above stood in one place, and swelling up like a mountain, that is called Adom, to the place of Sarthan: but those that were beneath, ran down into the sea of the wilderness (which now is called the Dead Sea) until they wholly failed.

And the people marched over against Jericho: and the priests that carried the ark of the covenant of the Lord, stood girded upon the dry ground in the midst of the Jordan, and all the people passed over through the channel that was dried up.

AND WHEN THEY WERE PASSED OVER, the Lord said to Josue:

Choose twelve men, one of every tribe: and command them to take from the middle of the channel of the Jordan, where the feet of the priests stood, twelve very hard stones, which you shall set in the place of the camp, where you shall pitch your tents this night.

And Josue called twelve men, whom he had chosen out of the children of Israel, one out of every tribe, and he said to them: Go before the ark of the Lord your God to the midst of the Jordan, and carry from thence every man a stone on your shoulders, according to the number of the children of Israel, that it may be a sign among you: and when your children shall ask you tomorrow, saying: What mean these stones? You shall answer them: The waters of the Jordan ran off before the ark of the covenant of the Lord, when it passed over the same: therefore were these stones set for a monument of the children of Israel for ever.

The children of Israel therefore did as Josue commanded them, carrying out of the channel of the Jordan twelve stones, as the Lord had commanded him, according to the number of the children of Israel, unto the place wherein they camped, and there they set them.

And Josue put other twelve stones in the midst of the channel of the Jordan, where the priests stood that carried the ark of the covenant: and they are there until this present day.

Now the priests that carried the ark, stood in the midst of the Jordan till all things were accomplished which the Lord had commanded Josue to speak to the people, and Moses had said to him. And the people made haste and passed over.

And when they had all passed over, the ark also of the Lord passed over, and the priests went before the people. The children of Ruben also and Gad, and half the tribe of Manasses, went armed before the children of Israel as Moses had commanded them.

And forty thousand fighting men by their troops, and bands, marched through the plains and fields of the city of Jericho.

In that day the Lord magnified Josue in the sight of all Israel, that they should fear him, as they had feared Moses, while he lived. And he said to him: Command the priests, that carry the ark of the covenant, to come up out of the Jordan.

And he commanded them, saying: Come ye up out of the Jordan.

And when they that carried the ark of the covenant of the Lord, were come up, and began to tread on the dry ground, the waters returned into the channel, and ran as they were wont before.

And the people came up out of the Jordan, the tenth day of the first month, and camped in Galgal . . . over against the east side of the city of Jericho.

And the twelve stones which they had taken out of the channel of the Jordan, Josue pitched in Galgal, and said to the children of Israel: When your children shall ask their fathers to-morrow, and shall say to them: What mean these stones?

You shall teach them and say: Israel passed over this Jordan through the dry channel, the Lord your God drying up the waters thereof in your sight, until you passed over: as he had done before in the Red Sea, which he dried up till we passed through: that all the people of the earth may learn the most mighty hand of the Lord, that you also may fear the Lord your God forever.

Now WHEN ALL THE KINGS OF THE AMORRHITES, who dwelt beyond the Jordan westward, and all the kings of Canaan, who possessed the places near the great sea, had heard that the Lord had dried up the waters of the Jordan before the Children of Israel till they passed over, their heart failed them, and there remained no spirit in them, fearing the coming in of the Children of Israel.

At the time the Lord said to Josue: Make thee knives of stone and circumcise the second time the children of Israel. He did what the Lord had commanded, and he circumcised the children of Israel in the hill of the foreskins. Now after they were all circumcised, they remained in the same place of the camp, until they were healed.

And the Lord said to Josue: This day have I taken away from you the reproach of Egypt. And the name of that place was called Galgal, until this present day.

And the children of Israel abode in Galgal, and they kept the phase on the fourteenth day of the month, at evening, in the plains of Jericho: and they ate on the next day unleavened bread of the corn of the land, and frumenty of the same year. And the manna ceased after they ate of the corn of the land, neither did the children of Israel use that food any more, but they ate of the corn of the present year of the land of Canaan.

And when Josue was in the field of the city of Jericho, he lifted up his eyes, and saw a man standing over against him, holding a drawn sword, and he went to him, and said: Art thou one of ours, or of our adversaries?

And he answered: No: but I am prince of the host of the Lord, and now I am come.

Josue fell on his face to the ground. And worshipping, said: What saith my Lord to his servant?

Loose, saith he, thy shoes from off thy feet: for the place whereupon thou standest is holy. And Josue did as was commanded him.

Now JERICHO was close shut up and fenced for fear of the children of Israel, and no man durst go out or come in.

And the Lord said to Josue: Behold I have given into thy hands Jericho, and the king thereof, and all the valiant men. Go about the city, all ye fighting men, once a day: so shall ye do for six days.

And on the seventh day the priests shall take the seven trumpets, which are used in the jubilee, and shall go before the ark of the covenant: and you shall go about the city seven times, and the priests shall sound the trumpets.

23

And when the voice of the trumpet shall give a longer and broken tune, and shall sound in your ears, all the people shall shout together with a very great shout, and the walls of the city shall fall to the ground, and they shall enter in every one at the place against which they shall stand.

Then Josue the son of Nun called the priests, and said to them: Take the ark of the covenant: and let seven other priests take the seven trumpets of the jubilee, and march before the ark of the Lord. And he said to the people: Go and compass the city, armed, marching before the ark of the Lord.

And when Josue had ended his words, and the seven priests blew the seven trumpets before the ark of the covenant of the Lord, and all the armed men went before, the rest of the common people followed the ark, and the sound of the trumpets was heard on all sides.

But Josue had commanded the people, saying: You shall not shout, nor shall your voice be heard, nor any word go out of your mouth: until the day come wherein I shall say to you: Cry and shout.

So the ark of the Lord went about the city once a day, and returning into the camp, abode there.

And Josue rising before day, the priests took the ark of the Lord, and seven of them seven trumpets, which are used in the jubilee: and they went before the ark of the Lord walking and sounding the trumpets: and the armed men went before them, and the rest of the common people followed the ark, and they blew the trumpets. And they went round about the city the second day once, and returned into the camp. So they did six days.

But the seventh day, rising up early, they went about the city, as it was ordered, seven times. And when in the seventh going about the priests sounded with the trumpets, Josue said to all Israel: Shout: for the Lord hath delivered the city to you: And let this city be an anathema, and all things that are in it, to the Lord. Let only Rahab the harlot live, with all that are with her in the house: for she hid the messengers whom we sent.

But beware ye lest you touch aught of those things that are forbidden, and you be guilty of transgression, and all the camp of Israel be under sin, and be troubled. But whatsoever gold or silver there shall be, or vessels of brass and iron, let it be consecrated to the Lord, laid up in his treasures.

So all the people making a shout, and the trumpets sounding, when the voice and the sound thundered in the ears of the multitude, the walls forthwith fell down: and every man went up by the place that was over against him: and they took the city. And killed all that were in it, man and woman, young and old. The oxen also and the sheep, and the asses, they slew with the edge of the sword.

But Josue said to the two men that had been sent for spies: Go into the harlot's house, and bring her out, and all things that are hers, as you assured her by oath. And the young men went in and brought out Rahab, and her parents, her brethren also and all her goods and her kindred, and made them to stay without the camp.

But they burned the city, and all things that were therein; except the gold and silver, and vessels of brass and iron, which they consecrated into the treasury of the Lord.

But Josue saved Rahab the harlot and her father's house, and all she had, and they dwelt in the midst of Israel until this present day: because she hid the messengers whom he had sent to spy out Jericho. At that time. Josue made an imprecation, saying: Cursed be the man before the Lord, that shall raise up and build the city of Jericho. In his firstborn may he lay the foundation thereof, and in the last of his children set up its gates.

And the Lord was with Josue, and his name was noised throughout all the land.

25

The Campaign That Crushed the Athenians

by Thucydides

In Greece about the middle of the fifth century, B.C., the military power of Sparta was challenged by the rising naval power of Athens. This resulted in the Peloponnesian War, the first ten years of which established Athens as a new and victorious empire. Pursuing a policy of expansion, the Athenians mounted an expedition against Sicily. Athenian forces landed at Syracuse and beseiged the city, and their fortunes began the final decline. In 413 B.C., Syracusans led by Gylippus moved to destroy the besiegers led by Nicias. What happened was described by Thucydides in his deathless *History of the Peloponnesian War*.

Gylippus and Sicanus returned to Syracuse.

Sicanus had not succeeded in his design upon Agrigentum; for while he was at Gela on his way the party inclined to friendship with the Syracusans had been driven out. But Gylippus brought back a large army, together with the hoplites who had been sent in merchant vessels from Poloponnesus in the spring, and had come by way of Libya to Selinus. They had been driven to Libya by stress of weather, and the Cyrenaeans had given them two trieremes and pilots. On their voyage they had made common cause with the Evesperitae, who were besieged by the Libyans. After defeating the Libyans they sailed on to Neapolis, a Carthaginian factory which is the nearest point to Sicily, the passage taking two days and a night only; thence they crossed and came to Selinus. On their arrival, the Syracusans immediately prepared to renew their attack upon the Athenians, both by land and sea.

And the Athenian generals, seeing that their enemy had been reinforced by a new army and that their own affairs, instead of improving, were daily growing worse in every respect, and being especially troubled by the sickness of their troops, repented that they had not gone before. Even Nicias now no longer objected, but only made the condition that there should be no open voting. So, maintaining such secrecy as they could, they gave orders for the departure of the expedition; the men were to prepare themselves against a given signal. The preparations were made and they were on the point of sailing, when the moon, being just then at the full, was eclipsed. The mass of the army was greatly moved, and called upon the generals to remain. Nicias himself, who was too much under the influence of divination and such like, refused even to discuss the question of their removal until they had remained thrice nine days, as the soothsayers prescribed. This was the reason why the departure of the Athenians was finally delayed.

And now the Syracusans, having heard what had happened, were more eager than ever to prosecute the war to the end; they saw in the intention of the Athenians to depart a confession that they were no longer superior to themselves, either by sea or land; and they did not want them to settle down in some other part of Sicily where they would be more difficult to manage, but sought to compel them forthwith to fight at sea under the disadvantages of their present position. So they manned their ships and exercised for as many days as they thought sufficient. When the time came they began by attacking the Athenian lines. A small number both of the hoplites and of the cavalry came out of some of the gates to meet them; they cut off however a portion of the hoplites, and, putting the main body to flight, drove them within their walls. The entrance was narrow, and the Athenians lost seventy horses and a few infantry.

The Syracusan army then retired. On the morrow their ships, in number seventy-six, sailed forth, and at the same time their land forces marched against the walls. The Athenians on their side put with eighty-six ships; and the two fleets met and fought. Eurymedon, who commanded the right wing of the Athenians, hoping to surround the enemy, extended his line too far toward the land, and was defeated by the Syracusans, who, after overcoming the Athenian center, cooped him up in the inner bay of the harbor. There he was slain, and the vessels which were under his command and had followed him were destroyed. The Syracusans now pursued and began to drive ashore the rest of the Athenian fleet.

Gylippus, observing the discomfiture of the enemy, who were being defeated and driven to land beyond their own palisade and the lines of their camp, hastened with a part of his army to the causeway which ran along the harbor, intending to kill all who landed, and to assist the Syracusans in capturing the ships, which could be more easily towed away if the shore was in the hands of their friends. The Tyrrhenians, who guarded this part of the Athenian lines, seeing Gylippus and his forces advance in disorder, rushed out, and attacking the foremost put them to flight and drove them into the marsh called Lysimelea. But soon the Syracusans and their allies came up in greater numbers. The Athenians in fear for their ships advanced to the support of the Tyrrhenians, and joined

29

in the engagement; the Syracusans were overcome and pursued, and a few of their heavy-armed slain. Most of the Athenian ships were saved and brought back to the Athenian station. Still the Syracusans and their allies took eighteen, and killed the whole of their crews. Then, hoping to burn the remainder of the fleet, they filled an old merchantman with faggots and brands; these they lighted, and as the wind blew right upon the enemy they let the ship go. The Athenians, alarmed for the safety of their fleet, contrived means by which they extinguished their flames, and succeeded in keeping the fireship at a distance. Thus the danger was averted.

The Syracusans now raised a trophy of their naval victory, and another marking their interception of the hoplites on the higher ground close to the wall at the place where they took the horses. The Athenians raised a trophy of the victory over the land forces whom the Tyrrhenians drove into the marsh, and another of that which they had themselves gained with the rest of the army.

The Syracusans, who up to this time had been afraid of the reinforcements of Demosthenes, had now gained a brilliant success by sea as well as by land; the Athenians were in utter despair. Great was their surprise at the result, and still greater their regret that they had ever come. The Sicilian were the only cities which they had ever encountered similar in character to their own, having the same democratic institutions and strong in ships, cavalry, and population. They were not able by holding out the prospect of a change of government to introduce an element of discord among them which might have gained them over, nor could they master them by a decided superiority of force. They had failed at almost every point, and were already in great straits, when the defeat at sea, which they could not have thought possible, reduced their fortunes to a still lower ebb.

The Athenians, seeing the closing of the harbor and inferring the intentions of the enemy, proceeded to hold a council. The generals and officers met and considered the difficulties of their position. The most pressing of all was the want of food. For they had already sent to Catana, when they intended to depart, and stopped the supplies for the present; and they could get no more in the future unless they recovered the command of the sea. They resolved therefore to quit their lines on the higher ground and to cut off by a cross-wall a space close to their ships, no greater than was absolutely required for their baggage and for their sick; after leaving a guard there they meant to put on board every other man, and to launch all their ships, whether fit for service or not; they would then fight a decisive battle, and, if they conquered, go to Catana; but if not, they would burn their ships, and retreat by land in good order, taking the nearest way to some friendly country, Barbarian or Hellenic. This design they proceeded to execute, and withdrawing quietly from the upper walls manned their whole fleet, compelling every man of any age at all suitable for service to embark. The entire number of the ships which they manned was about a hundred and ten. They put on board numerous archers and javelin-men, Acarnanians, and other foreigners, and made such preparations for action as their difficult situation and the nature of their plan allowed. . . .

Nicias gave orders to man the ships. Gylippus and the Syracusans could see clearly enough from the preparations which the Athenians were making that they were going to fight. But they had also previous notice, and had been told of the iron grapnels; and they took precautions against this as against all the other devices of the Athenians. They covered the prows of their vessels with hides, extending a good way along the upper part of their sides, so that the grapnels might slip and find no hold.

When Gylippus and the other Syracusan generals had, like Nicias, encouraged their troops, perceiving the Athenians to be manning their ships, they presently did the same. Nicias, overwhelmed by the situation, and seeing how great and how near the peril was (for the ships were on the very point of rowing out), feeling too, as men do on the eve of a great struggle, that all which he had done was nothing, and that he had not said half enough, again addressed the trierarchs, and calling each of them by his father's name, and his own name, and the name of his tribe, he entreated those who had made any reputation for themselves not to be false to it, and those whose ancestors were eminent not to tarnish their hereditary fame. He reminded them that they were the inhabitants of the freest country in the world, and how in Athens there was no interference with the daily life of any man. He spoke

31

to them of their wives and children and their father's gods, as men will at such a time; for then they do not care whether their commonplace phrases seem to be out of date or not, but loudly reiterate the old appeals, believing that they may be of some service at the awful moment. When he thought that he had exhorted them, not enough, but as much as the scanty time allowed, he retired, and led the land forces to the shore, extending the line as far as he could, so that they might be of the greatest use in encouraging the combatants on board ship. Demosthenes, Menander, and Euthydemus, who had gone on board the Athenian fleet to take the command, now quitted their own station, and proceeded straight to the closed mouth of the harbor, intending to force their way to the open sea where a passage was still left.

The Syracusans and their allies had already put out with nearly the same number of ships as before. A detachment of them guarded the entrance of the harbor; the remainder were disposed all round it in such a manner that they might fall on the Athenians from every side at once, and that their land forces might at the same time be able to cooperate wherever the ships retreated to the shore. Sicanus and Agatharchus commanded the Syracusan fleet, each of them a wing; Pythen and the Corinthians occupied the center. When the Athenians approached the closed mouth of the harbor the violence of their onset overpowered the ships which were stationed there; they then attempted to loosen the fastenings. Whereupon from all sides the Syracusans and their allies came bearing down upon them, and the conflict was no longer confined to the entrance, but extended throughout the harbor. No previous engagement had been so fierce and obstinate. Great was the eagerness with which the rowers on both sides rushed upon their enemies whenever the word of command was given; and keen was the contest between the pilots as they maneuvered one against another. The marines too were full of anxiety that, when ship struck ship, the service on deck should not fall short of the rest; everyone in the place assigned to him was eager to be foremost among his fellows. Many vessels meeting—and never did so many fight in so small a space, for the two fleets together amounted to nearly two hundred—they were seldom able to strike in the regular manner, because they had no opportunity of first retiring or

32

breaking the line; they generally fouled one another as ship dashed against ship in the hurry of flight or pursuit. All the time that another vessel was bearing down, the men on deck poured showers of javelins and arrows and stones upon the enemy; and when the two closed, the marines fought hand to hand, and endeavored to board. In many places, owing to the want of room, they who had struck another found that they were struck themselves; often two or even more vessels were unavoidably entangled about one, and the pilots had to make plans of attack and defense, not against one adversary only but against several coming from different sides. The crash of so many ships dashing against one another took away the wits of the crews, and made it impossible to hear the boat-swains, whose voices in both fleets rose high, as they gave directions to the rowers, or cheered them on in the excite-ment of the struggle. On the Athenian saide they were shout-ing to their men that they must force a passage and seize the opportunity now or never of returning in safety to their native land. To the Syracusans and their allies was represented the glory of preventing the escape of their enemies, and of a victory by which every man would exalt the honor of his own city. The commanders too, when they saw any ship backing without necessity, would call the captain by his name, and ask of the Athenians whether they were retreating be-cause they expected to be more at home upon the land of their bitterest foes than upon that sea which had been their own so long; on the Syracusan side whether, when they knew perfectly well that the Athenians were only eager to find some means of flight, they would themselves fly from the fugitives.

While the naval engagement hung in the balance the two armies on shore had great trial and conflict of soul. The Sicilian soldier was animated by the hope of increasing the glory which he had already won, while the invader was tormented by the fear that his fortunes might sink lower still. The last chance of the Athenians lay in their ships, and their anxiety was dreadful. The fortune of the battle varied; and it was not possible that the spectators on the shore should all receive the same impression of it. Being quite close and having different points of view, they would some of them see their own ships victorious; their courage would then revive, and

33

they would earnestly call upon the gods not to take from them their hope of deliverance. But others who saw their ships worsted cried and shrieked aloud, and were by the sight alone more utterly unnerved than the defeated combatants themselves. Others again, who had fixed their gaze on some part of the struggle which was undecided, were in a state of excitement still more terrible; they kept swaying their bodies to and fro in an agony of hope and fear as the stubborn conflict went on and on; for at every instant they were all but saved or all but lost. And while the strife hung in the balance you might hear in the Athenian army at once lamentation, shouting, cries of victory or defeat, and all the various sounds which are wrung from a great host in extremity of danger. Not less agonizing were the feelings of those on board. At length the Syracusans and their allies, after a protracted struggle, put the Athenians to flight, and triumphantly bearing down upon them, and encouraging one another with loud cries and exhortations, drove them to land. Then that part of the navy which had not been taken in the deep water fell back in confusion to the shore, and the crews rushed out of the ships into the camp. And the land forces, no longer now divided in feeling, but uttering one universal groan of intolerable anguish, ran, some of them to save the ships, others to defend what remained of the wall; but the greater number began to look to themselves and to their own safety. Never had there been a greater panic in an Athenian army than at that moment. They now suffered what they had done to others at Pylos. For at Pylos the Lacedaemonians, when they saw their ships destroyed, knew that their friends who had crossed over into the island of Sphacteria were lost with them. And so now the Athenians, after the rout of their fleet, knew that they had no hope of saving themselves by land unless events took some extraordinary turn.

Thus, after a fierce battle and a great destruction of ships and men on both sides, the Syracusans and their allies gained the victory. They gathered up the wrecks and bodies of the dead, and sailing back to the city, erected a trophy. The Athenians, overwhelmed by their misery, never so much as thought of recovering their wrecks or of asking leave to collect their dead. Their intention was to retreat that very night. Demosthenes came to Nicias and proposed that they

34

should once more man their remaining vessels and endeavor to force the passage at daybreak, saying that they had more ships fit for service than the enemy. For the Athenian fleet still numbered sixty, but the enemy had less than fifty. Nicias approved of his proposal, and they would have manned the ships, but the sailors refused to embark; for they were paralyzed by their defeat and had no longer any hope of succeeding. So the Athenians all made up their minds to escape by land.

Hermocrates the Syracusan suspected their intention, and dreading what might happen if their vast army, retreating by land and settling somewhere in Sicily, should choose to renew the war, he went to the authorities and represented to them that they ought not to allow the Athenians to withdraw by night (mentioning his own suspicion of their intentions), but that all the Syracusans and their allies should go out in advance, wall up the roads, and occupy the passes with a guard. They thought very much as he did, and wanted to carry out his plan, but doubted whether their men, who were too glad to repose after a great battle, and in time of festival—for there happened on that very day to be a sacrifice to Heracles—could be induced to obey. Most of them, in the exultation of victory, were drinking and keeping holiday, and at such a time how could they ever be expected to take up arms and go forth at the order of the generals? On these grounds the authorities decided that the thing was impossible. Whereupon Hermocrates himself, fearing lest the Athenians should gain a start and quietly pass the most difficult places in the night, contrived the following plan: when it was growing dark he sent certain of his own acquaintance, accompanied by a few horsemen, to the Athenian camp. They rode up within earshot, and pretending to be friends (there were known to be men in the city who gave information to Nicias of what went on) called to some of the soldiers and bade them tell him not to withdraw his army during the night, for the Syracusans were guarding the roads; he should make preparation at leisure and retire by day. Having delivered their message they departed, and those who had heard them informed the Athenian generals.

On receiving this message, which they supposed to be genuine, they remained during the night. And having once

35

given up the intention of starting immediately, they decided to remain during the next day, that the soldiers might, as well as they could, put together their baggage in the most convenient form, and depart, taking with them the bare necessaries of life, but nothing else.

Meanwhile the Syracusans and Gylippus, going forth before them with their land forces, blocked the roads in the country by which the Athenians were likely to pass, guarded the fords of the rivers and streams, and posted themselves at the best points for receiving and stopping them. Their sailors rowed up to the beach and dragged away the Athenian ships. The Athenians themselves had burned a few of them, as they had intended, but the rest the Syracusans towed away, unmolested and at their leisure, from the places where they had severally run aground, and conveyed them to the city.

On the third day after the sea fight, when Nicias and Demosthenes thought that their preparations were complete, the army began to move. They were in a dreadful condition; not only was there the great fact that they had lost their whole fleet, and instead of their expected triumph had brought the utmost peril upon Athens as well as upon themselves, but also the sights which presented themselves as they quitted the camp were painful to every eye and mind. The dead were unburied, and when anyone saw the body of a friend lying on the ground he was smitten with sorrow and dread, while the sick or wounded who still survived but had to be left were even a greater trial to the living, and more to be pitied than those who were gone. Their prayers and lamentations drove their companions to distraction; they would beg that they might be taken with them, and call by name any friend or relation whom they saw passing; they would hang upon their departing comrades and follow as far as they could, and, when their limbs and strength failed them, and they dropped behind, many were the imprecations and cries which they uttered. So that the whole army was in tears, and such was their despair that they could hardly make up their minds to stir, although they were leaving an enemy's country, having suffered calamities too great for tears already, and dreading miseries yet greater in the unknown future.

There was also a general feeling of shame and self-reproach—indeed they seemed not like an army but like the fugitive population of a city captured after a siege; and of a great city too. For the whole multitude who were marching together numbered not less than forty thousand. Each of them took with him anything he could carry which was likely to be of use. Even the heavy-armed and cavalry, contrary to their practice when under arms, conveyed about their persons their own food, some because they had no attendants, others because they could not trust them; for they had long been deserting and most of them had gone off all at once. Nor was the food which they carried sufficient; for the supplies of the camp had failed. Their disgrace and the universality of the misery, although there might be some consolation in the very community of suffering, were nevertheless at that moment hard to bear, especially when they remembered from what pride and splendor they had fallen into their present low estate.

Never had an Hellenic army experienced such a reverse. They had come intending to enslave others, and they were going away in fear that they would be themselves enslaved. Instead of the prayers and hymns with which they had put to sea, they were now departing amid appeals of another sort to heaven. They were no longer sailors but landsmen, depending not upon their fleet but upon their infantry. Yet in face of the great danger which still threatened them all these things appeared endurable.

Nicias, seeing the army disheartened at their terrible fall, went along the ranks and encouraged and consoled them as well as he could. . . . Nicias passed through the army, and wherever he saw gaps in the ranks or the men dropping out of line, he brought them back to their proper place. Demosthenes did the same for the troops under his command, and gave them similar exhortations. The army marched disposed in a hollow oblong, the division of Nicias leading and that of Demosthenes following; the hoplites enclosed within their ranks the baggage-bearers and the rest of the host. When they arrived at the ford of the river Anapus they found a force of the Syracusans and of their allies drawn up to meet them; these they put to flight, and getting command of the ford, proceeded on their march. The Syracusans continually harassed them, the cavalry riding alongside and the light-armed troops hurling darts at them. On this day the Athenians proceeded about four and a half miles and encamped at a hill. On the next day they started early, and, having advanced more than two miles, descended into a level plain, and encamped. The country was inhabited, and they were desirous of obtaining food from the houses, and also water which they might carry with them, as there was little to be had for many miles in the country which lay before them. Meanwhile the Syracusans had gone forward, and at a point where the road ascends a steep hill called the Acraean height, and there is a precipitous ravine on either side, were blocking up the pass by a wall. On the next day the Athenians advanced, although again impeded by the numbers of the enemy's cavalry who rode alongside, and of their javelin-men who threw darts at them. For a long time the Athenians maintained the struggle, but at last retired to their own encampment. Their supplies were now cut off, because the horsemen circumscribed their movements.

In the morning they started early and resumed their march. They pressed onward to the hill where the way was barred, and found in front of them the Syracusan infantry drawn up to defend the wall, in deep array, for the pass was narrow. Whereupon the Athenians advanced and assaulted the barrier, but the enemy, who were numerous and had the advantage of position, threw missiles upon them from the hill, which was steep, and so, not being able to force their way, they again retired and rested. During the conflict, as is often the case in the fall of the year, there came on a storm of rain and thunder, whereby the Athenians were yet more disheartened, for they thought that everything was conspiring to their destruction. While they were resting, Gylippus and the Syracusans dispatched a division of their army to raise a wall behind them across the road by which they had come; but the Athenians sent some of their own troops and frustrated their intention. They then retired with their whole army in the direction of the plain and passed the night.

On the following day they again advanced. The Syracusans now surrounded and attacked them on every side, and wounded many of them. If the Athenians advanced they retreated, but charged them when they retired, falling especially upon the hindermost of them, in the hope that, if they could put to flight a few at a time, they might strike a panic into the whole army. In this fashion the Athenians struggled on for a long time, and having advanced about three-quarters of a mile rested in the plain. The Syracusans then left them and returned to their own encampment.

The army was now in a miserable plight, being in want of every necessary; and by the continual assaults of the enemy great numbers of the soldiers had been wounded. Nicias and Demosthenes, perceiving their condition, resolved during the night to light as many watchfires as possible and to lead off their forces. They intended to take another route and march toward the sea in the direction opposite that from which the Syracusans were watching them. Now their whole line of march lay, not toward Catana, but toward the other side of Sicily, in the direction of Camarina and Gela, and the cities, Hellenic or Barbarian, of that region. So they lighted numerous fires and departed in the night. And then, as constantly happens in armies, especially in very great ones, and as might be expected when they were marching by night in an enemy's country, and with the enemy from whom they were flying not far off, there arose a panic among them, and they fell into confusion. The army of Nicias, which was leading the way, kept together, and got on considerably in advance, but that of Demosthenes, which was the larger half, was severed from the other division, and marched in worse order. At daybreak, however, they successded in reaching the sea, and striking into the Helorine road marched along it, intending as soon as they arrived at Cacyparis to follow up the course of the river through the interior of the island. They were expecting that the Sicels for whom they had sent would meet them on this road. When they had reached the river they found there also a guard of the Syracusans cutting off the passage by a wall and palisade. They forced their way through and, crossing the river, passed on toward another river which is called the Erineus, this being the direction in which their guides led them.

When daylight broke and the Syracusans and their allies saw that the Athenians had departed, most of them thought that Gylippus had let them go on purpose and were very angry with him. They easily found the line of their retreat, and quickly following, came up with them about the time of the midday meal. The troops of Demosthenes were last; they were marching slowly and in disorder, not having recovered from the panic of the previous night, when they were overtaken by the Syracusans, who immediately fell upon them and fought. Separated as they were from the others, they were easily hemmed in by the Syracusan cavalry and driven into a narrow space. The division of Nicias was now as much as six miles in advance, for he marched faster, thinking that their safety depended at such a time not in remaining and fighting, if they could avoid it, but in retreating as quickly as they could, and resisting only when they were positively compelled. Demosthenes, on the other hand, who had been more incessantly harassed throughout the retreat, because marching last he was first attacked by the enemy, now, when he saw the Syracusans pursuing him, instead of pressing onward, ranged his army in order of battle. Thus lingering he was surrounded, and he and the Athenians under his command were in the greatest confusion. For they were crushed into a walled enclosure, having a road on both sides and planted thickly with olive-trees, and missiles were hurled at them from all points. The Syracusans naturally preferred this mode of attack to a regular engagement. For to risk themselves against desperate men would have been only playing into the hands of the Athenians. Moreover, every one was sparing of his life; their good fortune was already assured, and they did not want to fall in the hour of victory. Even by this irregular mode of fighting they thought that they could overpower and capture the Athenians.

And so when they had gone on all day assailing them with missiles from every quarter, and saw that they were quite worn out with their wounds and all their other sufferings, Gylippus and the Syracusans made a proclamation, first of all to the islanders, that any of them who pleased might come over to them and have their freedom. But only a few cities accepted the offer. At length an agreement was made for the entire force under Demosthenes. Their arms were to be surrendered, but no one was to suffer death, either from violence or from imprisonment, or from want of the bare means of life. So they all surrendered, being in number six thousand, and gave up what money they had. This they threw into the hollows of shields and filled four. The captives were at once taken to the city. On the same day Nicias and his division reached the river Erineus, which he crossed, and halted his army on a rising ground.

On the following day he was overtaken by the Syracusans, who told him that Demosthenes had surrendered and bade him to do the same. He, not believing them, procured a truce while he sent a horseman to go and see. Upon the return of the horseman bringing assurance of the fact, he sent a herald to Gylippus and the Syracusans, saying that he would agree, on behalf of the Athenian state, to pay the expenses which the Syracusans had incurred in the war, on condition that they should let his army go; until the money was paid he would give Athenian citizens as hostages, a man for a talent. Gylippus and the Syracusans would not accept these proposals, but attacked and surrounded this division of the army as they had the other, and hurled missiles at them from every side until the evening. They too were grievously in want of food and necessaries. Nevertheless they meant to wait for the dead of the night and then to proceed. They were just resuming their arms when the Syracusans discovered them and raised the paean. The Athenians, perceiving that they were detected, laid down their arms again, with the exception of about three hundred men who broke through the enemy's guard and made their escape in the darkness as best they could.

When the day dawned Nicias led forward his army, and the Syracusans and their allies again assailed them on every side, hurling javelins and other missiles at them. The Athenians hurried on to the river Assinarus. They hoped to gain a little relief if they forded the river, for the mass of horsemen and other troops overwhelmed and crushed them; and they were worn out by fatigue and thirst. But no sooner did they reach the water than they lost all order and rushed in; every man was trying to cross first, and, the enemy pressing upon them at the same time, the passage of the river became hopeless. Being compelled to keep close together they fell one upon another and trampled each other under foot; some at once perished, pierced by their own spears, others got entangled in the baggage and were carried down the stream. The Syracusans stood upon the further bank of the river, which was steep, and hurled missiles from above on the Athenians, who were huddled together in the deep bed of the stream and for the most part were drinking greedily. The Peloponnesians

41

came down the bank and slaughtered them, falling chiefly upon those who were in the river. Whereupon the water at once became foul, but was drunk all the same, although muddy and dyed with blood, and the crowd fought for it.

At last, when the dead bodies were lying in heaps upon one another in the water and the army was utterly undone, some perishing in the river, and any who escaped being cut off by the cavalry, Nicias surrendered to Gylippus, in whom he had more confidence than in the Syracusans. He entreated him and the Lacedaemonians to do what they pleased with himself, but not to go on killing the men. So Gylippus gave the word to make prisoners. Thereupon the survivors, not including however a larger number whom the soldiers concealed, were brought in alive. As for the three hundred who had broken through the guard in the night, the Syracusans sent in pursuit and seized them. The total of the public prisoners when collected was not great; for many were appropriated by the soldiers, and the whole of Sicily was full of them, they not having capitulated like the troops under Demosthenes. A large number also perished; the slaughter at the river being very great, quite as great as any which took place in the Sicilian war; and not a few had fallen in the frequent attacks which were made upon the Athenians during their march. Still many escaped, some at the time, others ran away after an interval of slavery, and all these found refuge at Catana.

The Syracusans and their allies collected their forces and returned with the spoil, and as many prisoners as they could take with them, into the city. The captive Athenians and allies they deposited in the quarries, which they thought would be the safest place of confinement. Nicias and Demosthenes they put to the sword, although against the will of Gylippus. For Gylippus thought that to carry home with him to Lacedaemon the generals of the enemy, over and above all his other successes, would be a brilliant triumph. One of them, Demosthenes, happened to be the greatest foe, and the other the greatest friend of the Lacedaemonians, both in the same matter of Pylos and Sphacteria. For Nicias had taken up their cause, and had persuaded the Athenians to make the peace which set at liberty the prisoners taken in the island. The Lacedaemonians were grateful to him for the service, and this was the main reason why he trusted Gylippus and surrendered himself to him. But certain Syracusans, who had been in communication with him, were afraid (such was the report) that on some suspicion of their guilt he might be put to the torture and bring trouble on them in the hour of their prosperity. Others, and especially the Corinthians, feared that, being rich, he might by bribery escape and do them further mischief. So the Syracusans gained the consent of the allies and had him executed. For these or the like reasons he suffered death. No one of the Hellenes in my time was less deserving of so miserable an end, for he lived in the practice of every virtue.

Those who were imprisoned in the quarries were at the beginning of their captivity harshly treated by the Syracusans. There were great numbers of them, and they were crowded in a deep and narrow place. At first the sun by day was still scorching and suffocating, for they had no roof over their heads, while the autumn nights were cold, and the extremes of temperature engendered violent disorders. Being cramped for room they had to do everything on the same spot. The corpses of those who died from their wounds, exposure to heat and cold, and the like, lay heaped one upon another. The smells were intolerable; and they were at the same time afflicted by hunger and thirst. During eight months they were allowed only about half a pint of water and a pint of food a day. Every kind of misery which could befall man in such a place befell them. This was the condition of all the captives for about ten weeks. At length the Syracusans sold them, with the exception of the Athenians and of any Sicilian or Italian Greeks who had sided with them in the war. The whole number of the public prisoners is not accurately known, but they were not less than seven thousand.

Of all the Hellenic actions which took place in this war, or indeed, as I think, of all Hellenic actions which are on record, this was the greatest—the most glorious to the victors, the most ruinous to the vanquished; for they were utterly and at all points defeated, and their sufferings were prodigious. Fleet and army perished from the face of the earth; nothing was saved, and of the many who went forth few returned home.

Thus ended the Sicilian expedition.

Cyrus Dies in Battle

by Xenophon

The *Anabasis (March Upcountry)* of Xenophon,
written nearly four centuries before the birth of
Christ, remains one of the great firsthand accounts of
war adventure. An Athenian, Xenophon had joined the
ten thousand Greek soldiers recruited by Cyrus the
Younger of Persia for an expedition against his brother
Artaxerxes. The *Anabasis* tells of Cyrus' death on September 3, 401 B.C., in the battle of Cunaxa (a small
Babylonian town on the Euphrates). It records the
subsequent massacre of the Greek commanders by the
Persians and then tells how Xenophon himself, elected
general, led this mercenary band on history's greatest
march—1500 fighting miles over rivers and mountains
and deserts to final safety at Trebizond on the Black
Sea. In this selection, Xenophon writes of the battle
that cost the young Cyrus his life.

H ence Cyrus proceeded through Babylonia three days' march, a distance of twelve parasangs [40 to 50 miles]: and at the end of the third day's march, he reviewed his army, both Greeks and Barbarians, in the plain about midnight; for he expected that with the ensuing dawn the king would come up with his army to offer him battle. He desired Clearchus to take command of the right wing, and Menon the Thessalian that of the left, while he himself drew up his own troops.

After the review, at the dawn of day, some deserters from the Great King came and gave Cyrus information respecting the royal army. Cyrus, assembling the generals and captains of the Greeks, consulted with them how he should conduct the engagement, and then encouraged them with the following exhortations:

"It is not, O Greeks, from any want of Barbarian forces that I take you with me as auxiliaries; but it is because I think you more efficient and valuable than a multitude of Barbarians that I have engaged you in my service. See, then, that you prove yourselves worthy of the liberty of which you are possessed, and for which I esteem you fortunate; for be well assured that I should prefer that freedom to all that I possess, and to other possessions many times as great.

"But that you may know to what sort of encounter you are advancing, I, from my own experience, will inform you. The enemy's numbers are immense, and they make their onset with a loud shout; but if you are firm against this, I feel ashamed to think what sort of men, in other respects, you find those in the country to be. But if you are true men, and prove yourselves stout-hearted, I will enable those of you who may wish to go home to return thither the envy of their fellow countrymen; but I think that I shall induce most of you to prefer the advantages of remaining with me to those in your own country."

Upon this, Gaulites, an exile from Samos, a man in the confidence of Cyrus, being present said, "Yet some say,

46

O Cyrus, that you make many promises now because you are in such a situation of approaching danger; but that if things should turn out well, you will not remember them; and some, too, say, that even if you have both the memory and the will, you will not have the power of bestowing all that you promise."

Hearing this, Cyrus said, "We have before us, my friends, the empire that was my father's, extending on the south to the parts where men cannot live for heat; and on the north to the parts where they cannot live for cold; and over all that lies between these extremes, the friends of my brother are now satraps. But if we conquer, it will be proper for us to make our own friends masters of these regions. So that it is not this that I fear, that I shall not have enough to give to each of my friends, if things turn out successfully, but that I shall not have friends enough to whom I may give it. And to each of you Greeks, I will also give a golden crown."

The Greeks who were present, when they heard these assurances, were much encouraged, and reported what he had said to the rest. The captains, too, and some others of the Greeks, went into his tent, desiring to know for certain what would be their reward if they should be victorious; and he did not let them go without satisfying the minds of all.

But all who conversed with him urged him not to engage in the battle personally, but take his station behind their line. About this time, also, Clearchus put a question to Cyrus to this effect: "And do you think, Cyrus, that your brother will come to battle with you?" "By Jupiter," replied Cyrus, "if he be indeed the son of Darius and Parysatis, and my brother, I shall not gain possession of these dominions without a struggle."

In mustering the Greeks under arms, their numbers were found to be ten thousand four hundred heavy-armed men and two thousand four hundred peltasts; of Barbarian troops under Cyrus there were one hundred thousand, with about twenty chariots armed with scythes.

Of the enemy the number was said to be one million two hundred thousand, with two hundred scythed chariots. There were, besides, six thousand cavalry, of whom Artagerses had the command; these were drawn up in front of the king himself. Of the royal army there were four commanders, or generals, or leaders, over each three hundred thousand men; that is to say Abrocomas, Tissaphernes, Gobryas, and Arbaces. But of this number only nine hundred thousand were present at the battle, and one hundred fifty scythed chariots; for Abrocomas, who was marching from Phoenicia, did not arrive till five days after the battle.

This information was brought to Cyrus by some of the enemy who deserted from the Great King before the battle; and such of the enemy as were taken prisoners after the battle gave the same account.

Hence Cyrus proceeded one day's march, a distance of three parasangs, with all his forces, as well Greek as Barbarian, drawn up in order of battle: for he expected that on this day the king would give him battle as about the middle of the day's march, there was a deep trench dug; the breadth of it was five fathoms, and the depth three. This ditch extended up through the plain, to the distance of twelve parasangs, as far as the wall of Media. Here are the canals which are supplied from the river Tigris; there are four of them each a plethrum in breadth, and very deep; boats employed in conveying corn sail along them. They discharge themselves into the Euphrates, are distant from each other one parasang, and there are bridges over them. Near the Euphrates was a narrow passage between the river and the trench, about twenty feet in breadth. This trench the Great King had made to serve as a defense, when he heard that Cyrus was marching against him. By this passage Cyrus and his army made their way, and got within the trench.

On this day the king did not come to an engagement, but there were to be seen many traces of men and horses in retreat.

Cyrus sent for Silanus, the Ambracian soothsayer, and gave him three thousand darics, because on the eleventh day previous, while sacrificing, he had told Cyrus that the king would not fight for ten days; when Cyrus exclaimed, "He will not then fight at all, if he does not fight within that time; but if you shall prove to have spoken truly, I promise to give you ten talents." This money, therefore, he now paid him, the ten days having elapsed.

As the king made no attempt at the trench to prevent the passage of Cyrus's army, it was thought both by Cyrus and the rest that he had given up the intention of fighting so that on the day following Cyrus proceeded on his march with less caution. On the day succeeding that, he pursued his journey seated in his chariot and having but a small body of troops in line before him; while the far greater part of the army observed no order on their march, and many of the soldiers' arms were carried on the wagons and beasts of burden.

IT WAS NOW ABOUT THE TIME OF FULL MARKET, and the station where he intended to halt was not far off, when Pategyas, a Persian, one of Cyrus' confidential adherents, made his appearance, riding at his utmost speed, with his horse in a sweat, and straightway called out to all whom he met, both in Persian and Greek, that the king was approaching with a vast army, prepared as for battle.

Immediately great confusion ensued; for the Greeks and all the rest imagined that he would fall upon them suddenly, before they could form their ranks; and Cyrus, leaping from his chariot, put on his breastplate, and, mounting his horse, took his javelin in his hand, and gave orders for all the rest to arm themselves and to take their stations each in his own place. They accordingly formed with all expedition: Clearchus occupying the extremity of the right wing close to the Euphrates, Proxenus being next to him, and after him the other captains in succession. Menon and his troops occupied the left wing of the Greeks.

Of the Barbarian forces, about one thousand Paphlagonian cavalry were stationed near Clearchus, and the Grecian peltasts on the right; and on the left was Ariaeus, Cyrus' lieutenant, with the rest of the Barbarian troops.

In the center was Cyrus, and with him about six hundred cavalry, the men all armed with breastplates, defenses for the thighs, and helmets, except Cyrus alone; for Cyrus presented himself for battle with his head unprotected. (It is said, too, that the other Persians expose themselves in battle with their heads uncovered.) All the horses of the cavalry that were with Cyrus had defensive armor on the forehead and breast, and the horsemen had also Grecian swords.

It was now midday, and the enemy was not yet in sight. But when it was afternoon, there appeared a dust, like a white cloud, and not long after, a sort of blackness, extending

49

to a great distance over the plain. Presently, as they approached nearer, brazen armor began to flash, and the spears and ranks became visible. There was a body of cavalry, in white armor, on the left of the enemy's line (Tissaphernes was said to have the command of them); close by these were troops with wicker shields; and next to them, heavy-armed soldiers with long wooden shields reaching to their feet (these were said to be Egyptians); then other cavalry and bowmen. These all marched according to their nations, each nation separately in a solid oblong. In front of their line, at considerable intervals from each other, were stationed the chariots called scythed chariots; they had scythes projecting obliquely from the axletree, and others under the driver's seat, pointing to the earth, for the purpose of cutting through whatever came in their way; and the design of them was to penetrate and divide the ranks of the Greeks.

As to what Cyrus had said, however, when, on calling together the Greeks, he exhorted them to sustain unmoved the shout of the Barbarians, he was in this respect deceived; for they now approached, not with a shout but with all possible silence, and quietly, with an even and slow step.

Cyrus in the meantime, riding by with Pigres the interpreter and three or four others, called out to Clearchus to lead his troops against the enemy's center, for there was the king; "and if," said he, "we are victorious in that quarter, our object is fully accomplished." But though Clearchus saw that close collection of troops in the center of the enemy's line and heard from Cyrus that the king was beyond the left of the Greeks (for so much the superior was the king in numbers that, while occupying the middle of his own line, he was still beyond Cyrus' left), nevertheless he was unwilling to draw off his right wing from the river, fearing lest he should be hemmed in on both sides; and in answer to Cyrus he said that he would take care that all should go well.

During this time the Barbarian army advanced with a uniform pace; and the Grecian line, still remaining in the same place, was gradually forming from those who came up from time to time. Cyrus, riding by at a moderate distance from his army, surveyed from thence both the lines, looking as well toward the enemy as to his own men.

Xenophon, an Athenian, perceiving him from the Grecian

line, rode up to meet him and inquired whether he had any commands; when Cyrus stopped his horse and told him, and desired him to tell everybody, that the sacrifices and the appearances of the victims were favorable. As he was saying this, he heard a murmur passing through the ranks, and asked what noise that was. He answered that it was the watchword, passing now for the second time. At which Cyrus wondered who had given it, and asked what the word was. He replied that it was "JUPITER THE PRESERVER and VICTORY." When Cyrus heard it, "I accept it as a good omen," said he, "and let it be so." Saying this, he rode away to his own station; and the two armies were now not more than three or four stadia distant from each other, when the Greeks sang the paean, and began to march forward to meet the enemy. And as, while they proceeded, some part of their body fluctuated out of line, those who were thus left behind began to run; and at the same time they all raised just such a shout as they usually raise to Mars, and the whole of them took to a running pace. Some say that they made a noise with their spears against their shields, to strike terror into the horses.

But the Barbarians, before an arrow could reach them, gave way and took to flight. The Greeks then pursued them with all their force, calling out to each other not to run but to follow in order. The chariots, abandoned by their drivers, were hurried, some through the midst of the enemies themselves and others through the midst of the Greeks. The Greeks, when they saw them coming, opened their ranks to let them pass; some few, however, were startled and caught by them, as might happen in a racecourse; but these, they said, suffered no material injury; nor did any other of the Greeks receive any hurt in this battle, except that on the left of their army a man was said to have been shot with an arrow.

Cyrus, though he saw the Greeks victorious and pursuing those of the enemies who were opposed to them, and though he felt great pleasure at the sight and was already saluted as king by those about him, was not, however, led away to join in the pursuit; but keeping the band of six hundred cavalry that were with him, drew up in a close order around him, he attentively watched how the king would proceed; for he well knew that he occupied the center of the Persian army. All the commanders of the Barbarians, indeed, lead their troops to battle occupying the center of their own men; thinking that they will thus be most secure, if they have the strength of their force on either side of them, and that if they have occasion to issue orders, their army will receive them in half the time.

On the present occasion, the king, though he occupied the center of his own army, was nevertheless beyond Cyrus' left wing. But as no enemy attacked him in front, or the troops that were drawn up before him, he began to wheel round, as if to inclose his adversaries. Cyrus, in consequence, fearing that he might take the Greeks in the rear and cut them in pieces, moved directly upon him, and charging with his six hundred horses, routed the troops that were stationed in front of the king, and put the guard of six thousand to flight, and is said to have killed with his own hand Artagerses, their commander.

When this flight of the enemy took place, Cyrus' six hundred became dispersed in the eagerness of pursuit; only a very few remaining with him, chiefly those who were called "partakers of his table."

While accompanied by these, he perceived the king and the close guard around him; when he immediately lost his self-command, and exclaiming, "I see the man," rushed upon him, struck him on the breast, and wounded him through the breastplate, as Ctesias the physician relates, stating that he himself dressed the wound.

As Cyrus was in the act of striking, someone hit him violently with a javelin under the eye; and how many of those about the king were killed (while they thus fought—the king, and Cyrus, and their respective followers in defense of each), Ctesias relates; for he was with him; on the other side, Cyrus himself was killed and eight of his principal officers lay dead upon his body. Artapates, the most faithful servant to him of all his scepter-bearers, when he saw Cyrus fall, is said to have leaped from his horse and thrown himself upon the body of his master; and some say that the king ordered someone to kill him on the body of Cyrus; but others relate that he drew his scimeter and killed himself upon the body; for he had a golden scimeter by his side, and also wore a chain and bracelets and other ornaments, like the noblest of the Persians, since he was honored by Cyrus for his attachment and fidelity to him.

THUS THEN DIED CYRUS; a man who, of all the Persians since Cyrus the elder, was the most princely and most worthy of empire, as is agreed by all who appear to have had personal knowledge of him. In the first place, while he was yet a boy, and when he was receiving his education with his brother and the other youths, he was thought to surpass them all in everything. For all the sons of the Persian nobles are educated at the gates of the king, where they may learn many a lesson of virtuous conduct but can see or hear nothing disgraceful. Here the boys see some honored by the king and others disgraced, and hear of them; so that in their very childhood they learn to govern and to obey.

Here Cyrus, first of all, showed himself most remarkable for modesty among those of his own age and for paying more ready obedience to his elders than even those who were inferior to him in station; and next, he was noticed for his fondness for horses and for managing them in a superior manner. They found him, too, very desirous of learning, and most assiduous in practicing the warlike exercises of archery and hurling the javelin. When it suited his age, he grew extremely fond of the chase, and of braving dangers in encounters with wild beasts. On one occasion he did not shrink from a she-bear that attacked him, but, in grappling with her, was dragged from off his horse and received some wounds, the scars of which were visible on his body, but at last killed her. The person who first came to his assistance he made a happy man in the eyes of many.

When he was sent down by his father, as satrap of Lydia and Great Phrygia and Cappadocia, and was also appointed commander of all the troops whose duty it is to muster in the plain of Castolus, he soon showed that if he made a league or compact with anyone, or gave a promise, he deemed it of the utmost importance not to break his word. Accordingly the states that were committed to his charge, as well as individuals, had the greatest confidence in him; and if anyone had been his enemy, he felt secure that if Cyrus entered into a treaty with him, he should suffer no infraction of the stipulations. When, therefore, he waged war against Tissaphernes, all the cities, of their own accord, chose to adhere to Cyrus in preference to Tissaphernes, except the Milesians; but they feared him because he would not abandon the cause of the exiles; for he both showed by his deeds, and declared in words, that he would never desert them, since he had once become a friend to them, not even though they should grow still fewer in number and be in a worse condition than they were.

Whenever anyone did him a kindness or an injury, he showed himself anxious to go beyond him in those respects, and some used to mention a wish of his, that he desired to live long enough to outdo both those who had done him good, and those who had done him ill, in the requital that he should make. Accordingly to him alone of the men of our days were so great a number of people desirous of committing the disposal of their property, their cities, and their own persons.

Yet no one could with truth say this of him, that he suffered the criminal or unjust to deride his authority; for he of all men inflicted punishment most unsparingly; and there were often to be seen, along the most frequented roads, men deprived of their feet, or hands, or eyes; so that in Cyrus' dominions it was possible for any one, Greek or Barbarian, who did no wrong, to travel without fear whithersoever he pleased and having with him whatever might suit his convenience.

To those who showed ability for war, it is acknowledged that he paid distinguished honor. His first war was with the Pisidians and Mysians; and, marching in person into these countries, he made those whom he saw voluntarily hazarding their lives in his service governors over the territory that he subdued, and distinguished them with rewards in other ways. So that the brave appeared to be the most fortunate of men, while the cowardly were deemed fit only to be their slaves. There were, therefore, great numbers of persons who voluntarily exposed themselves to danger wherever they thought that Cyrus would become aware of their exertions.

With regard to justice, if any appeared to him inclined to display that virtue, he made a point of making such men richer than those who sought to profit by injustice. Accordingly, while in many other respects his affairs were administered judiciously, he likewise possessed an army worthy of the name. For it was not for money that generals and captains came from foreign lands to enter into his service, but because they were persuaded that to serve Cyrus well would be more profitable than any amount of monthly pay.

Besides, if anyone executed his orders in a superior

manner, he never suffered his diligence to go unrewarded; consequently, in every undertaking, the best-qualified officers were said to be ready to assist him.

If he noticed anyone that was a skillful manager, with strict regard to justice, stocking the land of which he had the direction and securing income from it, he would never take anything from such a person, but was ever ready to give him something in addition; so that men labored with cheerfulness, acquired property with confidence, and made no concealment from Cyrus of what each possessed; for he did not appear to envy those who amassed riches openly, but to endeavor to bring into use the wealth of those who concealed it.

Whatever friends he made, and felt to be well-disposed to him, and considered to be capable of assisting him in anything that he might wish to accomplish, he is acknowledged by all to have been most successful in attaching them to him. For, on the very same account on which he thought that he himself had need of friends—namely, that he might have cooperators in his undertakings—did he endeavor to prove an efficient assistant to his friends in whatever he perceived any of them desirous of effecting.

He received, for many reasons, more presents than perhaps any other single individual; and these he outdid everyone else in distributing among his friends, having a view to the character of each, and to what he perceived each most needed. Whatever presents anyone sent him of articles of personal ornament, whether for warlike accouterment or merely for dress, concerning these, they said he used to remark that he could not decorate his own person with them all, but that he thought friends well equipped were the greatest ornament a man could have.

That he should outdo his friends, indeed, in conferring great benefits is not at all wonderful, since he was so much more able; but that he should surpass his friends in kind attentions and anxious desire to oblige appears to me far more worthy of admiration. Frequently, when he had wine served him of a peculiarly fine flavor, he would send half-emptied flagons of it to some of his friends, with a message to this effect: "Cyrus has not for some time met with pleasanter wine than this; and he has therefore sent some of it to you, and begs you will drink it today, with those whom you love best." He would often, too, send geese partly eaten, and the halves of loaves and other such things, desiring the bearer to say, in presenting them, "Cyrus has been delighted with these, and therefore wishes you also to taste of them."

Wherever provender was scarce, but he himself, from having many attendants, and from the care which he took was able to procure some, he would send it about and desire his friends to give that provender to the horses that carried them, so that hungry steed might not carry his friends. Whenever he rode out, and many were likely to see him, he would call to him his friends and hold earnest conversation with them, that he might show whom he held in honor; so that, from what I have heard, I should think that no one was ever beloved by a greater number of persons, either Greeks or Barbarians. Of this fact the following is a proof; that no one deserted to the king from Cyrus, though only a subject (except that Orontes attempted to do so; but he soon found the person whom he believed faithful to him more a friend to Cyrus than to himself), while many came over to Cyrus from the king after they became enemies to each other, and these, too, men who were greatly beloved by the king; for they felt persuaded that if they proved themselves brave soldiers under Cyrus, they would obtain from him more adequate rewards for their services than from the king.

What occurred also at the time of his death is a great proof, as well that he himself was a man of merit as that he could accurately distinguish such as were trustworthy, well-disposed, and constant in their attachment. For when he was killed, all his friends and the partakers of his table who were with him fell fighting in his defense, except Ariaeus, who had been posted in command of the cavalry on the left; and, when he learned that Cyrus had fallen in the battle, he took to flight, with all the troops which he had under his command.

THE HEAD AND RIGHT HAND of Cyrus were then cut off. The king and the troops that were with him, engaging in pursuit, fell upon the camp of Cyrus; when the soldiers of Ariaeus no longer stood their ground but fled through their camp to the station whence they had last started, which was said to be four parasangs distant.

The king and his followers seized upon many other things, and also captured the Phocaean woman, the mistress of Cyrus, who was said to be both accomplished and beautiful. His younger mistress, a native of Miletus, being taken by some of the king's soldiers, fled for refuge, without her outer garment, to the party of Greeks, who were stationed under arms to guard the baggage, and who, drawing themselves up for defense, killed several of the pillagers; and some of their own number also fell; yet they did not flee, and saved not only the woman but all the rest of the property and people that were in their quarters.

The king and the main body of Greeks were now distant from each other about thirty stadia, the Greeks pursuing those that had been opposed to them, as if they had conquered all; the Persians engaged in plundering, as if they were wholly victorious. But when the Greeks found that the king with his troops was among their baggage; and the king, on the other hand, heard from Tissaphernes that the Greeks had routed that part of his line which had been opposed to them and were gone forward in pursuit, the king, on his part, collected his forces and formed them in line again; while Clearchus, on the other side, calling to him Proxenus, who happened to be nearest to him, consulted with him whether they should send a detachment to the camp or proceed, all of them together, to relieve it.

In the meantime, the king was observed again approaching them, as it seemed, in their rear. The Greeks, wheeling round, prepared to receive him in the belief that he would attack them on that quarter; the king, however, did not lead his troops that way, but led them off by the same route by which he had before passed on the outside of their left wing; taking with him both those who had deserted to the Greeks during the engagement and Tissaphernes with the troops under his command.

Tissaphernes had not fled at the commencement of the engagement, but had charged through the Greek peltasts, close to the banks of the river. In breaking through, however, he killed not a single man—for the Greeks, opening their ranks, struck his men with their swords and hurled their javelins at them. Episthenes of Amphipolis had the command of the peltasts and was said to have proved himself an able captain. Tissaphernes, therefore, when he thus came off with disadvantage, did not turn back again, but, proceeding onward to the Grecian camp, met the king there; and thence

57

they now returned together with their forces united in battle array. When they were opposite the left wing of the Greeks, the Greeks feared lest they should attack them on that wing, and, inclosing them on both sides, should cut them off; they therefore thought it advisable to draw back this wing and to put the river in their rear. While they were planning this maneuver, the king, having passed beyond them, presented his force opposite to them, in the same form in which he had at first come to battle; and when the Greeks saw their enemies close at hand and drawn up for fight, they again sang the paean, and advanced upon them with much greater spirit than before. The Barbarians, on the other hand, did not await their onset, but fled sooner than at first; and the Greeks pursued them as far as a certain village, where they halted; for above the village was a hill upon which the king's troops had checked their flight, and though there were no longer any infantry there, the height was filled with cavalry; so that the Greeks could not tell what was doing. They said that they saw the royal standard, a golden eagle upon a spear, with expanded wings.

But as the Greeks were on the point of proceeding thither, the cavalry too left the hill; not indeed in a body, but some in one direction and some in another; and thus the hill was gradually thinned of cavalry, till at last they were all gone. Clearchus, however, did not march up the hill, but, stationing his force at its foot, sent Lycius the Syracusan and another up the hill and ordered them, after taking a view from the summit, to report to him what was passing on the other side. Lycius accordingly rode thither, and having made his observations, brought word that the enemy were fleeing with precipitation. Just as these things took place, the sun set.

Here the Greeks halted and, piling their arms, took some rest; and at the same time they wondered that Cyrus himself nowhere made his appearance, and that no one else came to them from him; for they did not know that he was killed, but conjectured that he was either gone in pursuit of the enemy or had pushed forward to secure some post. They then deliberated whether they should remain in that spot and fetch their baggage thither or return to the camp; and it was resolved to return, and they arrived at the tents about suppertime.

Such was the conclusion of this day.

The Second Invasion of England

by Julius Caesar

With what his valor did enrich his wit,
His wit set down to make his valor live;
Death makes no conquest of this conqueror,
For now he lives in fame, though not in life.

—thus did William Shakespeare write of Julius Caesar. A contemporary American professor, Charles E. Bennett, puts it this way: "He was general, statesman, orator and man of letters; and in each of these fields he displayed consummate genius. His military campaigns have evoked the admiration of masters of the art of war. His statesmanship brought order out of anarchy. As an orator he was magnetic. As a man of letters he has left us accounts . . . admirable for their directness and luminous simplicity of statement. His essential qualities were those of a man of action—clearness of vision, promptness of decision, energy in execution and indefatigable perseverence. Needless cruelty and bloodshed at times stained his conduct, but these cannot obscure the greatness of his personality or essentially alter the measure of his achievements." In this selection, one of the great men of all time tells of his second invasion of Britain during the summer of 54 B.C.

In the consulship of Lucius Domitius and Appius Claudius, on the eve of my departure for Italy (a journey I had been making annually for the past few years), I directed my staff to arrange for the building of as many ships as possible during the winter and to have the old ones repaired. Detailed instructions were left for the dimensions and shape of these new vessels. To simplify loading and beaching they were to be constructed with a somewhat lower freeboard than that commonly used in the Mediterranean, especially as I had noticed that, owing to the frequent ebb and flow of tides, the waves in the Channel are comparatively small. To allow for heavy cargoes, including numerous pack-animals, they were to be rather wider in the beam than those used in other waters; and all were to be fitted with sails as well as oars, an arrangement which was greatly facilitated by their low freeboard. Materials for their equipment were ordered from Spain.

After concluding the assizes in northern Italy I started for Illyricum because of reports that the Pirustae were raiding over the adjacent frontier and causing serious damage in that province. On arrival I ordered the native states to levy troops, and named a place for their assembly; the Pirustae, however, got news of this and sent representatives to say that none of the raids had the authority of their government, which was ready to make full reparation. I accepted their assurance and demanded hostages, but made it quite clear that unless they were handed over by a fixed date it would mean war.

The hostages were punctually delivered, and arbitrators were then appointed to assess the damage suffered by the various tribes and to decide what reparation was due.

After disposing of that business and holding assizes, I returned to northern Italy and from there started back to rejoin the army. Soon after my arrival in Gaul I began a tour of the winter camps and found that, notwithstanding grave shortage of materials, the troops had worked so hard that there were about six hundred ships of the types described, including eighteen transports, ready for launching in a few days. After congratulating the men and those in charge of the work, I gave instructions that all vessels were to assemble at Boulogne, which had been found by experience to be the most convenient starting-point for the Channel crossing, being some twenty-eight miles from the coast of Britain. Sufficient troops were left to carry out these orders while I started with four legions in light marching order and eight hundred cavalry for the Moselle basin where, according to reports, the Treveri were defying orders by absenting themselves from the annual Gallic diets [legislative assemblies] and were making overtures to the Germans beyond the Rhine.

The Treveri, it will be remembered, are a Rhineland tribe: they have the most powerful cavalry corps in Gaul as well as strong forces of infantry, and two of their chieftains—Indutiomarus and Cingetorix—were at this time contending for supreme authority. Directly Cingetorix learned of our approach he paid me a visit, emphasized that he and his followers intended to support the Roman alliance, and gave me an account of the state of affairs in his country. Indutiomarus, on the other hand, began preparing for war: he assembled forces of cavalry and infantry and concealed all those above or below military age in the great forest of Ardennes, which stretches from the Rhine through Treveran territory to the eastern borders of Champagne. However, some of his most important followers, influenced by their personal friendship with Cingetorix and frightened by the approach of a Roman army, came to meet me. They said there was nothing they could do to help their country, and made certain requests with an eye to their personal interests. Indutiomarus now feared complete isolation: he sent representatives who apologized on behalf of their chief for his failure to put in an appearance, and explained that his presence at home was necessary to ensure the loyalty of his subjects. If every man of rank, the message went on, were to make this journey, there was danger that the ignorant masses might be led astray. As it was, he had everything under control and intended, subject to my approval, to visit me in camp, where he would place himself and his tribe under my protection.

The motive behind this statement was clear enough; it was obvious, too, what prevented him going ahead with his original design: but I did not want to have to spend the whole summer in that part of the world when arrangements for the British expedition were complete. I therefore ordered Indutiomarus to present himself with two hundred hostages, naming in particular his son and all his near relatives. They arrived in due course, and I told him he had nothing to fear so long as he remained loyal. At the same time, however, I summoned other dignitaries of the tribe and won them over individually to Cingetorix. He fully deserved this expression of confidence; but there were also diplomatic reasons for strengthening the authority of a man of such distinguished loyalty. Indutiomarus, however, was mortally offended by the gesture, which struck at his own power and fanned the flames of animosity which he already felt toward Rome.

After settling that matter we made our way back to Boulogne and found that sixty ships built on the lower Marne had been driven off their course by a storm and had returned to their starting point; the rest were in commission and ready to sail. The entire Gallic cavalry corps of four thousand horse now assembled at the port, as well as the most prominent citizens from every state. Being afraid of a rising in Gaul during my absence, I had decided to leave behind only a few of these men, whose loyalty was beyond question, and to take the others as hostages.

Among these Gallic leaders was the notorious Dumnorix. I was resolved from the start to keep this man with me, knowing him to be at heart a revolutionary, ambitious, brave, and highly respected by his fellow Gauls. Furthermore, he had stated in the Aeduan council that I had offered to make him ruler of the tribe, a claim which the Aedui strongly resented: they had not dared to send an open rejection of, or even to protest against, such a proposal, but I learned the truth from some friends at whose house I had stayed. At all events, Dumnorix began by pressing for leave to remain in Gaul: he said he was not used to sailing and was frightened of the sea; also that religious obligations made his presence at home absolutely essential. When he realized I was adamant and there was no chance of getting his own way, he approached the Gallic chiefs, talked with them privately one by one and urged them to remain on the Continent. He argued that I must have some ulterior motive in robbing Gaul of all her leading citizens: no doubt I shrank from putting them to death openly in their own country and therefore meant to do so as soon as I got them over to Britain. He suggested that they should all bind themselves by oath to work together for a better Gaul.

The foregoing information was derived from various sources; and because of my very high regard for the Aedui I came to the conclusion that Dumnorix must at all costs be restrained and prevented from achieving his ends. Since his fanaticism was going from bad to worse, precautions were necessary to forestall an attempt on my own life and possible damage to Roman interests. We were detained at Boulogne for just over three weeks by the prevailing northwest winds, and in the meantime I did my best to hold Dumnorix to his allegiance while keeping myself informed of his every move. The bad weather eventually lifted: all troops were ordered to embark, and while this operation was proceeding Dumnorix left camp without my knowledge at the head of some Aeduan horse. He made straight for home: but directly his escape was reported I postponed the sailing date, laid aside all other business, and sent a strong cavalry detachment in pursuit. Their orders were to bring him back alive unless he refused and offered resistance, in which case he was to be killed; for a man who flouted my authority to my face could clearly not be trusted to behave like a rational being behind my back. When called on to halt he resisted violently, appealing to the loyalty of his followers, and shouting over and over again: "I'm a free citizen of a free state!" The man was surrounded and killed according to instructions, and his Aeduan escort returned to camp.

Labienus remained on the Continent with three legions and two thousand cavalry: he was to guard the two ports, arrange food supplies, and keep an eye upon events in Gaul. Other measures were left to his discretion. Shortly before sunset [probably July 6, 54 B.C.] I sailed with five legions and two thousand cavalry; there was a light southwest wind, but about midnight it dropped. The tide carried us right off our course, and at dawn the coast of Britain appeared receding on our port quarter. As soon as the tide turned we rowed hard with it so as to make that part of the island where the best landing points were found last year. The soldiers worked splendidly, and by continuous rowing they enabled the heavily laden transports to keep up with the warships. The whole fleet reached Britain at about noon, but the enemy was nowhere to be seen. We therefore disembarked and chose a site for the camp. Some prisoners revealed that a large native force had originally concentrated on the beaches, but had withdrawn and hidden themselves at Bigbury Woods when they saw the numbers of our fleet. More than eight hundred ships, indeed, must have been visible at once, if one includes those which had survived last year's expedition and some privately owned vessels. We began moving inland just after midnight, leaving ten battalions and three hundred cavalry under Quintus Atrius to guard the fleet. No anxiety was felt about the ships, as they lay at anchor on a nice open shore. A night march of about twelve miles brought us to the Great Stour, within sight of the enemy forces. They came down with cavalry and war chariots and, by attacking from higher ground, tried to bar our passage of the river. Repulsed by our cavalry, they retired in the woods where they had a strongly fortified position of great natural strength. It had no doubt been prepared for some war among themselves, for every entrance was blocked by a mass of felled trees. Scattered parties of them came out to fight, and tried to prevent us breaking into the defenses; but troops of the Seventh Legion, working under cover of interlocked shields, piled up lumber against the fortifications, stormed the position, and drove them from the woods at the cost of only a few minor casualties. I would not allow them to pursue far; the ground was unfamiliar, and I was anxious to use the few remaining hours of daylight for entrenching the camp. Early next day, however, a light force of infantry and cavalry was sent out in three columns to overtake the fugitives. They had gone some way, and only their rearguard was visible, when some troopers arrived with news from Atrius. It appeared that a great storm overnight had wrecked nearly all the ships or cast them ashore: the anchors and cables had parted, seamen and pilots had been helpless, and heavy damage had been suffered as a result of collision.

After giving orders for the recall of our task force I went back to the coast, and found the news only too true: about forty ships were a total loss: the remainder could be repaired, but it would mean a very big job. Skilled workmen were called out from the legions, others were summoned from Gaul, and I wrote to Labienus directing him to build as many ships as he could with the troops at his disposal. Meanwhile it was decided to have all vessels beached and enclosed with the camp in a single line of fortifications: it seemed the best thing to do in spite of the enormous labor involved. Actually the work took ten days to complete with the men working day and night.

As soon as the ships were beached and the camp strongly fortified I returned inland, leaving the same guard as before, and on arrival discovered that larger British forces had assembled under Cassivellaunus. This chieftain's territory lies some seventy-five miles from the sea and is divided from the coastal districts by the river Thames. Until then he had been almost continually at war with the other tribes, but owing to the general alarm inspired by our arrival they had unanimously agreed to confer upon him the supreme command.

The enemy horse and chariots engaged in a fierce running fight with our cavalry, but we had the better of them everywhere and forced them back with heavy casualties into the woods and hills. We suffered a few losses, too, in consequence of a reckless pursuit.

It was not long, however, before the Britons caught us off our guard during the work of entrenchment. They rushed unexpectedly from the woods, attacked the outposts which were stationed in front of the camp, and some heavy fighting ensued. The first and second battalions of two legions went to the rescue and took up positions quite close together; but the troops were unnerved by these strange tactics, and the enemy with amazing dash broke through the gap and retreated to safety. They were eventually driven off by throwing in more battalions. That day Quintus Laberius Durus, one of our battalion commanders, lost his life.

Throughout this peculiar engagement, which took place in full view of the camp, it was evident that our troops were too heavily armed; they could not follow up when their opponents gave ground, and they dared not abandon their regular formation. The cavalry, too, had an extremely dangerous task. Every now and then the charioteers fell back on purpose, drew them away from the legions, then jumped down and re-engaged them on foot with the odds heavily in their own favor. Besides, they never fought in close order, but always in wide-open formation with reserves posted at strategic points, so that one unit covered another's retreat and fresh vigorous men took the place of their exhausted comrades.

Next day the enemy took up a position on the hills some considerable distance from the camp. Small groups appeared and began to harass our cavalry, though with not quite the same spirit as on the preceding day. However, I had sent out a foraging party consisting of three legions under a general officer, Caius Trebonius, and at midday the natives made a concerted attack, pressing right up to the companies on guard. The latter repulsed them in a furious counterattack and maintained pressure until the cavalry, heartened by the sight of the legions, who were moving up to their support, made a charge which drove the Britons in headlong flight and gave them no chance to close their ranks, to stand firm, or to jump from their chariots. In consequence of this defeat, reinforcements sent by the neighboring tribes dispersed, and the Britons never again fought us in a general action.

On learning the enemy's plan, we moved up in full strength to the Thames, preparatory to entering Cassivellaunus' dominions. The river can be forded at only one point and even there the crossing was difficult. Large native forces appeared in battle order on the far bank, which was also defended by a line of pointed stakes; and some deserters in our custody revealed that more of these obstacles were planted under water in the riverbed. The cavalry were sent over first, the infantry being ordered to follow soon afterward; but the legionaries dashed through with such speed (though only their heads were above water) that they were over as soon as the mounted troops. The Britons, overpowered by this combined attack, fled from the bank.

Cassivellaunus had now given up the idea of fighting a pitched battle. He disbanded most of his forces, and followed our line of march with some four thousand chariots. Keeping off the main route under cover of dense thickets, he drove the inhabitants and their cattle from the open country into the woods wherever he knew that we should pass. If our cavalry ranged too far to plunder and devastate the neighborhood they were in grave danger from native chariots sent out from the woods to engage them. In face of this threat they could not go far afield: I was obliged to keep them in touch with the main column and be content with such damage as we could do by ravaging and burning the countryside within reach of the legions.

Meanwhile envoys had arrived from the Trinovantes, who were about the strongest tribe in that area. One of their princes, a young man named Mandubracius, had come over to the Continent and put himself under my protection: he had fled for his life when his father, King of Trinovantes, was assassinated by Cassivellaunus. The envoys promised submission and obedience to my orders: they asked me to defend Mandubracius against the malice of Cassivellaunus, and to send him back an independent ruler of his people. I demanded forty hostages and a supply of grain for the troops. These were promptly delivered, and Mandubracius returned home.

When it became known that the Trinovantes were securely protected and suffered no harm from our troops, five more tribes from southern and eastern Britain sent delegations and submitted. They told me we were not far from Cassivellaunus' stronghold, which was strategically placed among woods and marshland, and that large numbers of men and cattle were gathered there.

Incidentally, the Britons call a "stronghold" any densely wooded spot fortified with a rampart and trench and used as a refuge against attack by marauding bands.

I started for this place with the legions, and notwithstanding its superb natural defenses, which had been improved by strong fortifications, we proceeded to the assault on two sides. After a very brief resistance the enemy gave way and escaped on another side. Great quantities of cattle were found there and many of the fugitives were overtaken and killed.

During these operations Cassivellaunus sent envoys to the four Kentish rulers: Cingetorix, Carvilius, Taximagulus, and Legovax, directing them to make a surprise assault on our naval base. As soon as their forces appeared the garrison attacked from the gates, killed many of them, took prisoner one of their leaders, a chieftain named Lugotorix, and retired without loss. The news of this engagement found Cassivellaunus already perturbed by his many reverses, by the devastation of his country, and above all by the defection of his allies. Acting through Commius, he sent a delegation to discuss terms of surrender. I had decided to winter on the Continent for fear of sudden risings in Gaul; besides, summer was nearly over, and it was clear that the enemy could easily hold out for the rest of the campaigning season: so I demanded hostages, fixed the annual tribute payable from Britain into the Roman treasure, and strictly forbade Cassivellaunus to interfere with Mandubracius and the Trinovantes. After receiving these hostages we returned to the coast. The ships had been repaired and were now launched; but since we had numerous prisoners, and some vessels had become a total loss in the recent storm, I decided to make the return voyage in two trips. It is worth noting that of the large fleets which had made so many voyages in the past twelve months not one ship with troops on board was lost. As for the empty vessels, which included those on their way back from Gaul after disembarking the first contingent, and the sixty ships newly constructed under Labienus' supervision, very few of them reached their destination: the majority were forced back to land by bad weather. We awaited them for some time in vain, until the approach of the equinox threatened to prevent our sailing at all, and there was nothing for it but to embark in what ships we had, though this necessitated a good deal of overloading. But a dead calm set in; we weighed anchor a little after 9 P.M., and the whole fleet reached land safely at dawn.

Saint Louis Goes on Crusade

by Jean de Joinville

Crusades is the name given those military expedi-
tions by which Medieval Christendom sought to recover the Holy Land from the Moslems. There were
eight crusades, covering a period of two centuries,
1096–1291, and though they commenced with true
spiritual zeal and with victory, they ended in political
or commercial venality and defeat. The last two were
led by Louis IX of France, one of the few kings canon-
ized by the Catholic Church. Here, in the words of
Jean de Joinville, the companion and biographer of
St. Louis, is the journal of that Seventh Crusade in the
years 1249–1250.

At Easter, in the year of grace that stood at 1248, I summoned my men, and all who held fiefs from me, to Joinville; and on the vigil of the said Easter, when all the people that I had summonded were assembled, was born my son John, Lord of Ancerville, by my first wife, the sister of the Count of Grandpré. All that week we feasted and danced, and my brother, the Lord of Vaucouleurs, and the other rich men who were there, gave feasts on the Monday, the Tuesday, the Wednesday and the Thursday.

On the Friday I said to them: "Lords, I am going oversea, and I know not whether I shall ever return. Now come forward; if I have done you any wrong, I will make it good, as I have been used to do, dealing, each in turn, with such as have any claim to make against me, or my people." So I dealt with each, according to the opinions of the men on my lands; and in order that I might not weigh upon their debate, I retired from the council, and agreed, without objection raised, to what they recommended.

Because I did not wish to take away with me one penny wrongfully gotten, therefore I went to Metz, in Lorraine, and placed in pawn the greater part of my land. And you must know that on the day when I left our country to go to the Holy Land, I did not hold more than one thousand livres [say $4000 of our money] a year in land, for my lady mother was still alive; and yet I went, taking with me nine knights and being the first of three knights-banneret. And I bring these things to your notice so that you may understand that if God, who never yet failed me, had not come to my help, I should hardly have maintained myself for so long a space as the six years that I remained in the Holy Land.

As I was preparing to depart, John, Lord of Apremont and Count of Sarrebruck in his wife's right, sent to tell me he had settled matters to go oversea, taking ten knights, and proposed, if I so willed, that we should hire a ship between him and me; and I consented. His people and mine hired a ship at Marseilles. . . .

In the month of August we entered into our ship at the Roche-de-Marseille. On the day that we entered into our ship, they opened the door of the ship and put therein all the horses we were to take oversea; and then they reclosed the door, and caulked it well, as when a cask is sunk in water, because, when the ship is on the high seas, all the said door is under water.

When the horses were in the ship, our master mariner called to his seamen, who stood at the prow, and said: "Are you ready?" and they answered, "Aye, sir—let the clerks and priests come forward!" As soon as these had come forward, he called to them, "Sing, for God's sake!" and they all, with one voice, chanted: *"Veni Creator Spiritus."*

Then he cried to his seamen, "Unfurl the sails, for God's sake!" and they did so.

In a short space the wind filled our sails and had borne us out of sight of land, so that we saw naught save sky and water, and every day the wind carried us further from the land where we were born. And these things I tell you, that you may understand how foolhardy is that man who dares, having other's chattels in his possession, or being in mortal sin, to place himself in such peril, seeing that, when you lie down to sleep at night on shipboard, you lie down not knowing whether, in the morning, you may find yourself at the bottom of the sea.

At sea a singular marvel befell us; for we came across a mountain, quite round, before the coast of Barbary. We came across it about the hour of vespers, and sailed all night, and thought to have gone about fifty leagues; and, on the morrow, we found ourselves before the same mountain; and this same thing happened to us some two or three times. When the sailors saw this, they were all amazed, and told us we were in very great peril; for we were nigh unto the land of the Saracens of Barbary.

Then spake a certain right worthy priest, who was called the Dean of Maurupt; and he told us that never had any mischance occurred in his parish—whether lack of water, or overplus of rain, or any other mischance—but so soon as he had made three processions, on three Saturdays, God and His mother sent them deliverance. It was then a Saturday. We made the first procession round the two masts of the ship. I

had myself carried in men's arms, because I was grievously
sick. Never again did we see the mountain; and on the third
Saturday we came to Cyprus. . . .

IT WAS SETTLED that the king should land on the Friday
before Trinity and do battle with the Saracens, unless they
refused to stand. The king ordered my Lord John of Beaumont to assign a galley to my Lord Everard of Brienne and
to myself, so as that we might land, we and our knights, because the great ships could not get close up to the shore.

As God so willed, when I returned to my ship, I found
a little ship that my Lady of Beyrout, who was cousin-german
to my Lord of Montbeliard and to myself, had given me, and
that carried eight of my horses.

When the Friday came I and my Lord Everard went,
fully armed, to the king and asked for the galley; whereupon
my Lord John of Beaumont told us that we should not have
it. When our people saw that they would get no galley, they
let themselves drop from the great ship into the ship's boat,
pell-mell, and as best they could, so that the boat began to
sink. The sailors saw that the boat was sinking, little by little,
and they escaped into the big ship and left my knights in the
boat. I asked the master how many more people there were in
the boat than the boat could hold. He told me twenty men-at-
arms; and I asked him whether he could take our people to
land if I relieved him of so many, and he said "Yes." So I relieved him in such sort that in three journeys he took them
to the ship that had carried my horses.

When I came back to my ship I put into my little boat
a squire whom I made a knight, and whose name was my
Lord Hugh of Vaucouleurs, and two very valiant bachelors—
of whom the one had name my Lord Villain of Versey, and
the other my Lord William of Dammartin—who were at bitter enmity the one against the other. Nor could any one make
peace between them, because they had seized each other by
the hair in Morea. And I made them forgive their grievances
and embrace, for I swore to them on holy relics that we should
not land in company of their enmity.

Then we set ourselves to get to land, and came alongside
of the barge belonging to the king's great ship, where the
king himself was. And his people began to cry out to us, be-

cause we were going more quickly than they, that I should land by the ensign of St. Denis, which was being borne in another vessel before the king. But I heeded them not, and caused my people to land in front of a great body of Turks, at a place where there were full six thousand men on horseback.

So soon as these saw us land, they came toward us, hotly spurring. We, when we saw them coming, fixed the points of our shields into the sand and the handles of our lances in the sand with the points set towards them. But when they were so near that they saw the lances about to enter into their bellies, they turned about and fled. . . .

When the king heard tell that the ensign of St. Denis was on shore he went across his ship with large steps; and maugre [in spite of] the legate who was with him he would not leave from following the ensign, but leapt into the sea, which was up to his armpits. So he went, with his shield hung to his neck, and his helmet on his head, and his lance in his hand, till he came to his people who were on the shore. When he reached the land, and looked upon the Saracens, he asked what people they were, and they told him they were Saracens; and he put his lance to his shoulder, and his shield before him, and would have run in upon the Saracens if the right worthy men who were about him would have suffered it.

The Saracens sent thrice to the soldan, by carrier-pigeons, to say that the king had landed, but never received any message in return, because the soldan's sickness was upon him. Wherefore they thought that the soldan was dead, and abandoned Damietta. The king sent a knight forward to know if it was sooth that Damietta was so abandoned. The knight returned to the king and said it was sooth and that he had been into the houses of the soldan. Then the king sent for the legate and all the prelates of the host, and all chanted with a loud voice *Te deum laudamus*. Afterwards the king mounted his horse, and we all likewise, and we went and encamped before Damietta.

Very unadvisedly did the Turks leave Damietta, in that they did not cut the bridge of boats, for that would have been a great hindrance to us; but they wrought us very much hurt in setting fire to the bazaar, where all the merchandise is collected, and everything that is sold by weight. The damage that followed from this was as great as if—which God forbid!—someone were, tomorrow, to set fire to the Petit-Pont in Paris.

Now let us declare that God Almighty was very gracious to us when He preserved us from death and peril on our disembarkation, seeing that we landed on foot and affronted our enemies who were mounted. Great grace did our Lord also show us when He delivered Damietta into our hands, for otherwise we could only have taken it by famine, and of this we may be fully assured, for it was by famine that King John had taken it in the days of our fathers [1219]. . . .

Now LET US GO BACK to the matter in hand, and tell how, shortly after we had taken Damietta, all the horsemen of the soldan came before the camp, and attacked it from the land side. The king and all the horsemen armed themselves. I, being in full armor, went to speak to the king, and found him fully armed, sitting on a settle, and round him were the right worthy knights belonging to his own division, all in full armor. I asked if he desired that I and my people should not fall upon our tents. When my Lord John of Beaumont heard my question, he cried to me in a very loud voice, and commanded me, in the king's name, not to leave my quarters till the king so ordered.

I have told you of the right worthy knights who were of the king's special following, for there were eight of them, all good knights who had won prizes for arms on the further or hither side of the seas, and such knights it was customary to call good knights. These are the names of the knights about the king:—my Lord Geoffry of Sargines, my Lord Matthew of Marly, my Lord Philip of Nanteuil, and my Lord Imbert of Beaujeu, Constable of France; but the last was not then present, he was outside the camp—he and the master of the crossbowmen, with most of the king's sergeants-at-arms—to guard the camp so that the Turks might not do any mischief thereto.

Now it happened that my Lord Walter of Autrèche got himself armed at all points in his pavilion; and when he was mounted upon his horse, with his shield at his neck and his helmet on his head, he caused the flaps of his pavilion to be lifted, and struck spurs into his horse to ride against the Turks;

and as he left his pavilion, all alone, all his men shouted with a loud voice, "*Chatillon.*" But so it chanced that or ever he came up to the Turks he fell, and his horse flew over his body; and the horse went on, covered with his arms, to our enemies, because the Saracens were, for the most part, mounted on mares, for which reason the horse drew to the side of the Saracens.

And those who looked on told us that four Turks came by Lord Walter, who lay upon the ground, and as they went by, gave him great blows with their maces there where he lay. Then did the Constable of France and several of the king's sergeants deliver him, and they brought him back in their arms to his pavilion. When he came there he was speechless. Several of the surgeons and physicians of the host went to him, and because it did not seem to them that he was in danger of death, they had him blooded in both arms.

That night, very late, my Lord Aubert of Narcy proposed that we should go and see him, for as yet we had not seen him, and he was a man of great name and of great valour. We entered into his pavilion, and the chamberlain came to meet us, and asked us to move quietly, so as not to wake his master. We found him lying on coverlets of miniver, and went to him very softly, and found him dead. When this was told to the king, he replied that he would not willingly have a thousand such men acting contrary to his orders as this man had done. . . .

AT THE BEGINNING OF ADVENT the king set out with his host to go towards Babylon, as the Count of Artois had advised. Pretty near to Damietta we found a stream that issued from the main stream, and it was decided that the host should remain there a day to dam up the said arm of the stream, so that we might pass. The thing was done pretty easily, for we dammed the said arm close to the main stream in such sort that the water flowed pretty easily along the main stream. At our passage over the arm, the soldan sent five hundred of his knights, the best mounted that he could find in all his host, to harass the host of the king, and delay our march.

On St. Nicholas Day (6th December 1249) the king commanded that we should prepare to ride forward, and forbade that anyone should be so bold as to attack the said Saracens.

Now it happened that when the host began to move forward, and the Saracens saw that no attack was to be made upon them—and they knew by their spies that the king had forbidden it—they waxed bold, and attacked the Templars who formed the van; and one of the Turks bore a knight of the Temple to the earth, right before the horse-hoofs of brother Renaud of Vichiers, who was then Marshal of the Temple. When the marshal saw this, he cried to his brother Templars: "Out on them for God's sake! I cannot brook this!" He struck his spurs into his horse, and all the host with him. The horses of our people were fresh, and the horses of the Turks already weary; and so, as I have heard tell, not one of them escaped, but all perished. Many of them had got into the river, and were drowned. . . .

ONE NIGHT when we were keeping guard over the towers that guarded the covered ways, it happened that the Saracens brought an engine called a petrary, which they had not hitherto done, and put Greek fire into the sling of the engine. When my Lord Walter of Ecurey, the good knight who was with me, saw it, he spoke thus: "Lords, we are in the greatest peril that we have ever been in, for if they set fire to our towers and we remain here we are but lost and burnt up; while if we leave these defenses which we have been set to guard, we are dishonored. Wherefore none can defend us in this peril save God alone. So my advice and counsel is, that every time they hurl the fire at us, we throw ourselves on our elbows and knees, and pray to our Saviour to keep us in this peril."

So soon as they hurled the first cast, we threw ourselves on our elbows and knees as he had taught us. That first cast fell between our two towers guarding the covered ways. It fell on the place in front of us, where the host had been working at the dam. Our firemen were ready to put out the fire; and because the Saracens could not shoot straight at them, because of two pavilion wings that the king had caused to be set up, they shot up into the clouds, so that the darts fell on the firemen's heads.

The fashion of the Greek fire was such that it came front-wise as large as a barrel of verjuice, and the tail of fire that issued from it was as large as a large lance. The noise it made

in coming was like heaven's thunder. It had the seeming of
a dragon flying through the air. It gave so great a light, because of the great foison of fire making the light, that one
saw as clearly throughout the camp as if it had been day.
Three times did they hurl Greek fire at us that night (from
the petraries), and four times with the swivel crossbow.

Every time that our saintly king heard them hurling the
Greek fire, he would raise himself in his bed, and lift up his
hands to our Saviour, and say, weeping: "Fair Lord God,
guard me my people!" And verily I believe that his prayers
did us good service in our need. At night, every time the fire
had fallen, he sent one of his chamberlains to ask how we
fared, and whether the fire had done us any hurt.

Once when they hurled it at us, the fire fell near the
tower which the people of my Lord of Courtenay were guarding, and struck the bank of the stream. Then, look you, a
knight, whose name was l'Aubigoiz, came to me, and said,
"Lord, if you do not come to our help we shall all be burned;
for the Saracens have shot so many of their shafts that it is as
if a great hedge were coming burning against our tower." We
sprang up, and went thither, and found he spoke sooth. We
put out the fire, and before we had put it out, the Saracens had
struck us all with shafts that they shot across the stream. . . .

. . . At the end of nine days the bodies of our people,
whom the Saracens had slain, came to the surface of the water;
and this was said to be because the gall had putrefied. The
bodies came floating to the bridge between our two camps,
and could not pass under because the bridge touched the
water. There was such great foison of them that all the river
was full of corpses, from the one bank to the other, and,
lengthwise, the cast of a small stone.

The king had hired a hundred vagabonds, who took full
eight days to clear the river. They cast the bodies of the Saracens, who were circumcised, on the other side of the bridge,
and let them go down with the stream; the Christians they
caused to be put in great trenches, one with another. I saw
there the chamberlains of the Court of Artois, and many
others, seeking for their friends among the dead; but never
did I hear tell that any was found [identified].

We ate no fish in the camp the whole of Lent save eels;

and the eels ate the dead people, for they are a gluttonous fish. And because of this evil, and for the unhealthiness of the land —where it never rains a drop of water—there came upon us the sickness of the host, which sickness was such that the flesh of our legs dried up, and the skin upon our legs became spotted, black and earth-color, like an old boot; and with us, who had this sickness, the flesh of our gums putrefied; nor could anyone escape from this sickness, but he had to die. The sign of death was this, that when there was bleeding of the nose, then death was sure.

A fortnight afterwards the Turks, in order to starve us— which very much astonished our people—took several of their galleys that were above our camp, and caused them to be dragged by land and put into the river, a full league below our camp. And these galleys brought famine upon us; for no one, because of these galleys, dared to come up the stream from Damietta and bring us provisions. We knew naught of these things till such time as a little ship, belonging to the Count of Flanders, escaped from them by force and told us of them, as also that the galleys of the soldan had taken full eighty of our galleys coming from Damietta, and put to death the people that were therein.

Thus there arose a great dearth in the camp, so that as soon as Easter was come an ox was valued at eighty livres, and a sheep at thirty livres, and an egg twelve deniers, and a measure of wine ten livres. . . .

Now I will leave off speaking of this matter, and tell you how the king was taken, as he himself related it to me. He told me how he had left his own division and placed himself, he and my Lord Geoffrey of Sargines, in the division that was under my Lord Gaucher of Châtillon, who commanded the rear guard.

And the king related to me that he was mounted on a little courser covered with a housing of silk; and he told me that of all his knights and sergeants there only remained behind with him my Lord Geoffrey of Sargines, who brought the king to a little village, there where the king was taken; and as the king related to me, my Lord Geoffrey of Sargines defended him from the Saracens as a good servitor defends his lord's drinking-cup from flies; for every time that the Saracens approached, he took his spear, which he had placed between himself and the bow of his saddle, and put it to his shoulder, and ran upon them, and drove them away from the king.

And thus he brought the king to the little village; and they lifted him into a house, and laid him, almost as one dead, in the lap of a burgher-woman of Paris, and thought he would not last till night. Thither came my Lord Philip of Montfort, and said to the king that he saw the emir with whom he had treated of the truce, and, if the king so willed, he would go to him, and renew the negotiation for a truce in the manner that the Saracens desired. The king begged him to go, and said he was right willing. So my Lord Philip went to the Saracen; and the Saracen had taken off his turban from his head, and took off the ring from his finger in token that he would faithfully observe the truce.

Meanwhile, a very great mischance happened to our people; for a traitor sergeant, whose name was Marcel, began to cry to our people: "Yield, lord knights, for the king commands you, and do not cause the king to be slain!" All thought that the king had so commanded, and gave up their swords to the Saracens. The emir saw that the Saracens were bringing in our people prisoners, so he said to my Lord Philip that it was not fitting that he should grant a truce to our people, for he saw very well that they were already prisoners.

So it happened to my Lord Philip that whereas all our people were taken captive, yet was not he so taken, because he was an envoy. But there is an evil custom in the land of paynimry that when the king sends envoys to the soldan, or the soldan to the king, and the king dies, or the soldan, before the envoys' return, then the envoys, from whithersoever they may come, and whether Christians or Saracens, are made prisoners and slaves. . . .

The counsellors of the soldan had tried the king in the same manner that they had tried us, in order to see if the king would promise to deliver over to them any of the castles of the Temple or the Hospital, or any of the castles belonging to the barons of the land; and, as God so willed, the king had answered. And they threatened him, and told him that as he would not do as they wished, they would cause him to be put in the *bernicles*. Now the *bernicles* are the most cruel torture that any one can suffer. They are made of two pieces of wood, pliable, and notched at the ends with teeth that enter the one into the other; and the pieces of wood are bound together at the end with strong straps of ox-hide; and when they want to set people therein, they lay them on their side, and put their legs between the teeth; and then they cause a man to sit on the pieces of wood. Hence it happens that, not half a foot of bone remains uncrushed. And to do the worst they can, at the end of three days, when the legs are swollen, they replace the swollen legs in the *bernicles*, and crush them all once more. To these threats the king replied that he was their prisoner, and that they could do with him according to their will.

When they saw they could not prevail over the good king by threats, they came back to him and asked how much money he would give to the soldan, besides surrendering Damietta. And the king replied that if the soldan would accept a reasonable sum, he would notify the queen to pay it for their deliverance. And they asked: "How is it that you will not tell us definitely that these things shall be done?" And the king replied that he did not know if the queen would consent, seeing she was his lady and the mistress of her actions. Then the counsellors returned and spoke to the soldan, and afterwards brought back word to the king that if the queen would pay a million besants of gold, which are worth five hundred thousand livres,* the soldan would release the king.

And the king asked them, on their oath, whether the soldan would release them, provided the queen consented. So they went back once more and spoke to the soldan, and on their return, made oath that the soldan would release the king on these conditions. And now that they had taken the oath, the king said and promised to the emirs, that he would willingly pay the five hundred thousand livres for the release of his own person, seeing it was not fitting that such as he should barter himself for coin. When the soldan heard this he said: "By my faith, this Frank is large-hearted not to have bargained over so great a sum! Now go and tell him," said he, "that I give him a hundred thousand livres towards the payment of the ransom." . . .

As God, who does not forget His own, so willed, it was

* M. de Wailly estimates this at 10,132,000 francs, of modern French money, or say, £405,000.

agreed, at about the setting of the sun, that we should be released. So we were brought back, and our four galleys drawn to the bank. We demanded to be let go. They said they would not let us go till we had eaten, "for it would be a shame to our emirs if you left our prisons fasting." So we told them to give us meat, and we would eat; and they said some had gone to fetch it in the camp. The food they gave us was fritters of cheese roasted in the sun so that worms should not come therein, and hard-boiled eggs cooked four or five days before; and these, in our honor, had been painted outside with divers colors.

They put us on land, and we went towards the king, whom they were leading to the river from the pavilion in which they had kept him; and there followed him full twenty thousand Saracens on foot, with their swords in their belts. On the river, before the place where the king stood, was a Genoese galley, and it seemed as if there were but one single man on board. As soon as he saw the king on the bank of the river, he sounded a whistle; and at the sound of the whistle, eighty crossbowmen leapt from the hold of the galley, all fully equipped, with their crossbows wound up, and in a moment they had the bolts in socket. As soon as the Saracens saw them, they took to flight like sheep, so that none remained with the king save two or three.

A plank was thrown to the land, so that the king might go on board, as also the Count of Anjou, his brother, and my Lord Geoffrey of Sargines, and my Lord Philip of Nemours, the Marshal of France, who was called of the Mez, and the Master of the Trinity, and I myself. The Count of Poitiers they kept in captivity, until such time as the king had paid the two hundred thousand livres, which he was to pay as a ransom before he left the river. . . .

A Thanksgiving to God for a Good Day's Work

by Oliver Cromwell

Oliver Cromwell could well have been the inspiration for the observation "In religion, what damned error did ever lack a sober brow to bless it and approve it with a text?" Never was there a man so quick with Bible or sword as he. Though he was indeed a great cavalry captain and an astute politician, though his religious fervor was genuine, the Lord High Protector of England—as Cromwell styled himself after the beheading of King Charles I—was possessed of an unpleasant habit of killing his brothers "for the greater glory of God." At Drogheda in Ireland in 1649, in what Thomas Carlyle called "a very handsome spell of work," Cromwell massacred the entire garrison. This is his report to the Speaker of the English House of Commons.

It hath pleased God to bless our endeavour at Drogheda. The enemy made a stout resistance, and near one thousand of our men being entered, the enemy forced them out again. But God, giving a new courage to our men, they attempted again, and entered, beating the enemy from their defences. The enemy had made three retrenchments, both to right and left, where we entered; all which they were forced to quit; being thus entered, we refused them quarter, having the day before summoned the town. I believe we put to the sword the whole number of the defendants. I do not think thirty of the whole number escaped with their lives; those that did are safe in custody for Barbadoes. I do not believe, neither do I hear, that any officer escaped with his life, save only one lieutenant. The enemy retreated, divers of them, into the Millmount, a place very strong and of difficult access, being exceeding high, having a good graft and strongly pallisadoed; the Governor, Sir Arthur Aston, and divers considerable officers being there, our men getting up to them, were ordered by me to put them all to the sword; and indeed being in the heat of action, I forbade them to spare any that were in arms in the town, and I think that night they put to the sword about two thousand men, divers of the officers and soldiers being fled over the bridge into the other part of the town, where about one hundred of them possessed St. Peter's Church steeple, some the West Gate, and others a round strong tower next the gate, called St. Sunday's. These being summoned to yield to mercy, refused; whereupon I ordered the steeple of St. Peter's Church to be fired. The next day the other two towers were summoned, in one of which were about six or seven score, but they refused to yield themselves; and we knowing that hunger must compel them, set only good guards to prevent them running away, until their stomachs were come down, from one of the said towers; notwithstanding their condition they killed and wounded some of our men; when they submitted, their officers were knocked on the head, and every tenth man of the soldiers killed, and the rest shipped for the Barbadoes. . . . This hath been a marvellous great victory. I wish that all honest hearts may give the glory of this to God alone, to whom indeed the praise of this mercy belongs.

Massacre At Fort Michilimackinac

by *Alexander Henry*

The chief result of the French and Indian War
(Seven Years' War) was that France lost her empire
in North America to Britain. A secondary result was
the Indian uprisings which followed the peace, for
those redmen who had been the allies of France dis-
liked the new British officials, feared the westward-
moving settlers, and hated the greedy traders. In 1763,
a loose federation of tribes led by Pontiac attacked
British posts along a thousand-mile frontier. At
Michilimackinac, on the tip of lower Michigan, a
young trader named Alexander Henry had the good
sense to decline to go see some Sacs and Chippewas
play lacrosse; the match was the ruse that lured the
British outside the fort.

Here is Alexander Henry's story:

The morning was sultry. A Chippewa came to tell me that his nation was going to play at baggatiway with the Sacs or Saäkies, another Indian nation, for a high wager. He invited me to witness the sport, adding that the commandant was to be there, and would bet on the side of the Chippewa. In consequence of this information I went to the commandant and expostulated with him a little, representing that the Indians might possibly have some sinister end in view; but the commandant only smiled at my suspicions.

Baggatiway, called by the Canadians *le jeu de la crosse*, is played with a bat and ball. The bat is about four feet in length, curved, and terminating in a sort of racket. Two posts are planted in the ground at a considerable distance from each other, as a mile or more. Each party has its post, and the game consists in throwing the ball up to the post of the adversary. The ball, at the beginning, is placed in the middle of the course and each party endeavors as well to throw the ball out of the direction of its own post as into that of the adversary's.

I did not go myself to see the match which was now to be played without the fort, because there being a canoe prepared to depart on the following day for Montreal I employed myself in writing letters to my friends; and even when a fellow trader, Mr. Tracy, happened to call upon me, saying that another canoe had just arrived from Detroit, and proposing that I should go with him to the beach to inquire the news, it so happened that I still remained to finish my letters, promising to follow Mr. Tracy in the course of a few minutes. Mr. Tracy had not gone more than twenty paces from my door when I heard an Indian war cry and a noise of general confusion.

Going instantly to my window I saw a crowd of Indians within the fort furiously cutting down and scalping every Englishman they found. In particular I witnessed the fate of Lieutenant Jemette.

I had in the room in which I was a fowling piece, loaded with swanshot. This I immediately seized and held it for a few minutes, waiting to hear the drum beat to arms. In this dreadful interval I saw several of my countrymen fall, and more than one struggling between the knees of an Indian, who holding him in this manner, scalped him while yet living.

At length, disappointed in the hope of seeing resistance made to the enemy, and sensible, of course, that no effort of my own unassisted arm could avail against four hundred Indians, I thought only of seeking shelter. Amid the slaughter which was raging I observed many of the Canadian inhabitants of the fort calmly looking on, neither opposing the Indians, nor suffering injury; and from this circumstance I conceived a hope of finding security in their houses.

Between the yard door of my own house and that of M. Langlade, my next neighbor, there was only a low fence, over which I easily climbed. At my entrance I found the whole family at the windows, gazing at the scene of blood before them. I addressed myself immediately to M. Langlade, begging that he would put me into some place of safety until the heat of the affair should be over; an act of charity by which he might perhaps preserve me from the general massacre; but while I uttered my petition M. Langlade, who had looked for a moment at me, turned again to the window, shrugging his shoulders and intimating that he could do nothing for me:— *"Que voudriez-vous que j'en ferais?"*

This was a moment for despair; but the next a Pani woman, a slave of M. Langlade's, beckoned me to follow her. She brought me to a door which she opened, desiring me to enter, and telling me that it led to the garret, where I must go and conceal myself. I joyfully obeyed her directions; and she, having followed me up to the garret door, locked it after me and with great presence of mind took away the key.

This shelter obtained, if shelter I could hope to find it, I was naturally anxious to know what might still be passing without. Through an aperture which afforded me a view of the area of the fort I beheld in shapes the foulest and most terrible, the ferocious triumphs of barbarian conquerors. The dead were scalped and mangled; the dying were writhing and shrieking under the unsatiated knife and tomahawk; and from the bodies of some, ripped open, their butchers were drinking the blood, scooped up in the hollow of joined hands and quaffed amid shouts of rage and victory. I was shaken not only with horror, but with fear. The sufferings which I witnessed I seemed on the point of experiencing. No long time elapsed before every one being destroyed who could be found, there was a general cry of "All is finished!" At the same instant I heard some of the Indians enter the house in which I was.

The garret was separated from the room below only by a layer of single boards, at once the flooring of the one and the ceiling of the other. I could therefore hear everything that passed; and the Indians no sooner came in than they inquired whether or not any Englishman were in the house. M. Langlade replied that he could not say—he did not know of any—answers in which he did not exceed the truth, for the Pani woman had not only hidden me by stealth, but kept my secret and her own. M. Langlade was therefore, as I presume, as far from a wish to destroy me as he was careless about saving me, when he added to these answers that they might examine for themselves, and would soon be satisfied as to the object of their question. Saying this, he brought them to the garret door.

The state of my mind will be imagined. Arrived at the door some delay was occasioned by the absence of the key and a few moments were thus allowed me in which to look around for a hiding place. In one corner of the garret was a heap of those vessels of birch bark used in maple-sugar making. . . .

The door was unlocked, and opening, and the Indians ascending the stairs, before I had completely crept into a small opening, which presented itself at one end of the heap. An instant after four Indians entered the room, all armed with tomahawks, and all besmeared with blood upon every part of their bodies.

The die appeared to be cast. I could scarcely breathe; but I thought that the throbbing of my heart occasioned a noise loud enough to betray me. The Indians walked in every direction about the garret, and one of them approached me so closely that at a particular moment, had he put forth his hand, he must have touched me. Still I remained undiscovered, a circumstance to which the dark color of my clothes and the want of light in a room which had no window, and in the corner in which I was, must have contributed. In a word, after taking several turns in the room, during which they told M. Langlade how many they had killed and how many scalps they had taken, they returned downstairs, and I with sensations not to be expressed, heard the door, which was the barrier between me and my fate, locked for the second time.

There was a feather bed on the floor, and on this, exhausted as I was by the agitation of my mind, I threw myself down and fell asleep. In this state I remained till the dusk of the evening, when I was awakened by a second opening of the door. The person that now entered was M. Langlade's wife, who was much surprised at finding me, but advised me not to be uneasy, observing that the Indians had killed most of the English, but that she hoped I might myself escape. A shower of rain having begun to fall, she had come to stop a hole in the roof. On her going away, I begged her to send me a little water to drink, which she did.

As night was now advancing I continued to lie on the bed, ruminating on my condition, but unable to discover a resource from which I could hope for life. A flight to Detroit had no probable chance of success. The distance from Michilimackinac was four hundred miles; I was without provisions; and the whole length of the road lay through Indian countries, countries of an enemy in arms, where the first man whom I should meet would kill me. To stay where I was threatened nearly the same issue. As before, fatigue of mind, and not tranquillity, suspended my cares and procured me further sleep.

The respite which sleep afforded me during the night was put an end to by the return of morning. I was again on the rack of apprehension. At sunrise I heard the family stirring, and presently after, Indian voices informing M. Langlade they had not found my hapless self among the dead, and that they supposed me to be somewhere concealed. M. Langlade appeared from what followed to be by this time acquainted with the place of my retreat, of which no doubt he had been informed by his wife. The poor woman, as soon as the Indians mentioned me, declared to her husband in the French tongue that he should no longer keep me in his house, but deliver me up to my pursuers, giving as a reason for this measure that should the Indians discover his instrumentality in my concealment, they might revenge it on her children, and that it was better that I should die than they. M. Langlade resisted at first this sentence of his wife's; but soon suffered her to prevail, informing the Indians that he had been told I was in his house, that I had come there without his knowledge, and that he would put me into their hands. This was no sooner expressed than he began to ascend the stairs, the Indians following upon his heels.

I now resigned myself to the fate with which I was menaced; and regarding every attempt at concealment as vain, I arose from the bed and presented myself full in view to the Indians who were entering the room. They were all in a state of intoxication, and entirely naked, except about the middle. One of them, named Wenniway, whom I had previously known, and who was upward of six feet in height, had his entire face and body covered with charcoal and grease, only that a white spot of two inches in diameter encircled either eye. This man, walking up to me, seized me with one hand by the collar of the coat while in the other he held a large carving knife, as if to plunge it into my breast; his eyes, meanwhile, were fixed steadfastly on mine. At length, after some seconds of the most anxious suspense, he dropped his arm, saying, "I won't kill you!" To this he added that he had been frequently engaged in wars against the English, and had brought away many scalps; that on a certain occasion he had lost a brother whose name was Musinigon, and that I should be called after him.

A reprieve upon any terms placed me among the living, and gave me back the sustaining voice of hope; but Wenniway ordered me downstairs, and there informing me that I was to be taken to his cabin, where, and indeed everywhere else, the Indians were all mad with liquor, death again was threatened, and not as possible only, but as certain. I mentioned my fears on this subject to M. Langlade, begging him to represent the danger to my master. M. Langlade in this instance did not withhold his compassion, and Wenniway immediately consented that I should remain where I was until he found another opportunity to take me away.

Thus far secure I reascended my garret stairs in order to place myself the furthest possible out of the reach of insult from drunken Indians; but I had not remained there more than an hour, when I was called to the room below in which was an Indian who said that I must go with him out of the fort, Wenniway having sent him to fetch me. This man, as well as Wenniway himself, I had seen before. In the preceding year I had allowed him to take goods on credit, for which he was still in my debt; and some short time previous to the surprise of the fort he had said upon my upbraiding him with want of honesty that he would pay me before long. This speech now came fresh into my memory and led me to suspect that the fellow had formed a design against my life. I communicated the suspicion to M. Langlade; but he gave for answer that I was not now my own master, and must do as I was ordered.

The Indian on his part directed that before I left the house I should undress myself, declaring that my coat and shirt would become him better than they did me. His pleasure in this respect being complied with, no other alternative was left me than either to go out naked, or to put on the clothes of the Indian, which he freely gave me in exchange. His motive for thus stripping me of my own apparel was no other as I afterward learned than this, that it might not be stained with blood when he should kill me.

I was now told to proceed; and my driver followed me close until I had passed the gate of the fort, when I turned toward the spot where I knew the Indians to be encamped. This, however, did not suit the purpose of my enemy, who seized me by the arm and drew me violently in the opposite direction to the distance of fifty yards above the fort. Here, finding that I was approaching the bushes and sand hills, I determined to proceed no farther, but told the Indian that I believed he meant to murder me, and that if so he might as well strike where I was as at any greater distance. He replied with coolness that my suspicions were just, and that he meant to pay me in this manner for my goods. At the same time he produced a knife and held me in a position to receive the intended blow. Both this and that which followed were necessarily the affair of a moment. By some effort, too sudden and too little dependent on thought to be explained or remembered, I was enabled to arrest his arm and give him a sudden push by which I turned him from me and released myself from his grasp. This was no sooner done than I ran toward the fort with all the swiftness in my power, the Indian following me, and I expecting every moment to feel his knife. I succeeded in my flight; and on entering the fort I saw Wenniway standing in the midst of the area, and to him I hastened for protection. Wenniway desired the Indian to desist; but the latter pursued me round him, making several strokes at me with his knife, and foaming at the mouth with rage at the repeated failure of his purpose. At length Wenniway drew near to M. Langlade's house; and, the door being open, I ran into it. The Indian followed me; but on my entering the house he voluntarily abandoned the pursuit.

Preserved so often and so unexpectedly as it had now been my lot to be, I returned to my garret with a strong inclination to believe that through the will of an overruling power no Indian enemy could do me hurt; but new trials, as I believed, were at hand when at ten o'clock in the evening I was roused from sleep and once more desired to descend the stairs. Not less, however, to my satisfaction than surprise, I was summoned only to meet Major Etherington, Mr. Bostwick, and Lieutenant Lesslie, who were in the room below.

These gentlemen had been taken prisoners while looking at the game without the fort and immediately stripped of all their clothes. They were now sent into the fort under the charge of Canadians, because, the Indians having resolved on getting drunk, the chiefs were apprehensive that they would be murdered if they continued in the camp. Lieutenant Jemette and seventy soldiers had been killed; and but twenty Englishmen, including soldiers, were still alive. These were all within the fort, together with nearly three hundred Canadians.

These being our numbers, myself and others proposed to Major Etherington to make an effort for regaining possession of the fort and maintaining it against the Indians. The Jesuit missionary was consulted on the project; but he discouraged us by his representations, not only of the merciless treatment which we must expect from the Indians should they regain their superiority, but of the little dependence which was to be placed upon our Canadian auxiliaries. Thus the fort and prisoners remained in the hands of the Indians, though through the whole night the prisoners and whites were in actual possession, and they were without the gates.

That whole night, or the greater part of it, was passed in mutual condolence, and my fellow prisoners shared my garret.

In the morning, being again called down, I found my master, Wenniway, and was desired to follow him. He led me to a small house within the fort, where in a narrow room and almost dark I found Mr. Ezekiel Solomons, an Englishman from Detroit, and a soldier, all prisoners. With these I remained in painful suspense as to the scene that was next to present itself till ten o'clock in the forenoon, when an Indian arrived, and presently marched us to the lakeside where a canoe appeared ready for departure, and in which we found that we were to embark.

Our voyage, full of doubt as it was, would have commenced immediately, but that one of the Indians who was to be of the party was absent. His arrival was to be waited for; and this occasioned a very long delay during which we were exposed to a keen northeast wind. An old shirt was all that covered me; I suffered much from the cold; and in this extremity M. Langlade coming down to the beach, I asked him for a blanket, promising if I lived to pay him for it at any price he pleased; but the answer I received was this, that he could let me have no blanket unless there were someone to be security for the payment. For myself, he observed, I had no longer any property in that country. I had no more to say to M. Langlade; but presently seeing another Canadian, named John Cuchoise, I addressed to him a similar request and was not refused. Naked as I was, and rigorous as was the weather, but for the blanket I must have perished. At noon our party was all collected, the prisoners all embarked, and we steered for the Isles du Castor in Lake Michigan.

The Shot Heard Round the World

by Jonas Clark

By the rude bridge that arched the flood,
  Their flag to April's breeze unfurled,
Here once th' embattled farmers stood
  And fired the shot heard round the world.

So wrote Ralph Waldo Emerson in the opening stanza of his "Concord Hymn," commemorating the famous fight at Concord Bridge. That skirmish, and the subsequent retreat of the British redcoats, was one of the memorable events of the historic year 1775. By then, although neither war nor American Independence had been declared, the relations between England and her colonies had reached the breaking point. The Boston Tea Party had taken place and King George had retaliated by closing Boston Harbor to shipping and stationing troops in the city. The colonists had meanwhile begun storing arms at Concord, some twenty miles northwest of Boston. On the night of April 18, 1775, seven hundred British regulars were sent to destroy the supplies. Paul Revere and William Dawes rode ahead of them to warn the colonists, who assembled the next day at Lexington, five miles to the east. What happened thereafter has been narrated by the Reverend Jonas Clark, a Lexington minister.

Between the hours of twelve and one, on the morning of the nineteenth of April, we received intelligence, by express, from the Honorable Joseph Warren Esq. at Boston, "that a large body of the king's troops (supposed to be a brigade of about 12, or 1500) were embarked in boats from Boston, and gone over to land on Lechmere's-Point (so called) in Cambridge: And that it was shrewdly suspected, that they were ordered to seize and destroy the stores, belonging to the colony, then deposited at Concord," in consequence of General Gage's unjustifiable seizure of the provincial magazine of powder at Medford, and other colony stores in several other places.

Upon this intelligence, as also upon information of the conduct of the officers as above-mentioned, the militia of this town were alarmed, and ordered to meet on the usual place of parade; not with any design of commencing hostilities upon the king's troops, but to consult what might be done for our own and the people's safety: And also to be ready for whatever service providence might call us out to, upon this alarming occasion, in case overt acts of violence, or open hostilities should be committed by this mercenary band of armed and bloodthirsty oppressors.

About the same time, two persons were sent express to Cambridge, if possible, to gain intelligence of the motions of the troops, and what route they took.

The militia met according to order; and waited the return of the messengers, that they might order their measures as occasion should require. Between three and four o'clock, one of the expresses returned informing, that there was no appearance of the troops, on the roads, either from Cambridge or Charlestown; and that it was supposed that the movements in the army the evening before, were only a feint to alarm the people. Upon this therefore, the militia company were dismissed for the present, but with orders to be within call of the drum,—waiting the return of the other messenger, who was expected in about an hour, or sooner, if any discovery should be made of the motions of the troops.—But he was prevented by their silent and sudden arrival at the place where he was, waiting for intelligence. So that, after all this precaution we had no notice of their approach, 'till the brigade was actually in the town, and upon a quick march within about a mile and a quarter of the meeting house and place of parade.

However, the commanding officer thought best to call the company together,—not with any design of opposing so superior a force, much less of commencing hostilities; but only with a view to determine what to do, when and where to meet, and to dismiss and disperse.

Accordingly, about half an hour after four o'clock, alarm guns were fired, and the drums beat to arms; and the militia were collecting together.—Some, to the number of about fifty, or sixty, or possibly more, were on the parade, others were coming towards it.—In the mean time, the troops, having thus stolen a march upon us, and to prevent any intelligence of their approach, having seized and held prisoners several persons whom they met unarmed upon the road, seemed to come determined for murder and bloodshed; and that whether provoked to it, or not!—When within about half a quarter of a mile of the meeting-house, they halted, and the command was given to prime and load; which being done, they marched on 'till they came up to the east end of said meeting-house, in sight of our militia (collecting as aforesaid) who were about 12, or 13 rods distant.—Immediately upon their appearing so suddenly, and so nigh, Capt. Parker, who commanded the militia company, ordered the men to disperse, and take care of themselves; and not to fire.—Upon this, our men dispersed; —but, many of them, not so speedily as they might have done, not having the most distant idea of such brutal barbarity and more than savage cruelty, from the troops of a British king, as they immediately experienced!–!—For, no sooner did they come in sight of our company, but one of them, supposed to be an officer of rank, was heard to say to the troops, "Damn them; we will have them!"—Upon which the troops shouted aloud, huzza'd, and rushed furiously towards our men.— About the same time, three officers (supposed to be Col. Smith, Major Pitcairn and another officer) advanced, on horseback, to the front of the body, and coming within 5 or 6 rods of the militia, one of them cried out, "ye villains, ye Rebels, disperse: Damn you disperse!"—or words to this effect. One of them (whether the same, or not, is not easily determined) said, "Lay down your arms; Damn you, why don't you lay down your arms!"—The second of these officers, about this time, fired a pistol towards the militia, as they were dispersing.— The foremost, who was within a few yards of our men, brandishing his sword, and then pointing towards them, with a loud voice said, to the troops, "Fire!—By God, fire!"— which was instantly followed by a discharge of arms from the said troops, succeeeded by a very heavy and close fire upon our party, dispersing, so long as any of them were within reach.—Eight were left dead upon the ground! Ten were wounded.—The rest of the company, through divine goodness, were (to a miracle) preserved unhurt in this murderous action!

   . . . Having thus vanquished the party in Lexington, the troops marched on for Concord, to execute their orders, in destroying the stores belonging to the colony, deposited there. —They met with no interruption in their march to Concord.— But by some means or other, the people of Concord had notice of their approach and designs, and were alarmed about break of day; and collecting as soon, and as many as possible, improved the time they had before the troops came upon them, to the best advantage, both for concealing and securing as many of the public stores as they could, and in preparing for defence.—By the stop of the troops at Lexington, many thousands were saved to the colony, and they were, in a great measure, frustrated in their design.

   When the troops made their approach to the easterly part of the town, the provincials of Concord and some neighbouring towns, were collected and collecting in an advantageous post, on a hill, a little distance from the meeting-house, north of the road, to the number of about 150, or 200: but finding the troops to be more than three times as many, they wisely retreated, first to a hill about 80 rods further north, and then over the north-bridge (so called) about a mile from the town: and there they waited the coming of the militia of the towns adjacent, to their assistance.

   In the meantime, the British detachment marched into

98

the center of the town. A party of about 200, was ordered to take possession of said bridge, other parties were dispatched to various parts of the town, in search of public stores, while the remainder were employed in seizing and destroying, whatever they could find, in the town-house, and other places, where stores had been lodged.—But before they had accomplished their design, they were interrupted by a discharge of arms, at said bridge.

It seems, that of the party above-mentioned, as ordered to take possession of the bridge, one half were marched on about two miles, in search of stores, at Col. Barret's and that part of the town: while the other half, consisting of towards 100 men, under Capt. Lawrie, were left to guard the bridge. The provincials, who were in sight of the bridge, observing the troops attempting to take up the planks of said bridge, thought it necessary to dislodge them, and gain possession of the bridge.—They accordingly marched, but with express orders not to fire, unless first fired upon by the king's troops. Upon their approach towards the bridge, Capt. Lawrie's party fired upon them, killed Capt. Davis and another man dead upon the spot, and wounded several others. Upon this our militia rushed on, with a spirit becoming freeborn Americans, returned the fire upon the enemy, killed 2, wounded several and drove them from the bridge, and pursued them towards the town, 'till they were covered by a reinforcement from the main body. The provincials then took post on a hill, at some distance, north of the town: and as their numbers were continually increasing, they were preparing to give the troops a proper discharge, on their departure from the town.

In the mean time, the king's troops collected; and having dressed their wounded, destroyed what stores they could find, and insulted and plundered a number of the inhabitants, prepared for a retreat.

While at Concord, the troops disabled two 24 pounders; destroyed their 2 carriages, and seven wheels for the same, with their limbers. Sixteen wheels for brass 3 pounders, and 2 carriages with limber and wheels for two 4 pounders. They threw into the river, wells, &c. about 500 weight of ball: and stove about 60 barrels of flour; but not having time to perfect their work, one half of the flour was afterwards saved.

The troops began a hasty retreat about the middle of

the day: and were no sooner out of the town, but they began
to meet the effects of the just resentments of this injured people. The provincials fired upon them from various quarters,
and pursued them (though without any military order) with
a firmness and intrepidity, beyond what could have been expected, on the first onset, and in such a day of confusion and
distress!—The fire was returned, for a time, with great fury,
by the troops as they retreated, though (through divine goodness) with but little execution.—This scene continued, with
but little intermission, till they returned to Lexington; when it
was evident, that, having lost numbers in killed, wounded, and
prisoners that fell into our hands, they began to be, not only
fatigued, but greatly disheartened. And it is supposed they
must have soon surrendered at discretion, had they not been
reinforced.—But Lord Percy's arrival with another brigade,
of about 1000 men, and 2 field pieces, about half a mile from
Lexington meeting-house, towards Cambridge, gave them a
seasonable respite.

The coming of the reinforcement, with the cannon,
which our people were not so well acquainted with then, as
they have been since put the provincials also to a pause, for a
time.—But no sooner were the king's troops in motion, but our
men renewed the pursuit with equal, and even greater ardor
and intrepidity than before, and the firing on both sides continued, with but little intermission, to the close of the day,
when the troops entered Charlestown, where the provincials
could not follow them, without exposing the worthy inhabitants of that truly patriotic town, to their rage and revenge.—
That night and the next day they were conveyed in boats,
over Charles-River to Boston, glad to secure themselves, under the cover of the shipping, and by strengthening and per-
fecting the fortifications, at every part, against the further
attacks of a justly incensed people, who, upon intelligence of
the murderous transactions of this fatal day, were collecting in
arms, round the town, in great numbers, and from every
quarter.

In the retreat of the king's troops from Concord to Lexington, they ravaged and plundered, as they had opportunity,
more or less, in most of the houses that were upon the road.—
But after they were joined by Percy's brigade, in Lexington,
it seemed as if all the little remains of humanity had left them;

100

and rage and revenge had taken the reins, and knew no bounds!—Cloathing, furniture, provisions, goods, plundered, broken, carried off, or destroyed!—Buildings (especially dwelling houses) abused, defaced, battered, shattered and almost ruined! And as if this had not been enough, numbers of them doomed to the flames!—Three dwelling houses, two shops and a barn, were laid in ashes, in Lexington!—Many others were set on fire, in this town, in Cambridge, &c. and all must have shared the same fate, had not the close pursuit of the provincials prevented, and the flames been seasonably quenched!—Add to all this; the unarmed, the aged and infirm, who were unable to flee, are inhumanly stabbed and murdered in their habitations! Yea, even women in child-bed, with their helpless babes in their arms, do not escape the horrid alternative, of being either cruelly murdered in their beds, burnt in their habitations, or turned into the streets to perish with cold, nakedness and distress!

   . . . Our loss, in the several actions of that day, was 49 killed, 34 wounded and 5 missing, who were taken prisoners, and have since been exchanged. The enemy's loss, according to the best accounts, in killed, wounded and missing, about 300.

Tom Paine Escapes the Guillotine

by Thomas Paine

Idealists are frequently indifferent to the sufferings their doctrines can inflict upon mankind—until the terror catches at their own coattails. Tom Paine was certainly one of these. The author of *Common Sense* and the *Rights of Man* did not raise his voice against the horrors of the French Revolution he had helped foster until it was too late. By then *la Guillotine* had kissed off the heads of so many of his friends that Tom could lament: "My heart was in distress . . . and my harp was hung upon the weeping willows." But for the fact of a door that swung outward, his head would also have been rolling in a bloody basket. This is Paine's account of that narrow escape.

In Paris, in 1793 I had lodgings in the Rue Faubourg St. Denis, No. 63. They were the most agreeable for situation of any I ever had in Paris, except that they were too remote from the Convention, of which I was then a member. But this was recompenced by their being also remote from the alarms and confusion into which the interior of Paris was then often thrown.

The news of those things used to arrive to us, as if we were in a state of tranquility in the country. The house, which was inclosed by a wall and gateway from the street, was a good deal like an old mansion farm-house, and the court-yard was like a farm-yard, stocked with fowls, ducks, turkeys, and geese; which, for amusement, we used to feed out of the parlour window on the ground floor. There were some hutches for rabbits, and a sty with two pigs. Beyond, was a garden of more than an acre of ground, well laid out, and stocked with excellent fruit-trees. The orange, apricot, and green-gage plum, were the best I ever tasted; and it is the only place where I saw the wild cucumber.

One day I went into my chamber to write and sign a certificate for two friends who were under arrest, which I intended to take to the guard-house to obtain their release. Just as I had finished it, a man came into my room, dressed in the Parisian uniform of a captain, and spoke to me in good English, and with a good address. He told me that two young men, Englishmen, were arrested, and detained in the guard-house, and that the section (meaning those who represented and acted for the section) had sent him to ask me if I knew them, in which case they would be liberated. This matter being soon settled between us, he talked to me about the Revolution, and something about the *Rights of Man*, which he had read in English; and at parting, offered me in a polite and civil manner his services. And who do you think the man was that offered me his services? It was no other than the public executioner *Samson*, who guillotined the king, and all who lived in the same section, and in the same street with me.

As to myself, I used to find some relief by walking alone in the garden after dark, and cursing, with hearty good-will, the authors of that terrible system that had turned the character of the revolution I had been proud to defend.

I went but little to the Convention, and then only to make my appearance; because I found it impossible to join in their tremendous decrees, and useless and dangerous to oppose them. My having voted and spoken extensively, more so than any other member, against the execution of the king, had already fixed a mark upon me: neither dared any of my associates in the Convention to translate, and speak in French for me, any thing I might have dared to have written.

Pen and ink were then of no use to me: no good could be done by writing, and no printer dared to print; and whatever I might have written for my private amusement, as anecdotes of the times, would have been continually exposed to be examined, and tortured into any meaning that the rage of party might fix upon it, and, as to softer subjects, my heart was in distress at the fate of my friends, and my harp was hung upon the weeping willows.

As it was summer, we spent most of our time in the garden, and passed it away in those childish amusements that serve to keep reflection from the mind; such as marbles, scotch-hops, battle-dores, etc. at which we were all pretty expert.

In this retired manner we remained about six or seven weeks; and our landlord went every evening into the city, to bring us the news of the day, and the evening journal.

Two days after, I heard a rapping at the gate; and looking out of the window of the bed-room, I saw the landlord going with a candle to the gate, which he opened and a guard with musquets and fixed bayonets entered. I went to bed again, and made up my mind for prison; for I was then the only lodger. It was a guard to take up ———, but, I thank God, they were out of their reach.

The guard came about a month after, in the night, and took away the landlord, Georgeit; and the scene in the house finished with the arrestation of myself.

I was one of the nine members that composed the first

105

Committee of Constitution. Six of them have been destroyed; Sièyes and myself have survived. He, by bending with the times; and I, by not bending. The other survivor joined Robespierre, and signed with him the warrant for my arrestation. After the fall of Robespierre, he was seized and imprisoned in his turn, and sentenced to transportation. He has since apologized to me for having signed the warrant, by saying, he felt himself in danger, and was obliged to do it. Herault Sechelles, an acquaintance of Mr. Jefferson's and a good patriot, was my *suppleant* as a member of the Committee of Constitution; that is, he was to supply my place, if I had not accepted or had resigned, being next in number of votes to me. He was imprisoned in the Luxembourg with me, and was taken to the tribunal, and to the guillotine; and I, his principal, was left.

There were but two foreigners in the Convention, Anarcharsis Cloots and myself. We were both put out of the Convention by the same vote, arrested by the same order, and carried to prison together the same night. He was taken to the guillotine, and I was again left. Joel Barlow was with us when we went to prison.

Joseph Lebon, one of the vilest characters that ever existed, and who made the streets of Arras run with blood, was my *suppleant* member of the Convention for the department of the Pays de Calais. When I was put out of the Convention, he came and took my place. When I was liberated from prison, and voted again into the Convention, he was sent to the same prison, and took my place there; and he went to the guillotine instead of me. He supplied my place all the way through.

One hundred and sixty-eight persons were taken out of the Luxembourg in one night, and a hundred and sixty of them guillotined the next day, of which I know I was to have been one; and the manner I escaped that fate is curious, and has all the appearance of accident.

The room in which I was lodged was on the ground-floor, and one of a long range of rooms under a gallery, and the door of it opened outward and flat against the wall; so that, when it was open, the inside of the door appeared outward, and the contrary, when it was shut. I had three comrades, fellow-prisoners with me: Joseph Vanhuile, of Bruges, since president of the municipality of that town, Michael Robins, and Bastini, of Louvain. When persons by scores and by hundreds were to be taken out of prison for the guillotine, it was always done in the night, and those who performed that office had a private mark or signal, by which they knew what rooms to go to, and what number to take.

We, as I said, were four, and the door of our room was marked, unobserved by us, with that number in chalk; but it happened, if *happening* is a proper word, the mark was put on the door when it was open and flat against the wall, and thereby came on the inside when we shut it at night,—and the destroying angel passed it by. A few days after this, Robespierre fell; and the American ambassador arrived and reclaimed me, and invited me to his house.

Napoleon's Greatest Victory

by Jean-Baptiste Marbot

On December 2, 1805, near the village of Austerlitz in what is now Czechoslovakia, Napoleon Bona-
parte won the victory dearest to his heart. Here he
defeated the Russians and Austrians led by Kutuzov—
and he won as a great general wishes to win: according to plan. At Austerlitz the Emperor of the French
set a trap for the enemy and the enemy fell into it,
whereupon the artillery Napoleon knew so well made
a great slaughter among them. The story of Austerlitz
—with a few astonishing asides—is told by Jean-Baptiste
Antoine Marcelin de Marbot, at Austerlitz a twenty-
three-year-old aide-de-camp, later to be a Napoleonic
general, and still later, having survived the Emperor's
misfortunes, a baron of France.

M ost military authors are apt to confuse the reader's mind by overcrowding their story with details. So much is this the case that, in the greater part of the works published on the wars of the Empire, I have been utterly unable to understand the history of many battles at which I was present and of which all the phases were well known to me. In order to preserve due clearness in relating a military action, I think one ought to be content with indicating the respective conditions of the two armies before the engagement, and reporting only such facts as affected the decision. That is what I shall try to do in order to give you an idea of the battle of Austerlitz, as it is called, though it took place short of the village of that name. On the eve of the battle, however, the Emperors of Austria and Russia had slept at the château of Austerlitz, and when Napoleon drove them from this, he wished to heighten his triumph by giving that name to the battle.

You will see on a map that the Goldbach brook, which rises on the other side of the Olmutz road, falls into the small lake of Monitz. This stream, flowing at the bottom of a little valley with pretty steep sides, separated the two armies. The Austro-Russian right rested on a hanging wood in the rear of the Posoritz post-house beyond the Olmutz road; their center occupied Pratzen and the wide plateau of that name; their left was near the pools of Satschan and the swampy ground in their neighborhood. The Emperor Napoleon rested his left on a hillock difficult of access, to which the Egyptian soldiers gave the name of the *Santon*, because it had on the top a little chapel with a spire like a minaret. The French center was near the marsh of Kobelnitz, the right was at Telnitz. But at this point the Emperor had placed very few people, in order to draw the Russians onto the marshy ground, where he had arranged to defeat them by concealing Davout's corps at Gross Raigern, on the Vienna road.

On the first of December, the day before the battle, Napoleon left Brunn early in the morning, spent the whole day in inspecting the positions, and in the evening fixed his headquarters in rear of the French center, at a point whence the view took in the bivouacs of both sides, as well as the ground which was to be their field of battle next day. There was no other building in the place than a poor barn. The Emperor's tables and maps were placed there, and he established himself in person by an immense fire, surrounded by his numerous staff and his guard. Fortunately there was no snow, and though it was very cold, I lay on the ground and went soundly to sleep. But we were soon obliged to remount and go the rounds with the Emperor. There was no moon, and the darkness of the night was increased by a thick fog which made progress very difficult. The *chasseurs* of the escort had the idea of lighting torches made of pine branches and straw, which proved very useful. The troops, seeing a group of horsemen thus lighted come toward them, had no difficulty in recognizing the imperial staff, and in an instant, as if by enchantment, we could see along the whole line all our bivouc fires lighted up by thousands of torches in the hands of the soldiers. The cheers with which, in their enthusiasm, they saluted Napoleon, were all the more animated for the fact that the morrow was the anniversary of his coronation, and the coincidence seemed of good omen. The enemies must have been a god deal surprised when, from the top of a neighboring hill, they saw in the middle of the night 60,000 torches lighted, and heard a thousand times repeated the cry of "Long live the Emperor!" accompanied by the sound of the many bands of the French regiments. In our camp all was joy, light, and movement, while on the side of the Austrians and Russians all was gloom and silence.

Next day, December 2, the sound of cannon was heard at daybreak. As we have seen, the Emperor had shown but few troops on his right; this was a trap for the enemy, with the view of allowing them to capture Telnitz easily, to cross the Goldbach there, then to go on to Gross Raigern and take possession of the road from Brunn to Vienna, and so to cut off our retreat. The Russians and Austrians fell into the snare perfectly, for, weakening the rest of their line, they clumsily crowded considerable forces into the bottom of Telnitz, and into the swampy valleys bordering on the pools of Satschan and Monitz. But as they imagined, for some not very apparent reason, that Napoleon had the intention of retreating without delivering battle, they resolved, by way of completing their success, to attack us on our left toward the *Santon,* and also on our center before Puntowitz. By this means our defeat would be complete when we had been forced back on these two points, and found the road to Vienna occupied in our rear by the Russians. As it befell, however, on our left Marshal Lannes not only repulsed all the attacks of the enemy upon the *Santon,* but drove him on the other side of the Olmutz road as far as Blasiowitz. There the ground became more level, and allowed Murat's cavalry to execute some brilliant charges, the results of which were of great importance, for the Russians were driven out of hand as far as the village of Austerlitz.

While this splendid success was being won by our left wing, the center, consisting of the troops under Soult and Bernadotte, which the Emperor had posted at the bottom of Goldbach ravine where it was concealed by a thick fog, dashed forward toward the hill on which stands the village of Pratzen. This was the moment when that brilliant sun of Austerlitz, the recollection of which Napoleon so delighted to recall, burst forth in all its splendor. Marshal Soult carried not only the village of Pratzen, but also the vast tableland of that name, which was the culminating point of the whole country, and consequently the key of the battlefield. There, under the Emperor's eyes, the sharpest of the fighting took place, and the Russians were beaten back. But one battalion, the 4th of the line, of which Prince Joseph, Napoleon's brother, was colonel, allowing itself to be carried too far in pursuit of the enemy, was charged and broken up by the Noble Guard and the Grand Duke Constantine's *cuirassiers,* losing its eagle. Several lines of Russian cavalry quickly advanced to support this momentary success of the guards, but Napoleon hurled against them the Mamelukes, the mounted *chasseurs,* and the mounted grenadiers of his guard, under Marshal Messières and General Rapp. The melee was of the most sanguinary kind; the Russian squadrons were crushed and driven back beyond the village of Austerlitz with immense loss. Our troopers captured many colors and prisoners, among the latter Prince Repnin, commander of the Noble Guard. This regiment, composed of the most brilliant of the young Russian nobility, lost heavily, because the swagger in which they had indulged against the French having come to the ears of our soldiers, these, and above all the mounted grenadiers, attacked them with fury, shouting as they passed their great sabers through their bodies: "We will give the ladies of St. Petersburg something to cry for!"

The painter Gérard, in his picture of the battle of Auster-litz, has taken for his subject the moment when General Rapp, coming wounded out of the fight and covered with his ene-mies' blood and his own, is presenting to the Emperor the flags just captured and his prisoner, Prince Repnin. I was present at this imposing spectacle, which the artist has repro-duced with wonderful accuracy. All the heads are portraits, even that of the brave *chasseur* who, making no complaint though he had been shot through the body, had the courage to come up to the Emperor and fall stone dead as he presented the standard which he had just taken. Napoleon, wishing to honor his memory, ordered the painter to find a place for him in his composition. In the picture may be seen also a Mame-luke, who is carrying in one hand an enemy's flag and holds in the other the bridle of his dying horse. This man, named Mustapha, was well known in the guard for his courage and ferocity. During the charge he had pursued the Grand Duke Constantine, who only got rid of him by a pistol shot, which severely wounded the Mameluke's horse. Mustapha, grieved at having only a standard to offer to the Emperor, said in his broken French as he presented it: "Ah, if me catch Prince Constantine, me cut him head off and bring it to emperor!" Napoleon, disgusted, replied: "Will you hold your tongue, you savage?" But to finish the account of the battle. While Marshals Lannes, Soult, and Murat, with the imperial guard, were beating the right and center of the allied army and driv-ing them back beyond the village of Austerlitz, the enemy's left, falling into the trap laid by Napoleon when he made a show of keeping close to the pools, threw itself on the village of Telnitz, captured it, and, crossing the Goldbach, prepared to occupy the road to Vienna. But the enemy had taken a false prognostic of Napoleon's genius when they supposed him capable of committing such a blunder as to leave undefended a road by which, in the event of disaster, his retreat was se-cured; for our right was guarded by the divisions under

113

Davout, concealed in the rear in the little town of Gross Raigern. From this point Davout fell upon the allies at the moment when he saw their masses entangled in the defiles between the lakes of Telnitz and Monitz and the stream.

The Emperor, whom we left on the plateau of Pratzen, having freed himself from the enemy's right and center, which were in flight on the other side of Austerlitz, descended from the heights of Pratzen with a small force of all arms, including Soult's corps and his guard, and went with all speed toward Telnitz, and took the enemy's columns in rear at the moment when Davout was attacking in front. At once the heavy masses of Austrians and Russians, packed on the narrow roadways which lead beside the Goldbach brook, finding themselves between two fires, fell into an indescribable confusion. All ranks were mixed up together, and each sought to save himself by flight. Some hurled themselves headlong into the marshes which border the pools; our cavalry charged them, and the butchery was frightful. Lastly, the greater part of the enemy, chiefly Russians, sought to pass over the ice. It was very thick, and five or six thousand men, keeping some kind of order, had reached the middle of the Satschan Lake, when Napoleon, calling up the artillery of his guard, gave the order to fire on the ice. It broke at countless points, and a mighty cracking was heard. The water, oozing through the fissures, soon covered the floes, and we saw thousands of Russians, with their horses, guns, and wagons, slowly settle down into the depths. It was a horribly majestic spectacle which I shall never forget. In an instant the surface of the lake was covered with everything that could swim. Men and horses struggled in the water among the floes. Some—a very small number—succeeded in saving themselves with the help of poles and ropes which our soldiers reached to them from the shore, but the greater part were drowned.

The number of combatants at the Emperor's disposal in this battle was 68,000 men; that of the allied army amounted to 82,000. Our loss in killed and wounded was about 8000; our enemies admitted that theirs, in killed, wounded, and drowned, reached 14,000. We had made 18,000 prisoners, captured 150 guns and a great quantity of standards and colors.

After giving the order to pursue the enemy in every direction, the Emperor betook himself to his new headquarters

114

at the post-house of Posoritz on the Olmutz road. As may be imagined, he was radiant, but frequently expressed regret that the very eagle we had lost should have belonged to the 4th regiment of the line, of which his brother Joseph was colonel, and should have been captured by the regiment of the Grand Duke Constantine, brother of the Emperor of Russia. The coincidence was, in truth, rather quaint, and made the loss more noticeable. But Napoleon soon received great consolation. Prince John of Lichtenstein came from the Emperor of Austria to request an interview, and Napoleon, understanding that this would result in a peace and would deliver him from the fear of seeing the Prussians march on his rear before he was clear of his present enemy, granted it.

Of all the divisions of the French imperial guard, it was the mounted *chasseurs* who suffered the heaviest loss in their great charge against the Russian guard on the Pratzen plateau. My poor friend, Captain Fournier, had been killed, and General Morland, too. The Emperor, always on the lookout for anything that might kindle the spirit of emulation among the troops, decided that General Morland's body should be placed in the memorial building which he proposed to erect on the Esplanade des Invalides at Paris. The surgeons, having neither the time nor the materials necessary to embalm the general's body on the battlefield, but it into a barrel of rum, which was transported to Paris. But subsequent events having delayed the construction of the monument destined for General Morland, the barrel in which he had been placed was still standing in one of the rooms of the School of Medicine when Napoleon lost the Empire in 1814. Not long afterward the barrel broke through decay, and people were much surprised to find that the rum had made the general's moustaches grow to such an extraordinary extent that they fell below his waist. The corpse was in perfect preservation, but, in order to get possession of it, the family was obliged to bring an action against some scientific man who had made a curiosity of it. Cultivate the love of glory and go and get killed, to let some oaf of a naturalist set you up in his library between a rhinoceros horn and a stuffed crocodile!

I did not receive any wound at the battle of Austerlitz, though I was often in a very exposed position; notably at the time of the cavalry melee on the Pratzen plateau. The Emperor had sent me with an order to General Rapp, whom I succeeded with great difficulty in reaching in the middle of that terrible hurlyburly of slaughterers and slaughtered. My horse came in contact with that of one of the Noble Guard, and our sabres were on the point of crossing when we were forced apart by the combatants, and I got off with a severe contusion. But the next day I incurred a much greater danger of a very different kind from those which one ordinarily meets on the field of battle. It happened in this way. On the morning of the third, the Emperor mounted and rode round the different positions where the fights of the day before had taken place. Having reached the shores of the Satschan Lake, Napoleon dismounted, and was chatting with several marshals round a campfire when he saw floating a hundred yards from the embankment a large isolated ice floe on which was stretched a poor Russian noncommissioned officer with a decoration. The poor fellow could not help himself, having got a bullet through his thigh, and his blood had stained the ice floe which supported him. It was a horrible sight. Seeing a numerous staff surrounded by guards, the man judged that Napoleon must be there; he raised himself as well as he could, and cried out that as soldiers of all countries became brothers when the fight was over, he begged his life of the powerful Emperor of the French. Napoleon's interpreter having translated this entreaty, he was touched by it, and ordered General Bertrand, his aide-de-camp, to do what he could to save the poor man. Straightway several men of the escort, and even two staff officers, seeing two great tree-trunks on the bank, pushed them into the water, and then, getting astride them, they thought that by moving their legs simultaneously they would drive these pieces of wood forward. But scarcely were they a fathom from the edge than they rolled over, throwing into the water the men who bestrode them. Their clothes were saturated in a moment, and as it was freezing very hard, the cloth of their sleeves and their trousers became stiff as they swam, and their limbs, shut up, as it were, in cases, could not move, so that several came near being drowned, and they only got back to land with great difficulty, by the help of ropes which were thrown to them.

I bethought me then of saying that the swimmers ought to have stripped; in the first place to preserve their freedom of movement, and secondly to avoid having to pass the night in wet clothes. General Bertrand, having heard this, repeated it to the Emperor, who declared that I was right and that the others had shown more zeal than discretion. I do not wish to make myself out better than I am, so I will admit that just having taken part in a battle where I had seen thousands of dead and dying, the edge had been taken off my sensibility and I did not feel philanthropic enough to run the risk of a bad cold by contesting with the ice floes the life of an enemy. I felt quite content with deploring his sad fate. But the Emperor's answer piqued me, and it seemed to me that I should be open to ridicule if I gave advice and did not dare to carry it into execution. So I leapt from my horse, and stripped myself naked and dashed into the water. I had gone fast in the course of the day and got hot, so that the chill struck me keenly, but I was young and vigorous and a good swimmer; the Emperor's presence encouraged me, and I struck out toward the Russian sergeant. At the same time my example, and probably the praise given me by the Emperor, determined a lieutenant of artillery, by name Roumestain, to imitate me.

While he was undressing I was advancing, but with a good deal more difficulty than I had foreseen. The older and stronger ice, which had been smashed to pieces the day before, had almost entirely disappeared, but a new skin had formed some line in thickness, the sharp edges of which scratched the skin of my arms, breast, and neck in a very unpleasant fashion. The artillery officer, who had caught me up halfway, had not perceived it at all, having profited by the path which I had opened in the new ice. He called my attention to this fact, and generously demanded to be allowed to take his turn at leading, to which I agreed, for I was cruelly cut up. At last we reached the huge floe of old ice on which the poor Russian was lying, and thought that the most laborious part of our enterprise was achieved. There we were quite wrong, for as soon as we began to push the floe forward the layer of new ice which covered the surface of the water, being broken by contact with it, piled itself up in front, so as in a short time to form a mass which not only resisted our efforts but began to break the edges of the big floe. The bulk of this got smaller every moment, and we began to fear that the poor man whom we were trying to save would be drowned before our eyes. The edges, moreover, of the floe were remarkably sharp, so that we had to choose spots on which to rest our hands and our chest as we pushed. We were at our last gasp. Finally, by way of a crowning stroke, as we got near the bank the ice split in several places, and the portion on which the Russian lay was reduced to a slab only a few feet in breadth, quite insufficient to bear his weight. He was on the point of sinking when my comrade and I, feeling bottom at length, slipped our shoulders under the ice slab and bore it to the shore. They threw us ropes, which we fastened round the Russian, and he was at last hoisted onto the beach. We had to use the same means to get out of the water, for we were wearied, torn, bruised, and bleeding, and could hardly stand. My kind comrade Massy, who had watched me with the greatest anxiety throughout my swim, had been so thoughtful as to have his horse-cloth warmed before the campfire, and as soon as I was out of the water he wrapped me in it. After a good rubdown I put on my clothes and wanted to stretch out by the fire, but this Dr. Larrey forbade, and ordered me to walk about, to do which I required the help of two *chasseurs*. The Emperor came and congratulated the artillery lieutenant and me on our courage in undertaking and achieving the rescue of the wounded Russian, and calling his Mameluke Rouston, who always carried refreshments with him on his horse, he poured us out a glass of excellent rum, and asked us, laughing, how we had liked our bath. As for the Russian sergeant, the Emperor directed Dr. Larrey to attend him, and gave him several pieces of gold. He was fed and put into dry clothes, and after being wrapped in warm rugs, he was taken to a house in Telnitz which was used as an ambulance, and transferred the next day to the hospital at Brunn. The poor lad blessed the Emperor as well as M. Roumestain and me, and would kiss our hands. He was Lithuanian, a native, that is, of a province of the old Poland now joined to Russia. As soon as he was well he declared that he would never serve any other than the Emperor Napoleon, so he returned to France with our wounded and was enrolled in the Polish legion. Ultimately he became a sergeant in the lancers of the guard, and whenever I came across him he testified his gratitude in broken but expressive language.

My icy bath, and the really superhuman efforts which I had had to make to save the poor man, might have cost me dear if I had been less young and vigorous. M. Roumestain, who did not possess the latter advantage to the same extent as I, was seized that same evening with violent congestion of the lungs, and had to be taken to the hospital, where he passed several months between life and death. He never, indeed, recovered completely, and had to leave the service invalided some years later. As for myself, though I was very weak, I got myself hoisted onto my horse when the Emperor left the lake to go to the château of Austerlitz, where his headquarters now were. Napoleon always went at a gallop, and in my shaken state this pace did not suit me; still, I kept up, because the night was coming on and I was afraid of straying; besides which, if I had gone at a walk the cold would have got hold of me. When I reached the château it took several men to help me to dismount, a shivering fit seized me, my teeth were chattering, and I was quite ill. Colonel Dahlmann, lieutenant-colonel of the mounted *chasseurs* who had just been promoted to general in place of Morland, grateful doubtless for the service I had rendered his late chief, took me into one of the outbuildings of the château, where he and his officers were established. After having given me some very hot tea, his surgeon rubbed me all over with warm oil; they swaddled me in many rugs and stuck me into a great heap of hay, leaving only my face outside. Gradually a pleasant warmth penetrated my numbed limbs. I slept soundly, and thanks to all this kind care, as well as to my twenty-three years, I found myself next morning fresh and in good condition, and was able to mount my horse and witness an extremely interesting spectacle.

The defeat the Russians had undergone had thrown their army into such disorder that all who escaped the disaster of Austerlitz made haste to reach Galicia and get out of the victor's power. The rout was complete; we took many prisoners and found the roads covered with deserted cannon and baggage. The Emperor of Russia, who had made sure of victory, went away in hopeless grief, authorizing his ally Francis II to make terms with Napoleon. On the very evening of the battle, the Emperor of Austria, to save his country from utter ruin, begged an interview of the French Emperor, and Napoleon agreeing, had halted at the village of Nasied-lowitz. The interview took place on the fourth, near the mill of Poleny, between the French and Austrian lines. I was present at this memorable meeting. Napoleon, starting very early from the château with his staff, was the first at the place of meeting. He dismounted and was strolling about when, seeing the Emperor of Austria approaching, he went toward him and embraced him cordially. A strange sight for the philosopher to reflect on! An Emperor of Germany come to humble himself by suing for peace to the son of a small Corsican family, not long ago a sublieutenant of artillery, whom his talents, his good fortune, and the courage of the French soldier had raised to the summit of power, and made the arbiter of the destinies of Europe!

The British Burn Washington

by George R. Glieg

In August 1814, as the War of 1812 neared its end, the British captured and burned the city of Washington. Forces led by General Robert Ross, having landed in Maryland from Chesapeake Bay, easily brushed past the Yankee militia at Bladensburg and entered the American capital on the heels of the fleeing President Madison. George R. Glieg, one of Ross's officers, described what happened.

As it was not the intention of the British government to attempt permanent conquests in this part of America; and as the General was well aware that, with a handful of men, he could not pretend to establish himself, for any length of time, in an enemy's capital, he determined to lay it under contribution, and to return quietly to the shipping. . . .

Such being the intention of General Ross, he did not march the troops immediately into the city, but halted them upon a plain in its immediate vicinity, whilst a flag of truce was sent in with terms. But whatever his proposal might have been, it was not so much as heard; for scarcely had the party bearing the flag entered the street, than they were fired upon from the windows of one of the houses, and the horse of the General himself, who accompanied them, killed. . . . All thoughts of accommodation were instantly laid aside; the troops advanced forthwith into the town, and having first put to the sword all who were found in the house from which the shots were fired, and reduced it to ashes, they proceeded, without a moment's delay, to burn and destroy everything in the most distant degree connected with government. In this general devastation were included the Senate-house, the President's palace, an extensive dock-yard and arsenal, barracks for two or three thousand men, several large store-houses filled with naval and military stores, some hundreds of cannon of different descriptions, and nearly twenty thousand stand of small arms. There were also two or three public rope-works which shared the same fate, a fine frigate pierced for sixty guns, and just ready to be launched, several gun-brigs and armed schooners, with a variety of gun-boats and small craft. The powder magazines were of course set on fire, and exploded with a tremendous crash, throwing down many houses in their vicinity, partly by pieces of the walls striking them, and partly by the concussion of the air; whilst quantities of shot, shell, and hand-grenades, which could not otherwise be rendered useless, were thrown into the river. . . .

Had the arm of vengeance been extended no farther, there would not have been room given for so much as a whisper of disapprobation. But, unfortunately, it did not stop here, a noble library, several printing offices, and all of the national archives were likewise committed to the flames, which, though no doubt the property of government, might better have been spared.

While the third brigade was thus employed, the rest of the army, having recalled its stragglers, and removed the wounded into Bladensburg, began its march towards Washington. Though the battle was ended by four o'clock, the sun had set before the different regiments were in a condition to move, consequently this short journey was performed in the dark. The work of destruction had also begun in the city, before they quitted their ground; and the blazing of houses, ships, and stores, the report of exploding magazines, and the crash of falling roofs, informed them, as they proceeded, of what was going forward. You can conceive nothing finer than the sight which met them as they drew near to the town. The sky was brilliantly illumined by the different conflagrations; and a dark red light was thrown upon the road, sufficient to permit each man to view distinctly his comrade's face. . . .

I need scarcely observe, that the consternation of the inhabitants was complete, and that to them this was a night of terror. So confident had they been of the success of their troops, that few of them had dreamt of quitting their houses, or abandoning the city; nor was it till the fugitives from the battle began to rush in, filling every place as they came with dismay, that the President himself thought of providing for his safety. The gentleman, as I was credibly informed, had gone forth in the morning with the army, and had continued among his troops till the British forces began to make their appearance. Whether the sight of his enemies cooled his courage or not, I cannot say, but, according to my informer, no sooner was the glittering of our arms discernible, than he began to discover that his presence was more wanted in the senate than with the army; and having ridden through the ranks, and exhorted every man to do his duty, he hurried back to his own house, that he might prepare a feast for the entertainment of his officers, when they should return victorious. For the truth of these details, I will not be answerable; but this much I know, that the feast was actually prepared, though, instead of being devoured by American officers it went to satisfy the less delicate appetites of a party of English soldiers. When the detachment, sent out to destroy Mr. Maddison's house, entered his dining parlour, they found a dinner-table spread, and covers laid for forty guests. Several kinds of wine, in handsome cut-glass decanters, were cooling on the sideboard; plate-holders stood by the fire-place, filled with dishes and plates; knives, forks and spoons, were arranged for immediate use; in short, everything was ready for the entertainment of a ceremonious party. Such were the arrangements in the dining-room, whilst in the kitchen were others answerable to them in every respect. Spits, loaded with joints of various sorts, turned before the fire; pots, saucepans, and other culinary utensils, stood upon the grate; and all the other requisites for an elegant and substantial repast, were exactly in a state which indicated that they had been lately and precipitately abandoned.

You will readily imagine, that these preparations were beheld, by a party of hungry soldiers, with no indifferent eye. An elegant dinner, even though considerably over-dressed, was a luxury to which few of them, at least for some time back, had been accustomed; and which, after the dangers and fatigues of the day, appeared peculiarly inviting. They sat down to it, therefore, not indeed in the most orderly manner, but with countenances which would not have disgraced a party of aldermen at a civic feast; and having satisfied their appetites with fewer complaints than would have probably escaped their rival *gourmands*, and partaken pretty freely of the wines, they finished by setting fire to the house which had so liberally entertained them. . . .

At day-break next morning, the light brigade moved into the city, while the reserve fell back to a height, about half a mile in the rear. Little, however, now remained to be done, because everything marked out for destruction, was already consumed. Of the senate-house, the President's palace, the barracks, the dock-yard, &c. nothing could be seen, except heaps of smoking ruins; and even the bridge, a noble structure upwards of a mile in length, was almost wholly demolished. There was, therefore, no farther occasion to scatter the troops, and they were accordingly kept together as much as possible on the Capitol hill.

Stonewall Jackson's Last Days

by Henry Kyd Douglas

On May 10, 1863, Major General Thomas Jonathan Jackson—the great "Stonewall" Jackson of the Confederate Army—died of wounds. The story of Stonewall's last days is told here by Henry Kyd Douglas, the youngest officer on Jackson's staff. Douglas completed the manuscript of his memoirs in 1899, at which time he wrote movingly: "My wounds have healed long ago and have left no hurt. While I cannot 'go back on' the boy soldier of '61, whose hair was as black as his coat is now and whose coat was as grey as his hair is now, I remember that in '99 he is wearing glasses, that few of his comrades are left, and that it behooves him to write soberly, discreetly, and fairly." This, as the reader will see, he did—and the reader will also discover the source of Ernest Hemingway's title *Across the River and into the Trees*. The place: Chancellorsville, Virginia. The time: May 1, 1863. The protagonists, the Confederates under Lee, the Union under Hooker—with Stonewall Jackson on the Confederate left wing.

The night was clear and cold. The General had neither overcoat nor blanket, for his wagon was far in the rear. Lieutenant J. P. Smith, aide-de-camp, offered him his cape, which the General at first refused and then, not to appear inconsiderate of Smith's persistent politeness, accepted. But he did not use it long. Waking up after a short doze, he observed Smith asleep near a tree and went up to him and placed the cape on its owner so quietly that he was not aroused and slept on in comfort. When Smith awoke, the General was asleep in his old position. It was a sad as well as tender incident for the General caught a cold that night, which predisposed his system to that attack of pneumonia which ended in his death.

But neither Lee nor Jackson had any idea of knocking the head of their troops against the breastworks of General Hooker. Major Jed Hotchkiss, Jackson's topographical engineer, had been sent out in the night to ascertain whether there was not a feasible route around the right flank of the enemy. His report with a map satisfied General Lee that it was practicable, and naturally Jackson was selected to make the movement. He then began his last and greatest flank movement; the one that for all time established his reputation—as said by a Federal officer, wounded at Chancellorsville, who had served fifteen years in an European army—as the "supremest flanker and rearer" the world had ever seen.

With General R. E. Rodes' division in front, covered on the flank and rear by Fitz Lee's cavalry, the column moved silently and rapidly in a semicircle by Catherine Furnace and the Brock road, until it came out again on the Plank road, which it had left on the other side of the enemy. Up to this point Jackson had marched about fifteen miles. His first intention was to turn at this point and move down the road against the enemy. But after a brief consultation with General Fitz Lee, he left the Stonewall Brigade with him to prevent any movement down that road and crossing it with the head of his column moved on to the Old Turnpike. He directed me to remain with General Lee and bring in person any report General Lee might wish to send. Thus having completely gained the rear of the Federal right wing, he put his first division in line and moved quickly against the enemy.

From my position with Lee and Paxton on the Plank road in advance of their commands, I witnessed the exciting spectacle. The surprise was complete. There was not even a skirmish line to give General Howard warning that the Rebels were upon him. Having no time for a formation, the retreat became a stampede. It was about six o'clock when the bugles of Rodes—Blackford in charge of them—sounded the advance, while the Eleventh Corps was preparing its evening meal with the sound of whistling and song. Following the bugles were a few scattering shots, then from the opening in the road the whiz of a shell, and, following after the wild game escaping from the wood, "Jackson's Foot Cavalry" were upon them. The grey line moved on regularly with whoop and yell and the rattle of musketry. There was, there could be, no effective attempt at resistance.

The Stonewall Brigade was not engaged. It was enjoying the novel sensation of watching a running fight without taking part in it. But it moved on in line toward the enemy, when uncovered by Jackson's advance, so as to unite with the division, for General Fitz Lee had no further use for it. I hurried on to the division to report for orders and to give a message to General Jackson. But I did not see General Jackson at all. It was getting dark—in fact, was dark—and, my brigade not being up, I joined General A. P. Hill at his request. He was busy getting his division into position to take the place of Rodes and Colston, whose divisions had become intermixed in the confusion of the charge and of the darkness.

During the advance of Jackson, General Lee was pressing McLaws' and Anderson's divisions against Hooker's front from the other side, and Early was watching and occupying Sedgwick with his usual skill. General Jackson was most impatient to "push on" and urged everyone to put forth his best efforts to that end. He wanted to get possession of the United States Ford road, which was the direct route from Hooker's rear.

Rumors came from the front that the enemy were mass-ing and were getting ready to make a charge down the road from Chancellorsville. General Jackson, determined to investigate for himself, put aside all warnings and rode directly to the front with Boswell, Morrison, and Wilbourn, of his staff, and several couriers and others. Crutchfield was already in the front, locating and directing some artillery. It does not seem likely that the General went directly along the road, but evidently went through our lines at another position. It seems now an unnecessary as well as a fatal thing for him to do. He was soon fired upon by a squad of the enemy and several horses were shot. I believed from what I heard at the time that by that volley General Jackson was shot through the right hand. Warned that they were actually in the lines of the enemy, the little cavalcade galloped off to the left and rear, into the shelter of the wood. Suddenly from the rear came a cry of, "Yankee Cavalry!" and a sharp volley (from Confederate guns) rang out on the night air and sent death among its friends.

General Jackson was shot through the left arm below the shoulder, and in the left wrist. Boswell, gallant, chivalric Boswell, fell from his horse, shot through the heart. Morrison had his horse shot under him. Captain Howard, a staff officer with Hill, was also wounded. Captain Forbes was killed and Sergeant Cunliffe mortally wounded. The courier just behind the General was killed, and another wounded; a number of horses were killed or wounded. "Little Sorrel" became frantic with fright, rushed first toward the enemy, then, being turned by the General with his wounded hand, broke again to the rear. The General was struck in the face by a hanging limb, his cap was knocked from his head, and when he was reeling from his saddle his horse was stopped by Captain Wilbourn into whose arms he fell. Suddenly the enemy's artillery opened on the scene and added to the confusion and horror of it. Others of the party were killed or wounded, and verily, in the language of General Sherman, "war was hell" that night.

Pendleton came and rode rapidly away for a surgeon. McGuire soon came and found that Dr. Barr of Hill's command had been doing what he could for the General. Colonel Crutchfield, Jackson's chief of artillery, had been badly injured by a shot in the leg which disabled him for a year.

130

Captain Benjamin Watkins Leigh, serving that day on Hill's staff, afterwards killed at Gettysburg, had his horse killed and was wounded slightly while helping Smith, who had come up, and Morrison to carry the General to the rear. It was a pandemonium of death and confusion, but above it all rose the iron purpose and commands of Jackson to General Pender and others to hold their positions.

And well was he seconded by Pendleton that night. At first, overcome by his personal grief and loss, as soon as he had seen McGuire and told him what had happened, he fell fainting from his horse. It was but a moment of weakness; he rallied, was soon in the saddle and during the night he remained there, knowing intuitively what should be done. A. P. Hill, having left Jackson when he was started for the hospital, was returning to his division to take command of Jackson's corps and issue orders when he, too, was wounded by a piece of a shell. I was with him at the time and a piece perhaps of the same shell cut through my boot and, cutting my stirrup leather, dropped the stirrup to the ground. He was temporarily disabled, and I immediately rode off to inform Pendleton. I met him on the road. He said General Rodes was next in command. At whose suggestion I do not know, but word was at once sent for General J. E. B. Stuart to come and take command of the Second Corps. When he arrived, both Hill and Rodes turned over the command to him. Everyone recognized at once that General Jackson would have suggested him as his choice to take command of the corps in that emergency. Certainly, as a matter of policy, for its effect upon the troops, the selection was a most judicious one. During the greater part of the night the troops were in great disorder, for in spite of the attempt to keep the wounding of Jackson from them it was very generally known throughout the corps. A gloom that was worse than night and disaster seemed to settle upon the army.

After rendering such assistance as I could to Pendleton in trying to communicate with the parts of the corps, I returned to General Paxton and the Stonewall Brigade, which had not been in the confusion that evening. I found General Paxton very much depressed; he had been so for several days. We had a long conversation late at night. At the conclusion, he repeated what he had stated to me in the beginning, that he was convinced he would not survive the next day's battle. He did not seem morbid or superstitious but he spoke with earnest conviction. He then told me exactly where certain private and personal papers were to be found in his desk, then in his headquarters wagon, and told me what some of them were. He requested me to see to it that they were not lost but sent to Lexington. He had the picture of his wife and his Bible with him. He concluded by asking me to write to his wife as soon as he was killed and to see that his body was sent to Lexington by Cox, his faithful orderly, who had recently been made his aide-de-camp. I was never so impressed by a conversation in my life. Paxton was not an emotional man but one of strong mind, cool action, and great force of character. He was the last man to give way to a superstition. When he finished I had no doubt of his sincerity and of his awful prescience. Coming upon the horrors of the evening, I need not say my night was a sleepless, cheerless vigil.

The next morning was Sunday and we were ordered to be ready to move forward at daylight. I had at that hour been along the line of the brigade, and the firing of artillery and of skirmishers had already begun in other parts of the line off to our right. I found General Paxton sitting some distance in rear of his line against a tree. He was reading his Bible. As I approached he closed it, greeted me cheerfully, and we conversed for a little while on indifferent subjects. In a short time the order came to get ready to move to the front. Paxton then recalled our conversation of the night before, asked if I remembered all he had said, and then added that when he fell, Colonel Funk would be the senior officer of the brigade and he would doubtless wish me to render him all the assistance I could in every way. He then said, "I will go to the right regiments of the Brigade—you look after the left," and we separated. We did not get into action for some little time.

After a while we became hotly engaged. For some time part of our brigade became separated and I feared Paxton was with it. We soon had some warm work and my time and attention were fully occupied. At the first lull, I was informed that General Paxton had been shot in the first movement and had died almost instantly. Very soon after, Captain R. J. Barton, Assistant Adjutant General, was wounded. I immediately sought Colonel Funk, directed him to take command,

and briefly told him what General Paxton had said to me.

I will not go into the particulars of the battle. So far as our brigade was involved, it seemed to me I never saw a hotter one. While we were lying behind some logs hastily thrown together, just before the final charge on the Chancellor House, General Stuart came down the line. He sent for me and gave me some specific instructions to communicate to Funk and others. When the charge was made it seemed to be a whirlwind, but Hooker's center was broken. The fight of the day was over for us. Our brigade suffered greatly, losing about 600 killed and wounded—which was a heavy per cent—but the proportion of killed was unusually small.

When the charge was over my attention was called to the new cap Lieutenant Ray had brought me from Richmond. A ball had entered just above the visor and had made its exit, bending a little upwards; and although it cut a lock of my hair, which fell off as I removed my cap, the shot had been such a clean one that I had not known it and had no idea when I received it. But remembering Boonsboro, I swore off from new hats in battle. I left that cap at home as a souvenir, en route to Gettysburg, but I fared no better there. I am indebted to both General Colston, commanding the division, and Colonel Funk for the special mention they made of me in their official reports of that day's battle.

The attack upon Hooker had been generally successful, except that Sedgwick's heavy column, moving from Fredericksburg, had driven Early's small force back and was following him toward Lee's right and rear. This made the position of the Confederate army a very precarious one if Sedgwick should be energetic and successful and if Hooker did his part.

After this Sunday's fight I rode to the brigade hospital and visited all the wounded. After doing that I went to see General Jackson and was with him for an hour. I found him not only cheerful but talkative—in fact, inquisitive. He seemed to be in excellent condition. He expressed great gratification that General Stuart had handled his corps so admirably. He asked about the positions of the divisions and even of the brigades and what news there was of Early. He asked me to describe as well as I could the movements of the several divisions during the battle and tell him what I knew of the losses.

He then began to enquire about individuals, mentioning a number of officers and asking if they were unhurt. He spoke most feelingly of the deaths of Paxton and Boswell. Then, saying he had heard I had been active with the Old Brigade that day, he asked me to tell him all about its movements. I described to him its different evolutions from the beginning: how Paxton was reading his Bible when the order came to advance, how the brigade assisted in the assault and capture of the first line of the enemy's works, how Paxton was mortally wounded, dying almost immediately, how the brigade then advanced and was repulsed, and how, when Stuart, in person, started it in its last grand charge, it broke over the field toward the enemy, shouting, louder than the din of musketry, "Remember Jackson!" and swept everything like a tempest before it. For a moment his face flushed with excitement and pride and lighted up with the fire of battle. But at once, with moist eyes and quivering voice, he said,

"It was just like them, just like them. They are a noble set of men. The name of Stonewall belongs to that brigade, not to me." This latter sentence he repeated several times before he died.

May 4th was spent by General Lee in punishing Sedgwick, and Hooker gave him no help. Our division did no fighting. I was occupied during the day paroling wounded prisoners at the hospital at Mr. Hatch's house. I wrote to Mrs. Paxton as I promised to do.

May 5th Hooker retreated at night and did not wait for the attack which General Lee had planned. He went back to his old camp.

It rained hard during the day, causing, doubtless, the death of many wounded soldiers. I was at the hospital looking after our wounded.

General Jackson was removed to Mr. Chandler's at Guinea Station, where Mrs. Jackson and Julia joined him.

On the 6th General A. P. Hill took command of our corps, relieving General Stuart. Captain Moore, Divisional Assistant Inspector General, and myself spent the day in company with Dr. Thad S. Gardner, Sixty-second Pennsylvania Volunteers, paroling prisoners. (Under his medical advice I exchanged my pipe for the Doctor's gold pen and holder.) I joined my brigade on the 8th and found it in General Henry Heth's division, and on the next day I had an interview with General Hill in regard to a commander for it.

Sunday, the 10th, was a beautiful day. Service was held by the Reverend Dr. Lacy at General Hill's Headquarters, and the text of his sermon was the hopeful one, "We know all things work together for good to them that fear God." It was an imposing service of the deepest solemnity.

Hope was expressed that the General was getting better, but private information gave no hope. I find this in my diary, "This afternoon my watch stopped at a quarter past three o'clock. At that moment the heart of Stonewall Jackson ceased to beat, and his soul departed for Heaven."

Stonewall Jackson had performed his greatest achievement and, from the hour he was struck down to the delirium of his last moments, his mind was upon it. He was virtually dying on the field, amid the trophies and ruins of his last victory. His spirit was riding on the whirlwind of the conflict.

"Order A. P. Hill to prepare for action!"

"Pass the infantry to the front ——" and his soul seemed ready to go out upon the storm.

And then the light of the eternal future broke upon him and after a pause he said, "No, no, let us cross over the river and rest under the shade of the trees."

That evening the news went abroad, and a great sob swept over the Army of Northern Virginia; it was the heartbreak of the Southern Confederacy.

A Hanging at Andersonville

by John McElroy

In our own time much has been written of the Civil War military prison the South maintained at Andersonville, Georgia—most of it is based on the personal experiences of a Union private named John McElroy. In the late autumn of 1863, McElroy was stationed at the Cumberland Gap near the Confederate-held Powell's Valley in Virginia. He was in high spirits, for he wrote: "Maj. C. H. Beer's Third Battalion, Sixteenth Illinois Cavalry—four companies, each about 75 strong—was sent on the errand of driving out the Rebels and opening up the Valley for our foraging teams. The writer was invited to attend the excursion. As he held the honorable, but not very lucrative position of 'high private' in Company L, of the Battalion, and the invitation came from the Captain, he did not feel at liberty to decline." A few days later Private McElroy was the prisoner of mounted Virginia riflemen and en route, with drooping spirits, for Andersonville. He describes what he found there and, in this excerpt, the execution of a fellow prisoner.

It began to be pretty generally understood through the prison that six men had been sentenced to be hanged, though no authoritative announcement of the fact had been made. There was much canvassing as to where they should be executed, and whether an attempt to hang them inside of the Stockade would not rouse their friends to make a desperate effort to rescue them, which would precipitate a general engagement of even larger proportions than that of the 3d. Despite the result of the affairs of that and the succeeding days, the camp was not yet convinced that the Raiders were really conquered, and the Regulators themselves were not thoroughly at ease on that score. Some five thousand or six thousand new prisoners had come in since the first of the month, and it was claimed that the Raiders had received large reinforcements from those—a claim rendered probable by most of the new-comers being from the Army of the Potomac.

Key and those immediately about him kept their own counsel in the matter, and suffered no secret of their intentions to leak out, until on the morning of the 11th, when it became generally known that the sentences were to be carried into effect that day, and inside the prison.

My first direct information as to this was by a messenger from Key with an order to assemble my company and stand guard over the carpenters who were to erect the scaffold. He informed me that all the Regulators would be held in readiness to come to our relief if we were attacked in force. I had hoped that if the men were to be hanged I would be spared the unpleasant duty of assisting, for, though I believed they richly deserved that punishment, I had much rather some one else administered it upon them. There was no way out of it, however, that I could see, and so "Egypt" and I got the boys together, and marched down to the designated place, which was an open space near the end of the street running from the South Gate, and kept vacant for the purpose of issuing

138

rations. It was quite near the spot where the Raiders' Big
Tent had stood, and afforded as good a view to the rest of
the camp as could be found.

Key had secured the loan of a few beams and rough
planks, sufficient to build a rude scaffold with. Our first duty
was to care for these as they came in, for such was the need
of wood, and plank for tent purposes, that they would scarcely
have fallen to the ground before they were spirited away, had
we not stood over them all the time with clubs.

The carpenters sent by Key came over and set to work.
The N'Yaarkers gathered around in considerable numbers,
sullen and abusive. They cursed us with all their rich vocabu-
lary of foul epithets, vowed that we should never carry out
the execution, and swore that they had marked each one for
vengeance. We returned the compliments in kind, and occasionally it seemed as if a general collision was imminent;
but we succeeded in avoiding this, and by noon the scaffold
was finished. It was a very simple affair. A stout beam was
fastened on the top of two posts, about fifteen feet high. At
about the height of a man's head a couple of boards stretched
across the space between the posts, and met in the center. The
ends at the posts laid on cleats; the ends in the center rested
upon a couple of boards, standing upright, and each having a
piece of rope fastened through a hole in it in such a manner
that a man could snatch it from under the planks serving as
the floor of the scaffold and let the whole thing drop. A rude
ladder to ascend by completed the preparations.

As the arrangements neared completion the excitement
in and around the prison grew intense. Key came over with
the balance of the Regulators, and we formed a hollow square
around the scaffold, our company making the line on the
East Side. There were now thirty thousand in the prison. Of
these about one-third packed themselves as tightly about our
square as they could stand. The remaining twenty thousand
were wedged together in a solid mass on the North Side.
Again I contemplated the wonderful, startling spectacle of
a mosaic pavement of human faces covering the whole broad
hillside.

Outside, the Rebel infantry was standing in the rifle pits,
the artillerymen were in place about their loaded and trained
pieces, the No. 4 of each gun holding the lanyard cord in his

hand, ready to fire the piece at the instant of command. The small squad of cavalry was drawn up on the hill near the Star Fort, and near it were the masters of the hounds, with their yelping packs.

All the hangers-on of the Rebel camp—clerks, teamsters, employes, negroes, hundreds of white and colored women, in all forming a motley crowd of between one and two thousand, were gathered together in a group between the end of the rifle pits and the Star Fort. They had a good view from there, but a still better one could be had a little farther to the right, and in front of the guns. They kept edging up in that direction, as crowds will, though they knew the danger they would incur if the artillery opened.

The day was broiling hot. The sun shot his perpendicular rays down with blistering fierceness, and the densely packed, motionless crowds made the heat almost insupportable.

Key took up his position inside the square to direct matters. With him were Limber Jim, Dick McCullough, and one or two others. Also, Ned Johnson, Tom Larkin, Sergeant Goody, and three others who were to act as hangmen. Each of these six was provided with a white sack, such as the Rebels brought in meal in. Two Corporals of my company—"Stag" Harris and Wat Payne—were appointed to pull the stays from under the platform at the signal.

A little after noon the South Gate opened, and Wirz rode in, dressed in a suit of white duck, and mounted on his white horse—a conjunction which had gained for him the appellation of "Death on a Pale Horse." Behind him walked the faithful old priest, wearing his Church's purple insignia of the deepest sorrow, and reading the service for the condemned. The six doomed men followed, walking between double ranks of Rebel guards.

All came inside the hollow square and halted. Wirz then said:

"Brizners, I return to you dese men so goot as I got dem. You haf tried dem yourselves, and found dem guilty. I haf had notting to do wit it. I vash my hands of eferyting connected wit dem. Do wit dem as you like, and may Gott haf mercy on you and on dem. Garts, about face! Vorwarts, march!"

With this he marched out and left us.

140

For a moment the condemned looked stunned. They seemed to comprehend for the first time that it was really the determination of the Regulators to hang them. Before that they had evidently thought that the talk of hanging was merely bluff. One of them gasped out:

"My God, men, you don't really mean to hang us up there?"

Key answered grimly and laconically.

"That seems to be about the size of it."

At this they burst out in a passionate storm of intercessions and imprecations, which lasted for a minute or so, when it was stopped by one of them saying imperatively:

"All of you stop now, and let the priest talk for us."

At this the priest closed the book upon which he had kept his eyes bent since his entrance, and facing the multitude on the North Side began a plea for mercy.

The condemned faced in the same direction, to read their fate in the countenances of those whom he was addressing. This movement brought Curtis—a low-statured, massively built man—on the right of their line, and about ten or fifteen steps from my company.

The whole camp had been as still as death since Wirz's exit. The silence seemed to become even more profound as the priest began his appeal. For a minute every ear was strained to catch what he said. Then, as the nearest of the thousands comprehended what he was saying they raised a shout of

"No! *no!! No!!*"

"Hang them! hang them!"

"Don't let them go! Never!"

"Hang the rascals! hang the villains!"

"Hang 'em! hang 'em! hang 'em!"

This was taken up all over the prison, and tens of thousands of throats yelled it in a fearful chorus.

Curtis turned from the crowd with desperation convulsing his features. Tearing off the broad-brimmed hat which he wore, he flung it on the ground with the exclamation:

"By God, I'll die this way first!" and, drawing his head down and folding his arms about it, he dashed forward for the center of my company, like a great stone hurled from a catapult.

"Egypt" and I saw where he was going to strike, and ran

141

down the line to help stop him. As he came up we rained blows on his head with our clubs, but so many of us struck at him at once that we broke each other's clubs to pieces, and only knocked him on his knees. He rose with an almost super-human effort, and plunged into the mass beyond.

The excitement almost became delirium. For an instant I feared that everything was gone to ruin. "Egypt" and I strained every energy to restore our lines, before the break could be taken advantage of by the others. Our boys behaved splendidly, standing firm, and in a few seconds the line was restored.

As Curtis broke through, Delaney, a brawny Irishman standing next to him, started to follow. He took one step. At the same instant Limber Jim's long legs took three great strides, and placed him directly in front of Delaney. Jim's right hand held an enormous bowie-knife, and as he raised it above Delaney he hissed out:

"If you dare move another step, you —— —— ——, I'll open you from one end to the other."

Delaney stopped. This checked the others till our lines reformed.

When Wirz saw the commotion he was panic-stricken with fear that the long-dreaded assault on the Stockade had begun. He ran down the headquarter steps to the Captain of the battery, shrieking

"Fire! fire! fire!"

The Captain, not being a fool, could see that the rush was not towards the Stockade, but away from it, and he refrained from giving the order.

But the spectators who had gotten before the guns, heard Wirz's excited yell, and remembering the consequences to themselves should the artillery be discharged, became frenzied with fear, and screamed, and fell down over and trampled upon each other in endeavoring to get away. The guards on that side of the Stockade ran down in a panic, and the ten thousand prisoners immediately around us, expecting no less than that the next instant we would be swept with grape and canister, stampeded tumultuously. There were quite a num-ber of wells right around us, and all of these were filled full of men that fell into them as the crowd rushed away. Many had legs and arms broken, and I have no doubt that several were killed.

142

It was the stormiest five minutes that I ever saw.

While this was going on two of my company, belonging to the Fifth Iowa Cavalry, were in hot pursuit of Curtis. I had seen them start and shouted to them to come back, as I feared they would be set upon by the Raiders and murdered. But the din was so overpowering that they could not hear me, and doubtless would not have come back if they had heard.

Curtis ran diagonally down the hill, jumping over the tents and knocking down the men who happened in his way. Arriving at the swamp he plunged in, sinking nearly to his hips in the fetid, filthy ooze. He forged his way through with terrible effort. His pursuers followed his example, and caught up to him just as he emerged on the other side. They struck him on the back of the head with their clubs, and knocked him down.

By this time order had been restored about us. The guns remained silent, and the crowd massed around us again. From where we were we could see the successful end of the chase after Curtis, and could see his captors start back with him. Their success was announced with a roar of applause from the North Side. Both captors and captured were greatly exhausted, and they were coming back very slowly. Key ordered the balance up on to the scaffold. They obeyed promptly. The priest resumed his reading of the service for the condemned. The excitement seemed to make the doomed ones exceedingly thirsty. I never saw men drink such inordinate quantities of water. They called for it continually, gulped down a quart or more at a time, and kept two men going nearly all the time carrying it to them.

When Curtis finally arrived, he sat on the ground for a minute or so, to rest, and then, reeking with filth, slowly and painfully climbed the steps. Delaney seemed to think he was suffering as much from fright as anything else, and said to him:

"Come on up, now, show yourself a man, and die game."

Again the priest resumed his reading, but it had no interest to Delaney, who kept calling out directions to Pete Donelly, who was standing in the crowd, as to dispositions to be made of certain bits of stolen property: to give a watch to this one, a ring to another, and so on. Once the priest stopped and said:

"My son, let the things of this earth go, and turn your attention toward those of heaven."

Delaney paid no attention to this admonition. The whole six of them began delivering farewell messages to those in the crowd. Key pulled a watch from his pocket and said:

"Two minutes more to talk."

Delaney said cheerfully:

"Well, good-by, b'ys; if I've hurted any of yez, I hope ye'll forgive me. Shpake up, now, any of yez that I've hurted, and say ye'll forgive me."

We called upon Marion Friend, whose throat Delaney had tried to cut three weeks before while robbing him of forty dollars, to come forward, but Friend was not in a forgiving mood, and refused with an oath.

Key said:

"Time's up!"

put the watch back in his pocket and raised his hand like an officer commanding a gun. Harris and Payne laid hold of the ropes to the supports of the planks. Each of the six hangmen tied a condemned man's hands, pulled a meal sack down over his head, placed the noose around his neck, drew it up tolerably close, and sprang to the ground. The priest began praying aloud.

Key dropped his hand. Payne and Harris snatched the supports out with a single jerk. The planks fell with a clatter. Five of the bodies swung around dizzily in the air. The sixth— that of "Mosby," a large, powerful, raw-boned man, one of the worst in the lot, and who, among other crimes, had killed Limber Jim's brother—broke the rope, and fell with a thud to the ground. Some of the men ran forward, examined the body, and decided that he still lived. The rope was cut off his neck, the meal sack removed, and water thrown in his face until consciousness returned. At the first instant he thought he was in eternity. He gasped out:

"Where am I? Am I in the other world?"

Limber Jim muttered that they would soon show him where he was, and went on grimly fixing up the scaffold anew. "Mosby" soon realized what had happened, and the unrelenting purpose of the Regulator Chiefs. Then he began to beg piteously for his life, saying:

"O for God's sake, do not put me up there again! God

144

has spared my life once. He meant that you should be merciful to me."

Limber Jim deigned him no reply. When the scaffold was rearranged, and a stout rope had replaced the broken one, he pulled the meal sack once more over "Mosby's" head, who never ceased his pleadings. Then picking up the large man as if he were a baby, he carried him to the scaffold and handed him up to Tom Larkin, who fitted the noose around his neck and sprang down. The supports had not been set with the same delicacy as at first, and Limber Jim had to set his heel and wrench desperately at them before he could force them out. Then "Mosby" passed away without a struggle.

After hanging till life was extinct, the bodies were cut down, the meal sacks pulled off their faces, and the Regulators formed two parallel lines, through which all the prisoners passed and took a look at the bodies. Pete Donelly and Dick Allen knelt down and wiped the froth off Delaney's lips, and swore vengeance against those who had done him to death.

The Battle at White Bird Canyon

by Chief Joseph

Of all the Indian leaders who resisted the white man's westward movement following the Civil War, none was more able or eloquent than Chief Joseph of the Nez Perce. Writes one of his biographers, Russell Davis: "With three hundred warriors he fought off the armed might of the United States Army while leading the women, children, and old people of his tribe over a tortuous eighteen-hundred-mile trail toward Canada. He fought eleven engagements with the Army, five of them major battles. Of these battles, Joseph won three, fought evenly in one, and lost only one—the last one." That single, devouring defeat came in Montana on October 5, 1877, after Generals Howard and Miles persuaded Chief Joseph to surrender. The white men had promised that the Nez Perce could return to their Wallowa Valley—Land of Winding Waters—in eastern Oregon; the pledge was never honored, much as Howard and Miles, both sincere and honest men, had been confident that it would be. Just before Chief Joseph died in 1904, after a single visit to his beloved Wallowa, he went to Washington to persuade the U.S. government to keep its promise. He said: "Let me be a free man—free to travel, to stop, free to work, free to trade where I choose, free to choose my own teachers, free to follow the religion of my fathers, free to think and talk and act for myself—and I will obey every law, or submit to the penalty." No more noble expression of human aspiration is possible, and yet, the pledge remained dishonored. But Chief Joseph never lost his own honor, as may be seen in his moving account of the events that brought him on the warpath in 1877.

Through all the years since the white man came to Wallowa we have been threatened and taunted by them and the treaty Nez Perces.* They have given us no rest. We have had a few good friends among white men, and they have always advised my people to bear these taunts without fighting. Our young men were quick-tempered, and I have had great trouble in keeping them from doing rash things. I have carried a heavy load on my back ever since I was a boy. I learned then that we were but few, while the white men were many, and that

* Chief Joseph's Nez Perces, who, incidentally, did not pierce their noses as the French phrase suggests, also did not sign the Treaty of 1863 under which the Wallowa lands were ceded to the U.S. Thus, they were known as the "nontreaty" Nez Perces.

we could not hold our own with them. We were like deer. They were like grizzly bears. We had a small country. Their country was large. We were contented to let things remain as the Great Spirit Chief made them. They were not; and would change the rivers and mountains if they did not suit them.

Year after year we have been threatened, but no war was made upon my people until General Howard came to our country two years ago and told us that he was the white war-chief of all that country. He said: "I have a great many soldiers at my back. I am going to bring them up here, and then I will talk to you again. I will not let white men laugh at me the next time I come. The country belongs to the Government, and I intend to make you go upon the reservation."

I remonstrated with him against bringing more soldiers to the Nez Percés country. He had one house full of troops all the time at Fort Lapwai.

The next spring the agent at Umatilla Agency sent an Indian runner to tell me to meet General Howard at Walla Walla. I could not go myself, but I sent my brother and five other head men to meet him, and they had a long talk.

General Howard said: "You have talked straight, and it is all right. You can stay at Wallowa." He insisted that my brother and his company should go with him to Fort Lapwai. When the party arrived there General Howard sent out runners and called all the Indians to a grand council. I was in that council. I said to General Howard, "We are ready to listen." He answered that he would not talk then, but would hold a council next day, when he would talk plainly. I said to General Howard: "I am ready to talk today. I have been in a great many councils, but I am no wiser. We are all sprung from a woman, although we are unlike in many things. We cannot be made over again. You are as you were made, and as you were made you can remain. We are just as we were made by the Great Spirit, and you cannot change us; then why should children of one mother and one father quarrel?—why should one try to cheat the other? I do not believe that the Great Spirit Chief gave one kind of men the right to tell another kind of men what they must do."

General Howard replied: "You deny my authority, do you? You want to dictate to me, do you?"

Then one of my chiefs—Too-hool-hool-suit—rose in the council and said to General Howard: "The Great Spirit Chief made the world as it is, and as He wanted it, and He made a part of it for us to live upon. I do not see where you get authority to say that we shall not live where He place us."

General Howard lost his temper and said: "Shut up! I don't want to hear any more of such talk. The law says you shall go upon the reservation to live, and I want you to do so, but you persist in disobeying the law" (meaning the treaty). "If you do not move, I will take the matter into my own hand, and make you suffer for your disobedience."

Too-hool-hool-suit answered: "Who are you, that you ask us to talk, and then tell me I shan't talk? Are you the Great Spirit? Did you make the world? Did you make the sun? Did you make the rivers to run for us to drink? Did you make the grass to grow? Did you make all these things that you talk to us as though we were boys? If you did, then you have the right to talk as you do."

General Howard replied: "You are an impudent fellow, and I will put you in the guard-house," and then ordered a soldier to arrest him.

Too-hool-hool-suit made no resistance. He asked General Howard: "Is this your order? I don't care. I have expressed my heart to you. I have nothing to take back. I have spoken for my country. You can arrest me, but you cannot change me or make me take back what I have said."

The soldiers came forward and seized my friend and took him to the guard-house. My men whispered among themselves whether they would let this thing be done. I counseled them to submit. I knew if we resisted that all the white men present, including General Howard, would be killed in a moment, and we would be blamed. If I had said nothing, General Howard would never have given order against my men. I saw the danger and while they dragged Too-hool-hool-suit to prison, I arose and said: "*I am going to talk now.* I don't care whether you arrest me or not." I turned to my people and said: "The arrest of Too-hool-hool-suit was wrong, but we will not resent the insult. We were invited to this council to express our hearts, and we have done so." Too-hool-hool-suit was prisoner for five days before he was released.

The council broke up that day. On the next morning

General Howard came to my lodge, and invited me to go with him and White Bird and Looking Glass, to look for land for my people. As we rode along we came to some good land that was already occupied by Indians and white people. General Howard, pointing to this land, said: "If you will come onto the reservation, I will give you these lands and move these people off."

I replied: "No. It would be wrong to disturb these people. I have no right to take their homes. I have never taken what did not belong to me. I will not now."

We rode all day upon the reservation, and found no good land unoccupied. I have been informed by men who do not lie that General Howard sent a letter that night telling the soldiers at Walla Walla to go to Wallowa Valley, and drive us out upon our return home.

In the council next day General Howard informed us in a haughty spirit that he would give my people *thirty days* to go back home, collect all their stock, and move onto the reservation, saying, "If you are not here in that time, I shall consider that you want to fight, and will send my soldiers to drive you on."

I said: "War can be avoided and it ought to be avoided. I want no war. My people have always been the friends of the white man. Why are you in such a hurry? I cannot get ready to move in thirty days. Our stock is scattered, and Snake River is very high. Let us wait until fall, then the river will be low. We want time to hunt our stock and gather our supplies for the winter."

General Howard replied, "If you let the time run over one day, the soldiers will be there to drive you onto the reservation, and all your cattle and horses outside of the reservation at that time will fall into the hands of the white men."

I knew I had never sold my country, and that I had no land in Lapwai; but I did not want bloodshed. I did not want my people killed. I did not want anybody killed. Some of my people had been murdered by white men, and the white murderers were never punished for it. I told General Howard about this, and again said I wanted no war. I wanted the people who live upon the lands I was to occupy at Lapwai to have time to gather their harvest.

I said in my heart that, rather than have war I would

151

give up my country. I would rather give up my father's grave. I would give up everything rather than have the blood of white men upon the hands of my people.

General Howard refused to allow me more than thirty days to move my people and their stock. I am sure that he began to prepare for war at once.

When I returned to Wallowa I found my people very much excited upon discovering that the soldiers were already in the Wallowa Valley. We held a council, and decided to move immediately to avoid bloodshed.

Too-hool-hool-suit, who felt outraged by his imprisonment, talked for war, and made many of my young men willing to fight rather than be driven like dogs from the land where they were born. He declared that blood alone would wash out the disgrace General Howard had put upon him. It required a strong heart to stand up against such talk, but I urged my people to be quiet, and not to begin a war.

We gathered all the stock we could find, and made an attempt to move. We left many of our horses and cattle in Wallowa, and we lost several hundred in crossing the river. All my people succeeded in getting across in safety. Many of the Nez Perces came together in Rocky Canyon to hold a grand council. I went with all my people. This council lasted ten days. There was a great deal of war talk and a great deal of excitement. There was one young brave present whose father had been killed by a white man five years before. This man's blood was bad against white men and he left the council calling for revenge.

Again I counseled peace, and I thought the danger was past. We had not complied with General Howard's order because we could not, but we intended to do so as soon as possible. I was leaving the council to kill beef for my family, when news came that the young man whose father had been killed had gone out with several hot-blooded young braves and killed four white men. He rode up to the council and shouted: "Why do you sit here like women? The war has begun already." I was deeply grieved. All the lodges were moved except my brother's and my own. I saw clearly that the war was upon us when I learned that my young men had been secretly buying ammunition. I heard then that Too-hool-hool-suit, who had been imprisoned by General Howard, had succeeded in organizing a war party. I knew that their acts would involve all my people. I saw that the war could not then be prevented. The time had passed. I counseled peace from the beginning. I knew that we were too weak to fight the United States. We had many grievances, but I knew that war would bring more. We had good white friends, who advised us against taking the war-path. My friend and brother, Mr. Chapman, who has been with us since the surrender, told us just how the war would end. Mr. Chapman took sides against us and helped General Howard. I do not blame him for doing so. He tried hard to prevent bloodshed. We hoped the white settlers would not join the soldiers. Before the war commenced we had discussed this matter all over, and many of my people were in favor of warning them that if they took no part against us they should not be molested in the event of war being begun by General Howard. This plan was voted down in the war-council.

There were bad men among my people who had quarreled with white men, and they talked of their wrongs until they roused all the bad hearts in the council. Still I could not believe that they would begin the war. I know that my young men did a great wrong, but I ask, Who was first to blame? They had been insulted a thousand times; their fathers and brothers had been killed; their mothers and wives had been disgraced; they had been driven to madness by the whiskey sold to them by the white men; they had been told by General Howard that all their horses and cattle which they had been unable to drive out of Wallowa were to fall into the hands of white men; and, added to all this, they were homeless and desperate.

I would have given my own life if I could have undone the killing of white men by my people. I blame my young men and I blame the white men. I blame General Howard for not giving my people time to get their stock away from Wallowa. I do not acknowledge that he had the right to order me to leave Wallowa at any time. I deny that either my father or myself ever sold that land. It is still our land. It may never again be our home, but my father sleeps there, and I love it as I love my mother. I left there, hoping to avoid bloodshed.

If General Howard had given me plenty of time to gather

153

up my stock, and treated Too-hool-hool-suit as a man should be treated, *there would have been no war*. My friends among white men have blamed me for the war. I am not to blame. When my young men began the killing, my heart was hurt. Although I did not justify them, I remembered all the insults I had endured, and my blood was on fire. Still I would have taken my people to the buffalo country without fighting, if possible.

I could see no other way to avoid a war. We moved over to White Bird Creek, sixteen miles away, and there encamped, intending to collect our stock before leaving; but the soldiers attacked us and the first battle was fought. We numbered in that battle sixty men, and the soldiers retreated before us for twelve miles. They lost thirty-three killed, and had seven wounded. When an Indian fights, he only shoots to kill; but soldiers shoot at random. None of the soldiers were scalped. We do not believe in scalping, nor in killing wounded men. Soldiers do not kill many Indians unless they are wounded and left upon the battle-field. Then they kill Indians.

Seven days after the first battle General Howard arrived in the Nez Perce country, bringing seven hundred more soldiers. It was now war in earnest. We crossed over Salmon River, hoping General Howard would follow. We were not disappointed. He did follow us, and we got between him and his supplies, and cut him off for three days. He sent out two companies to open the way. We attacked them, killing one officer, two guides, and ten men.

We withdrew, hoping the soldiers would follow, but they had got fighting enough for that day. They entrenched themselves, and next day we attacked again. The battle lasted all day, and was renewed next morning. We killed four and wounded seven or eight.

About this time General Howard found out that we were in his rear. Five days later he attacked us with three hundred and fifty soldiers and settlers. We had two hundred and fifty warriors. The fight lasted twenty-seven hours. We lost four killed and several wounded. General Howard's loss was twenty-nine men killed and sixty wounded.

The following day the soldiers charged upon us, and we retreated with our families and stock a few miles, leaving eighty lodges to fall into General Howard's hands.

154

Finding that we were outnumbered, we retreated to Bitter Root Valley. Here another body of soldiers came upon us and demanded our surrender. We refused. They said, "You cannot get by us." We answered, "We are going by you without fighting if you will let us, but we are going by you anyhow." We then made a treaty with these soldiers. We agreed not to molest anyone and they agreed that we might pass through the Bitter Root country in peace. We bought provisions and traded stock with white men there.

We understood that there was to be no war. We intended to go peaceably to the buffalo country, and leave the question of returning to our country to be settled afterward.

With this understanding we traveled on for four days, and thinking that the trouble was over, we stopped and prepared tent-poles to take with us. We started again, and at the end of two days we saw three white men passing our camp. Thinking that peace had been made, we did not molest them. We could have killed, or taken them prisoners, but we did not suspect them of being spies, which they were.

That night the soldiers surrounded our camp. About daybreak one of my men went out to look after his horses. The soldiers saw him and shot him down like a coyote. I have since learned that these soldiers were not those we had left behind. They had come upon us from another direction. The new white war-chief's name was Gibbon. He charged upon us while some of my people were still asleep. We had a hard fight. Some of my men crept around and attacked the soldiers from the rear. In this battle we lost nearly all our lodges, but we finally drove General Gibbon back.

Finding that he was not able to capture us, he sent to his camp a few miles away for his big guns [cannons], but my men had captured them and all the ammunition. We damaged the big guns all we could, and carried away the powder and lead. In the fight with General Gibbon we lost fifty women and children and thirty fighting men. We remained long enough to bury our dead. The Nez Perces never make war on women and children; we could have killed a great many women and children while the war lasted, but we would feel ashamed to do so cowardly an act.

We never scalp our enemies, but when General Howard

came up and joined General Gibbon, their Indian scouts dug up our dead and scalped them. I have been told that General Howard did not order this great shame to be done.

We retreated as rapidly as we could toward the buffalo country. After six days General Howard came close to us, and we went out and attacked him, and captured nearly all his horses and mules (about two hundred and fifty head). We then marched on to the Yellowstone Basin.

On the way we captured one white man and two white women. We released them at the end of three days. They were treated kindly. The women were not insulted. Can the white soldiers tell me of one time when Indian women were taken prisoners, and held three days and then released without being insulted? Were the Nez Perces women who fell into the hands of General Howard's soldiers treated with as much respect? I deny that a Nez Perce was ever guilty of such a crime.

A few days later we captured two more white men. One of them stole a horse and escaped. We gave the other a poor horse and told him that he was free.

Nine days' march brought us to the mouth of Clarke's Fork of the Yellowstone. We did not know what had become of General Howard, but we supposed that he had sent for more horses and mules. He did not come up, but another new war-chief [General Sturgis] attacked us. We held him in check while we moved all our women and children and stock out of danger, leaving a few men to cover our retreat.

Several days passed, and we heard nothing of General Howard, or Gibbon, or Sturgis. We had repulsed each in turn, and began to feel secure, when another army, under General Miles, struck us. This was the fourth army, each of which outnumbered our fighting forces, that we had encountered within sixty days.

We had no knowledge of General Miles' army until a short time before he made a charge upon us, cutting our camp in two, and capturing nearly all of our horses. About seventy men, myself among them, were cut off. My little daughter, twelve years of age, was with me. I gave her a rope, and told her to catch a horse and join the others who were cut off from the camp. I have not seen her since, but I have learned that she is alive and well.

156

I thought of my wife and children, who were now surrounded by soldiers, and I resolved to go to them or die. With a prayer in my mouth to the Great Spirit Chief who rules above, I dashed unarmed through the line of soldiers. It seemed to me that there were guns on every side, before and behind me. My clothes were cut to pieces and my horse was wounded, but I was not hurt. As I reached the door of my lodge, my wife handed me my rifle, saying: "Here's your gun. Fight!"

The soldiers kept up a continuous fire. Six of my men were killed in one spot near me. Ten or twelve soldiers charged into our camp and got possession of two lodges, killing three Nez Perces and losing three of their men, who fell inside our lines. I called my men to drive them back. We fought at close range, not more than twenty steps apart, and drove the soldiers back upon their main line, leaving their dead in our hands. We secured their arms and ammunition. We lost, the first day and night, eighteen men and three women. General Miles lost twenty-six killed and forty wounded. The following day General Miles sent a messenger into my camp under protection of a white flag. I sent my friend Yellow Bull to meet him.

Yellow Bull understood the messenger to say that General Miles wished me to consider the situation; that he did not want to kill my people unnecessarily. Yellow Bull understood this to be a demand for me to surrender and save blood. Upon reporting this message to me, Yellow Bull said he wondered whether General Miles was in earnest. I sent him back with my answer, that I had not made up my mind, but would think about it and send word soon. A little later he sent some Cheyenne scouts with another message. I went out to meet them. They said they believed that General Miles was sincere and really wanted peace. I walked on to General Miles' tent. He met me and we shook hands. He said, "Come, let us sit down by the fire and talk this matter over." I remained with him all night; next morning, Yellow Bull came over to see if I was alive, and why I did not return.

General Miles would not let me leave the tent to see my friend alone.

Yellow Bull said to me: "They have got you in their power, and I am afraid they will never let you go again. I have an officer in our camp, and I will hold him until they let you go free."

I said: "I do not know what they mean to do with me, but if they kill me you must not kill the officer. It will do no good to avenge my death by killing him."

Yellow Bull returned to my camp. I did not make any agreement that day with General Miles. The battle was renewed while I was with him. I was very anxious about my people. I knew that we were near Sitting Bull's camp in King George's land, and I thought maybe the Nez Percés who had escaped would return with assistance. No great damage was done to either party during the night.

On the following morning I returned to my camp by agreement, meeting the officer who had been held a prisoner in my camp at the flag of truce. My people were divided about surrendering. We could have escaped from Bear Paw Mountain if we had left our wounded, old women, and children behind. We were unwilling to do this. We had never heard of a wounded Indian recovering while in the hands of white men.

On the evening of the fourth day, General Howard came in with a small escort, together with my friend Chapman. We could now talk understandingly. General Miles said to me in plain words, "If you will come out and give up your arms, I will spare your lives and send you back to the reservation." I do not know what passed between General Miles and General Howard.

I could not bear to see my wounded men and women suffer any longer; we had lost enough already. General Miles had promised that we might return to our country with what stock we had left. I thought we could start again. I believed General Miles, *or I never would have surrendered.* I have heard that he has been censured for making the promise to return us to Lapwai. He could not have made any other terms with me at that time. I would have held him in check until my friends came to my assistance, and then neither of the generals nor their soldiers would have ever left Bear Paw Mountain alive.

On the fifth day I went to General Miles and gave up my gun, and said, "From where the sun now stands I will fight no more." My people needed rest—we wanted peace.

Marines Signalling Under Fire

by Stephen Crane

It is not widely known that Stephen Crane, author of *The Red Badge of Courage*, was a war correspondent as well as a writer of fiction, but he covered the Greco-Turkish War of 1897 and the Spanish-American War of 1898. In June 1898 Crane landed with U.S. Marines at Guantanamo Bay in Cuba, passing through such experiences as the following.

They were four Guantanamo marines, officially known for the time as signalmen, and it was their duty to lie in the trenches of Camp McCalla, that faced the water, and, by day, signal the *Marblehead* with a flag and, by night, signal the *Marblehead* with lanterns. It was my good fortune—at that time I considered it my bad fortune, indeed—to be with them on two of the nights when a wild storm of fighting was pealing about the hill; and, of all the actions of the war, none were so hard on the nerves, none strained courage so near the panic point, as those swift nights in Camp McCalla. With a thousand rifles rattling; with the field-guns booming in your ears; with the diabolic Colt automatics clacking; with the roar of the *Marblehead* coming from the bay, and, last, with Mauser bullets sneering always in the air a few inches over one's head, and with this enduring from dusk to dawn, it is extremely doubtful if any one who was there will be able to forget it easily. The noise; the impenetrable darkness; the knowledge from the sound of the bullets that the enemy was on three sides of the camp; the infrequent bloody stumbling and death of some man with whom, perhaps, one had messed two hours previous; the weariness of the body, and the more terrible weariness of the mind, at the endlessness of the thing, made it wonderful that at least some of the men did not come out of it with their nerves hopelessly in shreds.

But, as this interesting ceremony proceeded in the darkness, it was necessary for the signal squad to coolly take and send messages. Captain McCalla always participated in the defence of the camp by raking the woods on two of its sides with the guns of the *Marblehead*. Moreover, he was the senior officer present, and he wanted to know what was happening. All night long the crews of the ships in the bay would stare sleeplessly into the blackness toward the roaring hill.

The signal squad had an old cracker-box placed on top of the trench. When not signalling they hid the lanterns in this box; but as soon as an order to send a message was received, it became necessary for one of the men to stand up and expose the lights. And then—oh, my eye—how the guerillas hidden in the gulf of night would turn loose at those yellow gleams!

Signalling in this way is done by letting one lantern remain stationary—on top of the cracker-box, in this case—and moving the other over to the left and right and so on in the regular gestures of the wig-wagging code. It is a very simple system of night communication, but one can see that it presents rare possibilities when used in front of an enemy who, a few hundred yards away, is overjoyed at sighting so definite a mark.

How, in the name of wonders, those four men at Camp McCalla were not riddled from head to foot and sent home more as repositories of Spanish ammunition than as marines is beyond all comprehension. To make a confession—when one of these men stood up to wave his lantern, I, lying in the trench, invariably rolled a little to the right or left, in order that, when he was shot, he would not fall on me. But the squad came off scatheless, despite the best efforts of the most formidable corps in the Spanish army—the *Escuadra de Guantanamo*. That it was the most formidable corps in the Spanish army of occupation has been told me by many Spanish officers and also by General Menocal and other insurgent officers. General Menocal was Garcia's chief-of-staff when the latter was operating busily in Santiago province. The regiment was composed solely of *practicos*, or guides, who knew every shrub and tree on the ground over which they moved.

Whenever the adjutant, Lieutenant Draper, came plunging along through the darkness with an order—such as: "Ask the *Marblehead* to please shell the woods to the left"—my heart would come up into my mouth, for I knew then tha one of my pals was going to stand up behind the lanterns and have all Spain shoot at him.

The answer was always upon the instant:

"Yes, sir." Then the bullets began to snap, snap, snap, at his head while all the woods began to crackle like burning straw. I could lie near and watch the face of the signalman, illumined as it was by the yellow shine of lantern light, and the absence of excitement, fright, or any emotion at all on his countenance, was something to astonish all theories out of one's mind. The face was in every instance merely that of a man intent upon his business, the business of wig-wagging into the gulf of night where a light on the *Marblehead* was seen to move slowly.

These times on the hill resembled, in some ways, those terrible scenes on the stage—scenes of intense gloom, blinding lightning, with a cloaked devil or assassin or other appropriate character muttering deeply amid the awful roll of the thunder-drums. It was theatric beyond words: one felt like a leaf in this booming chaos, this prolonged tragedy of the night. Amid it all one could see from time to time the yellow light on the face of a preoccupied signalman.

Possibly no man who was there ever before understood the true eloquence of the breaking of the day. We would lie staring into the east, fairly ravenous for the dawn. Utterly worn to rags, with our nerves standing on end like so many bristles, we lay and watched the east—the unspeakably obdurate and slow east. It was a wonder that the eyes of some of us did not turn to glass balls from the fixity of our gaze.

Then there would come into the sky a patch of faint blue light. It was like a piece of moonshine. Some would say it was the beginning of daybreak; others would declare it was nothing of the kind. Men would get very disgusted with each other in these low-toned arguments held in the trenches. For my part, this development in the eastern sky destroyed many of my ideas and theories concerning the dawning of the day; but then I had never before had occasion to give it such solemn attention.

This patch widened and whitened in about the speed of a man's accomplishments if he should be in the way of painting Madison Square Garden with a camel's hair brush. The guerillas always set out to whoop it up about this time, because they knew the occasion was approaching when it would be expedient for them to elope. I, at least, always grew furious with this wretched sunrise. I thought I could have walked around the world in the time required for the old thing to get up above the horizon.

One midnight, when an important message was to be sent to the *Marblehead*, Colonel Huntington came himself to the signal place with Adjutant Draper and Captain McCauley, the quartermaster. When the man stood up to signal, the colonel stood beside him. At sight of the lights, the Spaniards performed as usual. They drove enough bullets into that immediate vicinity to kill all the marines in the corps.

Lieutenant Draper was agitated for his chief. "Colonel, won't you step down, sir?"

"Why, I guess not," said the grey old veteran in his slow, sad, always-gentle way. "I am in no more danger than the man."

"But, sir—" began the adjutant.

"Oh, it's all right, Draper."

So the colonel and the private stood side to side and took the heavy fire without either moving a muscle.

Day was always obliged to come at last, punctuated by a final exchange of scattering shots. And the light shone on the marines, the dumb guns, the flag. Grimy yellow face looked into grimy yellow face, and grinned with weary satisfaction. Coffee!

Usually it was impossible for many of the men to sleep at once. It always took me, for instance, some hours to get my nerves combed down. But then it was great joy to lie in the trench with the four signalmen, and understand thoroughly that that night was fully over at last, and that, although the future might have in store other bad nights, that one could never escape from the prison-house which we call the past.

AT THE WILD LITTLE FIGHT AT CUSCO there were some splendid exhibitions of wig-wagging under fire. Action began when an advanced detachment of marines under Lieutenant Lucas with the Cuban guides had reached the summit of a ridge overlooking a small valley where there was a house, a well, and a thicket of some kind of shrub with great broad, oily leaves. This thicket, which was perhaps an acre in extent, contained the guerillas. The valley was open to the sea. The distance from the top of the ridge to the thicket was barely two hundred yards.

The *Dolphin* had sailed up the coast in line with the marine advance, ready with her guns to assist in any action. Captain Elliott, who commanded the two hundred marines in this fight, suddenly called out for a signalman. He wanted a man to tell the *Dolphin* to open fire on the house and the

163

thicket. It was a blazing, bitter hot day on top of the ridge with its shrivelled chaparral and its straight, tall cactus plants. The sky was bare and blue, and hurt like brass. In two minutes the prostrate marines were red and sweating like so many hull-buried stokers in the tropics.

Captain Elliott called out:

"Where's a signalman? Who's a signalman here?"

A red-headed "mick"—I think his name was Clancy—at any rate, it will do to call him Clancy—twisted his head from where he lay on his stomach pumping his Lee, and saluting, said that he was a signalman.

There was no regulation flag with the expedition, so Clancy was obliged to tie his blue polka-dot neckerchief on the end of his rifle. It did not make a very good flag. At first Clancy moved a ways down the safe side of the ridge and wig-wagged there very busily. But what with the flag being so poor for the purpose, and the background of ridge being so dark, those on the *Dolphin* did not see it. So Clancy had to return to the top of the ridge and outline himself and his flag against the sky.

The usual thing happened. As soon as the Spaniards caught sight of his silhouette, they let go like mad at it. To make things more comfortable for Clancy, the situation demanded that he face the sea and turn his back to the Spanish bullets. This was a hard game, mark you—to stand with the small of your back to volley firing. Clancy thought so. Everybody thought so. We all cleared out of his neighborhood. If he wanted sole possession of any particular spot on that hill, he could have it for all we would interfere with him.

It cannot be denied that Clancy was in a hurry. I watched him. He was so occupied with the bullets that snarled close to his ears that he was obliged to repeat the letters of his message softly to himself. It seemed an intolerable time before the *Dolphin* answered the little signal. Meanwhile, we gazed at him, marvelling every second that he had not yet pitched headlong. He swore at times.

Finally the *Dolphin* replied to his frantic gesticulation, and he delivered his message. As his part of the transaction was quite finished—whoop!—he dropped like a brick into the firing line and began to shoot; began to get "hunky" with all those people who had been plugging at him. The blue polka-dot neckerchief still fluttered from the barrel of his rifle. I am quite certain that he let it remain there until the end of the fight.

The shells of the *Dolphin* began to plough up the thicket, kicking the bushes, stones, and soil into the air as if somebody was blasting there.

Meanwhile, this force of two hundred marines and fifty Cubans and the force of—probably—six companies of Spanish guerillas were making such an awful din that the distant Camp McCalla was all alive with excitement. Colonel Huntington sent out strong parties to critical points on the road to facilitate, if necessary, a safe retreat, and also sent forty men under Lieutenant Magill to come up on the left flank of the two companies in action under Captain Elliott. Lieutenant Magill and his men had crowned a hill which covered entirely the flank of the fighting companies, but when the *Dolphin* opened fire, it happened that Magill was in the line of the shots. It became necessary to stop the *Dolphin* at once. Captain Elliott was not near Clancy at this time, and he called hurriedly for another signalman.

Sergeant Quick arose, and announced that he was a signalman. He produced from somewhere a blue polka-dot neckerchief as large as a quilt. He tied it on a long, crooked stick. Then he went to the top of the ridge, and turning his back to the Spanish fire, began to signal to the *Dolphin*. Again we gave a man sole possession of a particular part of the ridge. We didn't want it. He could have it and welcome. If the young sergeant had had the smallpox, the cholera, and the yellow fever, we could not have slid out with more celerity.

As men have said often, it seemed as if there was in this war a God of Battles who held His mighty hand before the Americans. As I looked at Sergeant Quick wig-wagging there against the sky, I would not have given a tin tobacco-tag for his life. Escape for him seemed impossible. It seemed absurd to hope that he would not be hit; I only hoped that he would be hit just a little, little, in the arm, the shoulder, or the leg.

I watched his face, and it was as grave and serene as that of a man writing in his own library. He was the very embodiment of tranquillity in occupation. He stood there amid the animal-like babble of the Cubans, the crack of rifles, and the whistling snarl of the bullets, and wig-wagged what-

165

ever he had to wig-wag without heeding anything but his business. There was not a single trace of nervousness or haste.

To say the least, a fight at close range is absorbing as a spectacle. No man wants to take his eyes from it until that time comes when he makes up his mind to run away. To deliberately stand up and turn your back to a battle is in itself hard work. To deliberately stand up and turn your back to a battle and hear immediate evidences of the boundless enthusiasm with which a large company of the enemy shoot at you from an adjacent thicket is, to my mind at least, a very great feat. One need not dwell upon the detail of keeping the mind carefully upon a slow spelling of an important code message.

I saw Quick betray only one sign of emotion. As he swung his clumsy flag to and fro, an end of it once caught on a cactus pillar, and he looked sharply over his shoulder to see what had it. He gave the flag an impatient jerk. He looked annoyed.

The Execution of Rodriguez

by Richard Harding Davis

Born at the end of the Civil War, correspondent and author Richard Harding Davis covered six wars before his death in 1916 at the age of 52. He was, after Winston Churchill, probably the most dashing of that colorful band of international journalists who rushed from country to country to report the numerous conflicts which brought the starry-eyed nineteenth-century to a sputtering close. In 1896, Richard Harding Davis covered the Cuban revolt against Spain—the prelude to the Spanish-American War. It was then that he witnessed the execution of which he wrote so movingly.

Adolfo Rodriguez was the only son of a Cuban farmer, who lived nine miles outside of Santa Clara, beyond the hills that surround that city to the north.

When the revolution in Cuba broke out young Rodriguez joined the insurgents, leaving his father and mother and two sisters at the farm. He was taken, in December of 1896, by a force of the *Guardia Civile,* the *corps d'élite* of the Spanish army, and defended himself when they tried to capture him, wounding three of them with his machete.

He was tried by a military court for bearing arms against the government, and sentenced to be shot by a fusillade some morning before sunrise.

Previous to execution he was confined in the military prison of Santa Clara with thirty other insurgents, all of whom were sentenced to be shot, one after the other, on mornings following the execution of Rodriguez.

His execution took place the morning of the 19th of January, 1897, at a place a half-mile distant from the city, on the great plain that stretches from the forts out to the hills, beyond which Rodriguez had lived for nineteen years. At the time of his death he was twenty years old.

I witnessed his execution, and what follows is an account of the way he went to his death. The young man's friends could not be present, for it was impossible for them to show themselves in that crowd and that place with wisdom or without distress, and I like to think that, although Rodriguez could not know it, there was one person present when he died who felt keenly for him, and who was a sympathetic though unwilling spectator.

There had been a full moon the night preceding the execution, and when the squad of soldiers marched from town it was still shining brightly through the mists. It lighted a plain two miles in extent, broken by ridges and gullies and covered with thick, high grass, and with bunches of cactus

168

and palmetto. In the hollow of the ridges the mist lay like broad lakes of water, and on one side of the plain stood the walls of the old town. On the other rose hills covered with royal palms that showed white in the moonlight, like hundreds of marble columns. A line of tiny camp-fires that the sentries had built during the night stretched between the forts at regular intervals and burned clearly.

But as the light grew stronger and the moonlight faded these were stamped out, and when the soldiers came in force the moon was a white ball in the sky, without radiance, the fires had sunk to ashes, and the sun had not yet risen.

So even when the men were formed into three sides of a hollow square, they were scarcely able to distinguish one another in the uncertain light of the morning.

There were about three hundred soldiers in the formation. They belonged to the volunteers, and they deployed upon the plain with their band in front playing a jaunty quickstep, while their officers galloped from one side to the other through the grass, seeking a suitable place for the execution. Outside the line the band still played merrily.

A few men and boys, who had been dragged out of their beds by the music, moved about the ridges behind the soldiers, half-clothed, unshaven, sleepy-eyed, yawning, stretching themselves and shivering in the cool, damp air of the morning.

Either owing to discipline or on account of the nature of their errand, or because the men were still but half awake, there was no talking in the ranks, and the soldiers stood motionless, leaning on their rifles, with their backs turned to the town, looking out across the plain to the hills.

The men in the crowd behind them were also grimly silent. They knew that whatever they might say would be twisted into a word of sympathy for the condemned man or a protest against the government. So no one spoke; even the officers gave their orders in gruff whispers, and the men in the crowd did not mix together, but looked suspiciously at one another and kept apart.

As the light increased a mass of people came hurrying from the town with two black figures leading them, and the soldiers drew up at attention, and part of the double line fell back and left an opening in the square.

With us a condemned man walks only the short distance

169

from his cell to the scaffold or the electric chair, shielded from sight by the prison walls, and it often occurs even then that the short journey is too much for his strength and courage.

But the Spaniards on this morning made the prisoner walk for over a half-mile across the broken surface of the fields. I expected to find the man, no matter what his strength at other times might be, stumbling and faltering on this cruel journey; but as he came nearer I saw that he led all the others, that the priests on either side of him were taking two steps to his one, and that they were tripping on their gowns and stumbling over the hollows in their efforts to keep pace with him as he walked, erect and soldierly, at a quick step in advance of them.

He had a handsome, gentle face of the peasant type, a light, pointed beard, great wistful eyes, and a mass of curly black hair. He was shockingly young for such a sacrifice, and looked more like a Neapolitan than a Cuban. You could imagine him sitting on the quay at Naples or Genoa lolling in the sun and showing his white teeth when he laughed. Around his neck, hanging outside his linen blouse, he wore a new scapular.

It seems a petty thing to have been pleased with at such a time, but I confess to have felt a thrill of satisfaction when I saw, as the Cuban passed me, that he held a cigarette between his lips, not arrogantly nor with bravado, but with the nonchalance of a man who meets his punishment fearlessly, and who will let his enemies see that they can kill but cannot frighten him.

It was very quickly finished, with rough and, but for one frightful blunder, with merciful swiftness. The crowd fell back when it came to the square, and the condemned man, the priests, and the firing squad of six young volunteers passed in and the line closed behind them.

The officer who had held the cord that bound the Cuban's arms behind him and passed across his breast, let it fall on the grass and drew his sword, and Rodriguez dropped his cigarette from his lips and bent and kissed the cross which the priest held up before him.

The elder of the priests moved to one side and prayed rapidly in a loud whisper, while the other, a younger man, walked behind the firing squad and covered his face with his hands. They had both spent the last twelve hours with Rodriguez in the chapel of the prison.

The Cuban walked to where the officer directed him to stand, and turning his back on the square, faced the hills and the road across them, which led to his father's farm.

As the officer gave the first command he straightened himself as far as the cords would allow, and held up his head and fixed his eyes immovably on the morning light, which had just begun to show above the hills.

He made a picture of such pathetic helplessness, but of such courage and dignity, that he reminded me on the instant of the statue of Nathan Hale which stands in the City Hall Park, above the roar of Broadway. The Cuban's arms were bound, as are those of the statue, and he stood firmly, with his weight resting on his heels like a soldier on parade, and with his face held up fearlessly, as is that of the statue. But there was this difference, that Rodriguez, while probably as willing to give six lives for his country as was the American rebel, being only a peasant, did not think to say so, and he will not, in consequence, live in bronze during the lives of many men, but will be remembered only as one of thirty Cubans, one of whom was shot at Santa Clara on each succeeding day at sunrise.

The officer had given the order, the men had raised their pieces, and the condemned man had heard the clicks of the triggers as they were pulled back, and he had not moved. And then happened one of the most cruelly refined, though unintentional, acts of torture that one can very well imagine. As the officer slowly raised his sword, preparatory to giving the signal, one of the mounted officers rode up to him and pointed out silently that, as I had already observed with some satisfaction, the firing squad were so placed that when they fired they would shoot several of the soldiers stationed on the extreme end of the square.

Their captain motioned his men to lower their pieces, and then walked across the grass and laid his hand on the shoulder of the waiting prisoner.

It is not pleasant to think what that shock must have been. The man had steeled himself to receive a volley of bullets. He believed that in the next instant he would be in another world;

171

he had heard the command given, had heard the click of the Mausers as the locks caught—and then, at that supreme moment, a human hand had been laid upon his shoulder and a voice spoke in his ear.

You would expect that any man, snatched back to life in such a fashion, would start and tremble at the reprieve, or would break down altogether, but this boy turned his head steadily, and followed with his eyes the direction of the officer's sword, then nodded gravely, and, with his shoulders squared, took up the new position, straightened his back, and once more held himself erect.

As an exhibition of self-control this should surely rank above feats of heroism performed in battle, where there are thousands of comrades to give inspiration. This man was alone, in sight of the hills he knew, with only enemies about him, with no source to draw on for strength but that which lay within himself.

The officer of the firing squad, mortified by his blunder, hastily whipped up his sword, the men once more levelled their rifles, the sword rose, dropped, and the men fired. At the report the Cuban's head snapped back almost between his shoulders, but his body fell slowly, as though someone had pushed him gently forward from behind and he had stumbled.

He sank on his side in the wet grass without a struggle or sound, and did not move again.

It was difficult to believe that he meant to lie there, that it could be ended so without a word, that the man in the linen suit would not rise to his feet and continue to walk on over the hills, as he apparently had started to do, to his home; that there was not a mistake somewhere, or that at least someone would be sorry or say something or run to pick him up.

But, fortunately, he did not need help, and the priests returned—the younger one with the tears running down his face—and donned their vestments and read a brief requiem for his soul, while the squad stood uncovered, and the men in the hollow square shook their accoutrements into place, and shifted their pieces and got ready for the order to march, and the band began again with the same quickstep which the fusillade had interrupted.

The figure still lay on the grass untouched, and no one seemed to remember that it had walked there of itself, or noticed that the cigarette still burned, a tiny ring of living fire, at the place where the figure had first stood.

The figure was a thing of the past, and the squad shook itself like a great snake, and then broke into little pieces and started off jauntily, stumbling in the high grass and striving to keep step to the music.

The officers led it past the figure in the linen suit, and so close to it that the file closers had to part with the column to avoid treading on it. Each soldier as he passed turned and looked down on it, some craning their necks curiously, others giving a careless glance, and some without any interest at all, as they would have looked at a house by the roadside, or a hole in the road.

One young soldier caught his foot in a trailing vine, just opposite to it, and fell. He grew very red when his comrades giggled at him for his awkwardness. The crowd of sleepy spectators fell in on either side of the band. They, too, had forgotten it, and the priests put their vestments back in the bag and wrapped their heavy cloaks about them, and hurried off after the others.

Everyone seemed to have forgotten it except two men, who came slowly towards it from the town, driving a bullock-cart that bore an unplaned coffin, each with a cigarette between his lips, and with his throat wrapped in a shawl to keep out the morning mists.

At that moment the sun, which had shown some promise of its coming in the glow above the hills, shot up suddenly from behind them in all the splendor of the tropics, a fierce, red disk of heat, and filled the air with warmth and light.

The bayonets of the retreating column flashed in it, and at the sight a rooster in a farm-yard nearby crowded vigorously, and a dozen bugles answered the challenge with the brisk, cheery notes of the reveille, and from all parts of the city the church bells jangled out the call for early mass, and the little world of Santa Clara seemed to stretch itself and to wake to welcome the day just begun.

But as I fell in at the rear of the procession and looked back, the figure of the young Cuban, who was no longer a part of the world of Santa Clara, was asleep in the wet grass, with his motionless arms still tightly bound behind him, with the scapular twisted awry across his face, and the blood from his breast sinking into the soil he had tried to free.

173

The Cavalry Charge at Omdurman

by *Winston S. Churchill*

During the eighth decade of the nineteenth century, an Arab of the Sudan who styled himself the Mahdi—guide of Islam—led an uprising which, carried on after his death by another such chieftain called the Khalifa, resulted in the end of Egyptian rule there. But Egypt was then occupied by Britain, and the British, both outraged by the excesses of mahdism and motivated by economic motives, organized an Anglo-Egyptian expedition to recover the Sudan. This force, commanded by Lord Kitchener, struck its decisive blow against the Khalifa at Omdurman in the Sudan September 2, 1898, a battle Winston Churchill, then a cavalry officer of twenty-four, recalled in memorable detail.

175

Long before the dawn we were astir, and by five o'clock the 21st Lancers were drawn up mounted outside the zeriba. My squadron leader Major Finn, an Australian by birth, had promised me some days before that he would give me "a show" when the time came; I was afraid that he would count my mission to Lord Kitchener the day before as quittance; but I was now called out from my troop to advance with a patrol and reconnoitre the ridge between the rocky peak of Jebel Surgham and the river. Other patrols from our squadron and from the Egyptian cavalry were also sent hurrying forward in the darkness. I took six men and a corporal. We trotted fast over the plain and soon began to breast the unknown slopes of the ridge. There is nothing like the dawn. The quarter of an hour before the curtain is lifted upon an unknowable situation is an intense experience of war. Was the ridge held by the enemy or not? Were we riding through the gloom into thousands of ferocious savages? Every step might be deadly; yet there was no time for overmuch precaution. The regiment was coming on behind us, and dawn was breaking. It was already half light as we climbed the slope. What should we find at the summit? For cool, tense excitement I commend such moments.

Now we are near the top of the ridge. I make one man follow a hundred yards behind, so that whatever happens, he may tell the tale. There is no sound but our own clatter. We have reached the crest line. We rein in our horses. Every minute the horizon extends; we can already see 200 yards. Now we can see perhaps a quarter of a mile. All is quiet; no life but our own breathes among the rocks and sand hummocks of the ridge. No ambuscade, no occupation in force! The farther plain is bare below us: we can now see more than half a mile.

So they have all decamped! Just what we said! All bolted off to Kordofan; no battle! But wait! The dawn is growing fast. Veil after veil is lifted from the landscape. What is this

176

shimmering in the distant plain? Nay—it is lighter now—what are these dark markings beneath the shimmer? *They are there!* These enormous black smears are thousands of men; the shimmering is the glinting of their weapons. It is now daylight. I slip off my horse; I write in my field service notebook "The Dervish army is still in position a mile and a half south-west of Jebel Surgham." I send this message by the corporal direct as ordered to the Commander-in-Chief. I mark it *XXX*. In the words of the drill book "with all despatch" or as one would say "Hell for leather."

A glorious sunrise is taking place behind us; but we are admiring something else. It is already light enough to use field-glasses. The dark masses are changing their values. They are already becoming lighter than the plain; they are fawn-coloured. Now they are a kind of white, while the plain is dun. In front of us is a vast array four or five miles long. It fills the horizon till it is blocked out on our right by the serrated silhouette of Surgham Peak. This is an hour to live. We mount again, and suddenly new impressions strike the eye and mind. These masses are not stationary. They are advancing, and they are advancing fast. A tide is coming in. But what is this sound which we hear: a deadened roar coming up to us in waves? They are cheering for God, his Prophet and his holy Khalifa. They think they are going to win. We shall see about that presently. Still I must admit that we check our horses and hang upon the crest of the ridge for a few moments before advancing down its slopes.

But now it is broad morning and the slanting sun adds brilliant colour to the scene. The masses have defined themselves into swarms of men, in ordered ranks bright with glittering weapons, and above them dance a multitude of gorgeous flags. We see for ourselves what the Crusaders saw. We must see more of it. I trot briskly forward to somewhere near the sandhills where the 21st Lancers had halted the day before. Here we are scarcely 400 yards away from the great masses. We halt again and I make four troopers fire upon them, while the other two hold their horses. The enemy come on like the sea. A crackle of musketry breaks out on our front and to our left. Dust spurts rise among the sandhills. This is no place for Christians. We scamper off; and luckily no man or horse is hurt. We climb back on to the ridge, and almost at this moment there returns the corporal on a panting horse. He comes direct from Kitchener with an order signed by the Chief of Staff. "Remain as long as possible, and report how the masses of attack are moving." Talk of Fun! Where will you beat this! On horseback, at daybreak, within shot of an advancing army, seeing everything, and corresponding direct with Headquarters.

So we remained on the ridge for nearly half an hour and I watched close up a scene which few have witnessed. All the masses except one passed for a time out of our view beyond the peak of Surgham on our right. But one, a division of certainly 6000 men, moved directly over the shoulder of the ridge. Already they were climbing its forward slopes. From where we sat on our horses we could see both sides. There was our army ranked and massed by the river. There were the gunboats lying expectant in the stream. There were all the batteries ready to open. And meanwhile on the other side, this large oblong gay-coloured crowd in fairly good order climbed swiftly up to the crest of exposure. We were about 2500 yards from our own batteries, but little more than 200 from the approaching target. I called these Dervishes "The White Flags." They reminded me of the armies in the Bayeux tapestries, because of their rows of white and yellow standards held upright. Meanwhile the Dervish centre far out in the plain had come within range, and one after another the British and Egyptian batteries opened upon it. My eyes were riveted by a nearer scene. At the top of the hill "The White Flags" paused to rearrange their ranks and drew out a broad and solid parade along the crest. Then the cannonade turned upon them. Two or three batteries and all the gunboats, at least thirty guns, opened an intense fire. Their shells shrieked towards us and burst in scores over the heads and among the masses of the White Flag-men. We were so close, as we sat spellbound on our horses, that we almost shared their perils. I saw the full blast of Death strike this human wall. Down went their standards by dozens and their men by hundreds. Wide gaps and shapeless heaps appeared in their array. One saw them jumping and tumbling under the shrapnel bursts; but none turned back. Line after line they all streamed over the shoulder and advanced toward our zeriba, opening a heavy rifle fire which wreathed them in smoke.

178

Hitherto no one had taken any notice of us; but I now saw Baggara horsemen in twos and threes riding across the plain on our left towards the ridge. One of these patrols of three men came within pistol range. They were dark, cowled figures, like monks on horseback—ugly, sinister brutes with long spears. I fired a few shots at them from the saddle, and they sheered off. I did not see why we should not stop out on this ridge during the assault. I thought we could edge back towards the Nile and so watch both sides while keeping out of harm's way. But now arrived a positive order from Major Finn, whom I had perforce left out of my correspondence with the Commander-in-Chief, saying "Come back at once into the zeriba as the infantry are about to open fire." We should in fact have been safer on the ridge, for we only just got into the infantry lines before the rifle-storm began.

It is not my purpose in this record of personal impressions to give a general account of the Battle of Omdurman. The story has been told so often and in such exact military detail that everyone who is interested in the subject is no doubt well acquainted with what took place. I shall only summarise the course of the battle so far as may be necessary to explain my own experiences.

The whole of the Khalifa's army, nearly 60,000 strong, advanced in battle order from their encampment of the night before, topped the swell of ground which hid the two armies from one another, and then rolled down the gently sloping amphitheatre in the arena of which, backed upon the Nile, Kitchener's 20,000 troops were drawn up shoulder to shoulder to receive them. Ancient and modern confronted one another. The weapons, the methods and the fanaticism of the Middle Ages were brought by an extraordinary anachronism into dire collision with the organisation and inventions of the nineteenth century. The result was not surprising. As the successors of the Saracens descended the long smooth slopes which led to the river and their enemy, they encountered the rifle fire of two and a half divisions of trained infantry, drawn up two deep and in close order and supported by at least 70 guns on the river bank and in the gunboats, all firing with undisturbed efficiency. Under this fire the whole attack withered and came to a standstill, with a loss of perhaps six or seven

179

thousand men, at least 700 yards away from the British–
Egyptian line. The Dervish army, however, possessed nearly
20,000 rifles of various kinds, from the most antiquated to
the most modern, and when the spearmen could get no farther,
these riflemen lay down on the plain and began a ragged, un-
aimed but considerable fusillade at the dark line of the thorn-
fence zeriba. Now for the first time they began to inflict losses
on their antagonists, and in the shot space that this lasted perhaps two hundred casualities occurred among the British and
Egyptian troops.

Seeing that the attack had been repulsed with great
slaughter and that he was nearer to the city of Omdurman
than the Dervish army, Kitchener immediately wheeled his
five brigades into his usual echelon formation, and with his
left flank on the river proceeded to march south towards the
city, intending thereby to cut off what he considered to be
the remnants of the Dervish army from their capital, their
base, their food, their water, their home, and to drive them
out into the vast deserts which stared on every side. But the
Dervishes were by no means defeated. The whole of their
left, having overshot the mark, had not even been under fire.
The Khalifa's reserve of perhaps 15,000 men was still intact.
All these swarms now advanced with undaunted courage to
attack the British and Egyptian forces, which were no longer
drawn up in a prepared position, but marching freely over
the desert. This second shock was far more critical than the
first. The charging Dervishes succeeded everywhere in coming to within a hundred or two hundred yards of the troops,
and the rear brigade of Soudanese, attacked from two directions, was only saved from destruction by the skill and firmness of its commander, General Hector Macdonald. However,
discipline and machinery triumphed over most desperate
valour, and after an enormous carnage, certainly exceeding
20,000 men, who strewed the ground in heaps and swathes
"like snowdrifts," the whole mass of the Dervishes dissolved
into fragments and into particles and streamed away into the
fantastic mirages of the desert.

The Egyption cavalry and the camel corps had been protecting the right flank of the zeriba when it was attacked, and
the 21st Lancers were the only horsemen on the left flank
nearest to Omdurman. Immediately after the first attack had

been repulsed we were ordered to leave the zeriba, ascertain what enemy forces, if any, stood between Kitchener and the city, and if possible drive these forces back and clear the way for the advancing army. Of course as a regimental officer one knows very little of what is taking place over the whole field of battle. We waited by our horses during the first attack close down by the river's edge, sheltered by the steep Nile bank from the bullets which whistled overhead. As soon as the fire began to slacken and it was said on all sides that the attack had been repulsed, a General arrived with his staff at a gallop with instant orders to mount and advance. In two minutes the four squadrons were mounted and trotting out of the zeriba in a southerly direction. We ascended again the slopes of Jebel Surgham which had played its part in the first stages of the action, and from its ridges soon saw before us the whole plain of Omdurman with the vast mud city, its minarets and domes, spread before us six or seven miles away. After various halts and reconnoiterings we found ourselves walking forward in what is called "column of troops." There are four troops in a squadron and four squadrons in a regiment. Each of these troops now followed the other. I commanded the second troop from the rear, comprising between twenty and twenty-five Lancers.

Everyone expected that we were going to make a charge. That was the one idea that had been in all minds since we had started from Cairo. Of course there would be a charge. In those days, before the Boer War, British cavalry had been taught little else. Here was clearly the occasion for a charge. But against what body of enemy, over what ground, in which direction or with what purpose, were matters hidden from the rank and file. We continued to pace forward over the hard sand, peering into the mirage-twisted plain in a high state of suppressed excitement. Presently I noticed 300 yards away on our flank and parallel to the line on which were were advancing, a long row of blue-black objects, two or three yards apart. I thought there were about a hundred and fifty. Then I became sure that these were men—enemy men—squatting on the ground. Almost at the same moment the trumpet sounded "Trot," and the whole long column of cavalry began to jingle and clatter across the front of these crouching figures. We were in the lull of the battle and there was perfect silence. Forthwith from every blue-black blob came a white puff of smoke, and a loud volley of musketry broke the odd stillness. Such a target at such a distance could scarcely be missed, and all along the column here and there horses bounded and a few men fell.

The intentions of our Colonel had no doubt been to move round the flank of the body of Dervishes he had now located, and who, concealed in a fold of the ground behind their riflemen, were invisible to us, and then to attack them from a more advantageous quarter; but once the fire was opened and losses began to grow, he must have judged it inexpedient to prolong his procession across the open plain. The trumpet sounded "Right wheel into line," and all the sixteen troops swung round towards the blue-black riflemen. Almost immediately the regiment broke into a gallop, and the 21st Lancers were committed to their first charge in war!

I propose to describe exactly what happened to me: what I saw and what I felt. I recalled it to my mind so frequently after the event that the impression is as clear and vivid as it was a quarter of a century ago. The troop I commanded was, when we wheeled into line, the second from the right of the regiment. I was riding a handy, sure-footed grey Arab polo pony. Before we wheeled and began to gallop, the officers had been marching with drawn swords. On account of my shoulder I had always decided that if I were involved in hand-to-hand fighting, I must use a pistol and not a sword. I had purchased in London a Mauser automatic pistol, then the newest and the latest design. I had practised carefully with this during our march and journey up the river. This then was the weapon with which I determined to fight. I had first of all to return my sword into its scabbard, which is not the easiest thing to do at a gallop. I had then to draw my pistol from its wooden holster and bring it to full cock. This dual operation took an appreciable time, and until it was finished, apart from a few glances to my left to see what effect the fire was producing, I did not look up at the general scene.

Then I saw immediately before me, and now only half the length of a polo ground away, the row of crouching blue figures firing frantically, wreathed in white smoke. On my right and left my neighbouring troops leaders made a good line. Immediately behind was a long dancing row of lances

182

couched for the charge. We were going at a fast but steady gallop. There was too much trampling and rifle fire to hear any bullets. After this glance to the right and left and at my troop, I looked again towards the enemy. The scene appeared to be suddenly transformed. The blue-black men were still firing, but behind them there now came into view a depression like a shallow sunken road. This was crowded and crammed with men rising up from the ground where they had hidden. Bright flags appeared as if by magic, and I saw arriving from nowhere Emirs on horseback among and around the mass of the enemy. The Dervishes appeared to be ten or twelve deep at the thickets, a great grey mass gleaming with steel, filling the dry watercourse. In the same twinkling of an eye I saw also that our right overlapped their left, that my troops would just strike the edge of their array, and that the troop on my right would charge into air. My subaltern comrade on the right, Wormald of the 7th Hussars, could see the situation too; and we both increased our speed to the very fastest gallop and curved inwards like the horns of the moon. One really had not time to be frightened or to think of anything else but these particular necessary actions which I have described. They completely occupied mind and senses.

The collision was now very near. I saw immediately before me, not ten yards away, the two blue men who lay in my path. They were perhaps a couple of yards apart. I rode at the interval between them. They both fired. I passed through the smoke conscious that I was unhurt. The trooper immediately behind me was killed at this place and at this moment, whether by these shots or not I do not know. I checked my pony as the ground began to fall away beneath his feet. The clever animal dropped like a cat four or five feet down on to the sandy bed of the watercourse, and in this sandy bed I found myself surrounded by what seemed to be dozens of men. They were not thickly packed enough at this point for me to experience any actual collision with them. Whereas Grenfell's troop, next but one on my left, was brought to a complete standstill and suffered very heavy losses, we seemed to push our way through as one has sometimes seen mounted policemen break up a crowd. In less time than it takes to relate, my pony had scrambled up the other side of the ditch. I looked round.

Once again I was on the hard, crisp desert, my horse at a trot. I had the impression of scattered Dervishes running to and fro in all directions. Straight before me a man threw himself on the ground. The reader must remember that I had been trained as a cavalry soldier to believe that if ever cavalry broke into the mass of infantry, the latter would be at their mercy. My first idea therefore was that the man was terrified. But simultaneously I saw the gleam of his curved sword as he drew it back from a hamstringing cut. I had room and time enough to turn my pony out of his reach, and leaning over on the off side I fired two shots into him at about three yards. As I straightened myself in the saddle, I saw before me another figure with uplifted sword. I raised my pistol and fired. So close were we that the pistol itself actually struck him. Man and sword disappeared below and behind me. On my left, ten yards away, was an Arab horseman in a bright-coloured tunic and steel helmet, with chain-mail hangings. I fired at him. He turned aside. I pulled my horse into a walk and looked around again.

In one respect a cavalry charge is very like ordinary life. So long as you are all right, firmly in your saddle, your horse in hand, and well armed, lots of enemies will give you a wide berth. But as soon as you have lost a stirrup, have a rein cut, have dropped your weapon, are wounded, or your horse is wounded, then is the moment when from all quarters enemies rush upon you. Such was the fate of not a few of my comrades in the troops immediately on my left. Brought to an actual standstill in the enemy's mass, clutched at from every side, stabbed at and hacked at by spear and sword, they were dragged from their horses and cut to pieces by the infuriated foe. But this I did not at the time see or understand. My impressions continued to be sanguine. I thought we were masters of the situation, riding the enemy down, scattering them and killing them. I pulled my horse up and looked about me. There was a mass of Dervishes about forty or fifty yards away on my left. They were huddling and clumping themselves together, rallying for mutual protection. They seemed wild with excitement, dancing about on their feet, shaking their spears up and down. The whole scene seemed to flicker. I have an impression, but it is too fleeting to define, of brown-clad Lancers mixed up here and there with this surging mob. The scattered individuals in my immediate neighbourhood made no attempt to molest me. Where was my troop? Where were the other troops of the squadron? Within a hundred yards of me I could not see a single officer or man. I looked back at the Dervish mass. I saw two or three riflemen crouching and aiming their rifles at me from the fringe of it. Then for the first time that morning I experienced a sudden sensation of fear. I felt myself absolutely alone. I thought these riflemen would hit me and the rest devour me like wolves. What a fool I was to loiter like this in the midst of the enemy! I crouched over the saddle, spurred my horse into a gallop and drew clear of the *mêlee*. Two or three hundred yards away I found my troop already faced about and partly formed up.

The other three troops of the squadron were reforming close by. Suddenly in the midst of the troop up sprang a Dervish. How he got there I do not know. He must have leaped out of some scrub or hole. All the troopers turned upon him thrusting with their lances: but he darted to and fro causing for the moment a frantic commotion. Wounded several times, he staggered towards me raising his spear. I shot him at less than a yard. He fell on the sand, and lay there dead. How easy to kill a man! But I did not worry about it. I found I had fired the whole magazine of my Mauser pistol, so I put in a new clip of ten cartridges before thinking of anything else.

I was still prepossessed with the idea that we had inflicted great slaughter on the enemy and had scarcely suffered at all ourselves. Three or four men were missing from my troop. Six men and nine or ten horses were bleeding from spear thrust or sword cuts. We all expected to be ordered immediately to charge back again. The men were ready, though they all looked serious. Several asked to be allowed to throw away their lances and draw their swords. I asked my second sergeant if he had enjoyed himself. His answer was "Well, I don't exactly say I enjoyed it, Sir; but I think I'll get more used to it next time." At this the whole troop laughed.

But now from the direction of the enemy there came a succession of grisly apparitions; horses spouting blood, struggling on three legs, men staggering on foot, men bleeding from terrible wounds, fish-hook spears stuck right through them, arms and faces cut to pieces, bowels protruding, men gasping, crying, collapsing, expiring. Our first task was to succour these; and meanwhile the blood of our leaders cooled. They remembered for the first time that we had carbines. Everything was still in great confusion. But trumpets were sounded and orders shouted, and we all moved off at a trot towards the flank of the enemy. Arrived at a position from which we could enfilade and rake the watercourse, two squadrons were dismounted and in a few minutes with their fire at three hundred yards compelled the Dervishes to retreat. We therefore remained in possession of the field. Within twenty minutes of the time when we had first wheeled into line and began our charge, we were halted and breakfasting in the very watercourse that had so nearly proved our undoing. There one could see the futility of the much-vaunted *Arme Blanche*. The Dervishes had carried off their wounded, and the corpses of thirty or forty enemy were all that could be counted on the ground. Among them lay the bodies of over twenty Lancers, so hacked and mutilated as to be mostly unrecognisable. In all out of 310 officers and men the regiment had lost in the space of about two or three minutes five officers and sixty-five men killed and wounded, and 120 horses—nearly a quarter of its strength.

Such were my fortunes in this celebrated episode. It is very rarely that cavalry and infantry, while still both unshaken, are intermingled as the result of an actual collision. Either the infantry keep their heads and shoot the cavalry down, or they break into confusion and are cut down or speared as they run. But the two or three thousand Dervishes who faced the 21st Lancers in the watercourse at Omdurman were not in the least shaken by the stress of battle or afraid of cavalry. Their fire was not good enough to stop the charge, but they had no doubt faced horsemen many a time in the wars with Abyssinia. They were familiar with the ordeal of the charge. It was the kind of fighting they thoroughly understood. Moreover, the fight was with equal weapons, for the British too fought with sword and lance as in the days of old.

A white gunboat seeing our first advance had hurried up the river in the hopes of being of assistance. From the crow's nest, its commander, Beatty, watched the whole event with breathless interest. Many years passed before I met this officer or knew that he had witnessed our gallop. When we met, I was First Lord of the Admiralty and he the youngest Admiral in the Royal Navy. "What did it look like?" I asked him. "What was your prevailing impression?" "It looked," said Admiral Beatty, "like plum duff: brown currants scattered about in a great deal of suet." With this striking, if somewhat homely, description my account of this adventure may fittingly close.

Combat Fatigue

by Mark Twain

It is regrettable in some ways that Mark Twain's experience of the military did not go beyond his first encounter with tedium and snafu as practiced during the Civil War. If it had, there might be a Confederate comedy to lighten the great grim lump of war literature based on that savage struggle. But the soldiering career of Samuel Langhorne Clemens turned out to be very brief—and furnished him only just enough material for this speech, made before the Ancient and Honorable Artillery Company of Massachusetts.

The last time I had the privilege of breaking bread with soldiers was some years ago, with the oldest military organization in England, the Ancient and Honorable Artillery Company of London, somewhere about its six hundredth anniversary; and now I have enjoyed this privilege with its eldest child, the oldest military organization in America, the Ancient and Honorable Artillery Company of Massachusetts, on this your two hundred and fortieth anniversary. Fine old stock, both of you—and if you fight as well as you feed, God protect the enemy.

I did not assemble at the hotel parlors today to be received by a committee as a mere civilian guest; no, I assembled at the headquarters of the Putnam Phalanx and insisted upon my right to be escorted to this place as one of the military guests. For I, too, am a soldier! I am inured to war. I have a military history. I have been through a stirring campaign, and there is not even a mention of it in any history of the United States or of the Southern Confederacy—to such length can the envy and malignity of the historian go! I will unbosom myself here, where I cannot but find sympathy; I will tell you about it, and appeal through you to justice.

In the earliest summer days of the war I slipped out of Hannibal, Missouri, by night, with a friend, and joined a detachment of the rebel General Tom Harris's army (I find myself in a minority here), up a gorge behind an old barn in Rolls County. Colonel Rolls swore us in. He made us swear to uphold the flag and Constitution of the United States, and to destroy any other military organization that we caught doing the same thing. In other words, we were to repel invasion. Well, you see, this mixed us up. We couldn't really tell which side we were on, but we went into camp and left it to the God of Battles (for that was the term then). I was made second lieutenant and chief mogul of a company of eleven men, for we had no captain. My friend, who was nineteen years old, six feet high, three feet wide, some distance through, and just out of infant school, was made orderly sergeant. His name was

Ben Tupper. He had a hard time. When he was mounted and on the march he used to go to sleep, and his horse would reach around and bite his leg, and then he would cry and curse, and want to go home. The other men pestered him a good deal, too. When they were dismounted they said they couldn't march in double file with him because his feet took up so much room. One night when we were around the camp-fire, a fellow on the outside of the circuit said, "Ben Tupper, put down that newspaper; it casts a shadow like a blanket." Ben said, "I ain't got any newspaper." Then that other fellow said, "Oh, I see—'twas your ear!" We all slept in a corn-crib, on the corn, and the rats were very thick. Ben Tupper had been rightly reared, and when he was ready for bed he would start to pray and a rat would bite him on the heel, and then he would sit up and swear all night and keep everybody awake. He was town-bred and did not seem to have any correct idea of military discipline. If I commanded him to shut up, he would say, "Who was your nigger last year?" One evening I ordered him to ride out on picket duty about three miles, to the beginning of a prairie. Said he, "What—in the night!—and them blamed Union soldiers likely to be prowling around there any time!" So he wouldn't go. Next morning I ordered him again. Said he, "In the rain—I think I see myself!" He didn't go. Next day I ordered him on picket duty once more. This time he looked hurt. Said he, "What! on Sunday?—you must be a damn fool!" Picketing was impracticable, so I dropped it from my military system.

We had a good enough time there at that barn, barring the rats and the mosquitoes and the rain. We levied on both parties impartially; and both parties hated us impartially. But one day we heard that the invader was approaching; so we had to pack up and move, of course. Inside of twenty-four hours he was coming again. So we moved again. Next day he was after us once more. We didn't like it much, but we moved rather than make trouble. This went on for a week or ten days, and we saw considerable scenery. Then Ben Tupper lost patience. Said he, "War ain't what it's cracked up to be; I'm going home if I can't ever get a chance to sit down. Why do those people keep us a-humping around so? Blame their skins, do they think this is an excursion?" Some of the other town boys began to grumble; they complained that there was

191

an insufficiency of umbrellas. So I sent around to the farmers and borrowed what I could. Then they complained that the Worcestershire sauce was out. There was mutiny and dissatisfaction all around, and of course here came the enemy pestering us again—as much as two hours before breakfast, too, when nobody wanted to turn out, of course. This was a little too much. The whole command felt insulted. I sent an aid to the brigadier, and asked him to assign us a district where there wasn't so much bother going on. The history of our campaign was laid before him, but instead of being touched by it, what did he do? He sent back an indignant message. He said, "You have had a dozen chances inside of two weeks to capture the enemy, and he is still at large. Feeling bad? Stay where you are this time, or I will court-martial and hang the whole of you."

I submitted this rude message to my command, and asked their advice. Said the orderly sergeant, "If Tom Harris wants the enemy, let him come and get him; I ain't got any use for my share. And who's Tom Harris, anyway, that's putting on so many frills? Why, I knew him when he wasn't nothing but a darn telegraph operator. Gentlemen, you can do as you choose; as for me I've got enough of this sashshaying around so's 't you can't get a chance to pray because the time's all required for cussing. So off goes my war-paint—you hear me!" The whole regiment said, "That's the talk for me!" So then and there my brigade disbanded itself and tramped off home, I at the tail of it. I hung up my sword and returned to the arts of peace. We were the first men that went into the service in Missouri; were the first that went out of it anywhere.

This, gentlemen, is the history of the part which my division took in the great rebellion, and such is the military record of its commander-in-chief. And this is the first time that the deeds of those eleven warriors have been brought officially to the notice of mankind. Treasure these things in your hearts, and so shall the dejected and truculent historians of this land be brought to shame and confusion. I ask you to fill your glasses and drink with me to the reverent memory of the Orderly Sergeant and those other neglected and forgotten heroes, my footsore and travel-stained paladins, who were first in war, first in peace, and were not idle during the interval that lay between.

The Private War of Captain Douglas MacArthur

by Douglas MacArthur

In April 1914, during President Wilson's dispute
with President Huerta of Mexico, U.S. troops occupied the Mexican port city of Vera Cruz. However,
the Americans were under strict orders to refrain from
acts which might provoke war with Mexico. Meanwhile, the Secretary of the Army sent Captain Douglas MacArthur down to Vera Cruz as his personal
observer. MacArthur was a soldier who combined energy and daring with fondness for the bold stroke.
Besides, he had found that "the command at Vera
Cruz was practically immobile." So he undertook a
personal reconnaissance which might have changed
things a bit more than President Wilson desired. Here
is his report:

September 30, 1914

From: Capt. Douglas MacArthur, General Staff
To: Major General Leonard Wood
Subject: Detailed report of reconnaissance from Vera Cruz
          to Alvarado on the night of May 6, 1914.

1. This report is supplementary to the general one made to you under date of May 9, 1914. It has not been rendered before as I did not realize the matter was under consideration.

2. The general purpose of the reconnaissance was the location of locomotives suitable for road use on the narrow-gauge line of the Inter-Oceanic Railroad. Due to the great shortage of animal transportation, the command at Vera Cruz was practically immobile. Freight and passenger cars were in abundance, but no road motive power. Every effort was being made to remedy this state of affairs so that in case of field operations, which appeared imminent, the command would not be tied to Vera Cruz.

3. Through the maudlin talk of a drunken Mexican, I received an inkling that a number of engines were hidden somewhere on the line connecting Vera Cruz and Alvarado. This man was sobered up and found to be a railroad fireman and engineer on the Vera Cruz and Alvarado R.R. He consented, after certain financial inducements had been offered, to assist me in accurately locating the engines.

4. At this time I occupied at Vera Cruz a unique and rather difficult status. I had been ordered there before the Fifth Brigade left Galveston as one of the prospective Assistant Chiefs of Staff of the First Field Army. My orders were defined in a letter from the Secretary of War to the Secretary of the Navy under date of April 23, 1914, in the following words:

"I am very desirous of sending down for purposes of observation and reconnaissance a representative of the War Department. This officer is Captain Douglas MacArthur, of

194

the General Staff, who, in case of any aggressive movement by the Army in regard to Mexico, will function as one of the General Staff officers of the Commanding General. In order to facilitate his observations and his passage to Vera Cruz, I would appreciate very much if the Admiral Commanding be requested to extend such privileges to him as may be possible and that the Battleship *Nebraska* which it is expected will touch at New York tomorrow be directed to take him on board as a passenger."

On arrival at Vera Cruz, the headquarters of the Fifth Brigade did not recognize me as an official member of their command, as I had no orders assigning me thereto. They took the attitude that I was an independent staff officer functioning directly under you. I was permitted to exercise my own judgment in regard to fulfilling my general orders and instructions, subject to only such limitations as were prescribed by the Military Governor for all those domiciled in Vera Cruz. In undertaking this reconnaissance, therefore, I was thrown entirely on my own responsibility, as it was not feasible or safe to communicate the question to you for decision. The object of the trip not being aggressive, but merely for the purpose of obtaining information, my general instructions as given above seemed to cover the very contingency, and I accordingly made my plans.

5. The Alvarado Railroad is a narrow-gauge road connecting Vera Cruz and Alvarado, distant about 42 miles. The principal towns en route are Tejar, Medallin, Paso del Toro, Laguna, La Piedra, and Salinas. We held the line as far as Tejar, nine miles out. About four miles beyond Tejar, at Paso del Toro, the Alvarado line is crossed by the broad-gauge line connecting Vera Cruz and the Isthmus of Tehuantepec. This latter line after leaving Vera Cruz passes through the town of Boca del Rio, where it crosses the Jamapa River, before reaching Paso del Toro. From Vera Cruz to Paso del Toro, therefore, these two railroad lines formed roughly the two halves of an ellipse. We did not hold the Isthmus line beyond the outskirts of Vera Cruz.

6. Mexican troops in force were reported near Tejar and in order to avoid them I determined to proceed along the Isthmus line as far as Paso del Toro and then change to the Alvarado line. My general plan was to leave Vera Cruz alone

195

on foot at dusk and to join my Mexican engineer, who was to have a hand-car on the Alvarado line manned by two Mexicans. From there we were to push along the line until the engines were located and their condition ascertained. All three of the Mexicans were railroad men and their affiliations and experience enabled them to obtain the hand-cars and have them at their appointed places. For their services I agreed to give them $150.00 gold, payable only after my safe return to Vera Cruz. Captain Cordier of the 4th Infantry was the only person outside of these men who knew of the plan.

7. The night was squally and overcast. At dusk I crossed our line unseen near the wireless stations, where a detachment of the 7th Infantry was encamped. I was in military uniform with no attempt to disguise and with absolutely nothing on me in addition to my clothes except my identification tag and my automatic revolver with ammunition. I found my engineer with a broad-gauge hand-car in the appointed place. I carefully searched him and after some demur on his part removed his weapons, a .38-caliber revolver and a small dirk knife. As a further precaution against his possible treachery I had him search me so that he might better realize that there being nothing of value on me my death would afford him no monetary return. The essence of the transaction for him, therefore, became my safe return to Vera Cruz when he would receive his pay.

8. We proceeded as far as Boca del Rio without incident, but at the Jamapa River found the railroad bridge down. I decided to leave the hand-car, concealing it as well as possible. After searching the bank of the river for a short distance, we discovered a small native boat by means of which we paddled across, landing well above the town so as to escape observation. On landing we located, after some search, two ponies near a small shack and mounted on them we followed the trail along the railway until near Paso del Toro. We then made a detour and hit the Alvarado line below the town. The two Mexican firemen were awaiting us with the hand-car. We secreted our ponies and after I had searched the two newcomers and found them unarmed we pushed on. Mile after mile was covered with no sign of the engines. The line is studded with bridges and culverts and my crew protested violently at crossing them without investigating their

196

condition. Time was so short, however, that I dared not stop for such steps, and had to take them in our stride. I was obliged to threaten my men to the point of covering them with a revolver at the first bridge, but after that I had no further trouble with them. In fact, after getting into the spirit of the thing their conduct was most admirable. At every town we reached I took one man and left the car which was run through to the far side by the other two. I fastened myself by a lashing to the man acting as my guide so as to insure us against separation and together we made a circuit of the town, joining the car on the far side. This took time, but was the only way I could avoid detection.

9. We reached Alvarado shortly after one o'clock and there found five engines. Two of these were switch engines and worthless for our purpose. The other three were just what we needed—fine big road pullers in excellent condition except for a few minor parts which were missing. I made a careful inspection of them and then started back.

10. At Salinas, while moving around the town with one of my men as described above, we were halted by five armed men. They were on foot and wore no uniforms. They were not soldiers and were evidently one of the marauding bands that infest the country with brigandage as a trade. We started to run for it and they opened fire and followed us. We outdistanced all but two and in order to preserve our own lives I was obliged to fire upon them. Both went down. I was fearful lest the firing might have frightened away my hand-car men, but after some search we found them awaiting us about a mile beyond the town.

11. At Piedra, under somewhat similar circumstances and in a driving mist, we ran flush into about fifteen mounted men of the same general type. We were among them before I realized it and were immediately the center of a melee. I was knocked down by the rush of horsemen and had three bullet holes through my clothes, but escaped unscathed. My man was shot in the shoulder, but not seriously injured. At least four of the enemy were brought down and the rest fled. After bandaging up my wounded man we proceeded north with all speed possible.

12. Near Laguna we were again encountered and fired upon by three mounted men who kept up a running fight with

the hand-car. I did not return this fire. All but one of these men were distanced, but this one man, unusually well mounted, overhauled and passed the car. He sent one bullet through my shirt and two others that hit the car within six inches of me, and I then felt obliged to bring him down. His horse fell across the front of the car and on the track and we were obliged to remove the carcass before proceeding.

13. At Paso del Toro we abandoned the hand-car, found the two ponies where we had left them and made the best of our way back to Boca del Rio where we returned the animals from whence we had procured them.

14. We found the boat where we had left it and started to cross the Jamapa River, but when near the shore the boat struck a snag in the darkness and sank. Fortunately the water at this point was something less than five feet deep, for in our exhausted physical condition I do not believe we would have been capable of swimming. As it was I was hard put to it to keep my wounded man's head above water. Day was breaking when we reached the bank, but so wearied were we that we were unable to move on for nearly half an hour. We then located our first hand-car and ran in close to Vera Cruz where we crossed the American lines unobserved.

15. None of the men we encountered were Mexican troops. All were guerillas undoubtedly bent on general mischief. Owing to the darkness I was not recognized as an American soldier and in consequence no alarm was ever felt for the engines. Months later when traffic was partially resumed I saw one of them running to Tejar from Alvarado.

(Signed)
Douglas MacArthur
Captain, General Staff

Blowing Up a Train

by T. E. Lawrence

At the outbreak of World War I, Thomas Edward Lawrence was in the British service in Egypt. Already known as Lawrence of Arabia for his profound knowledge of the desert, it became his mission to organize the Arabs in a revolt against Turkey, which had entered the war on the German side. With Feisal, one of the sons of the Emir Hussein Ibn Ali, Lawrence conducted one of history's most successful guerrilla campaigns—and his techniques in such niceties as train-blowing were described by him in a book published after he lost his life in a motorcycle accident in 1935, *The Seven Pillars of Wisdom.*

Blowing up trains was an exact science when done deliberately, by a sufficient party, with machine-guns in position. If scrambled at it might become dangerous. The difficulty this time was that the available gunners were Indians; who, though good men fed, were only half-men in cold and hunger. I did not propose to drag them off without rations on an adventure which might take a week. There was no cruelty in starving Arabs; they would not die of a few days' fasting, and would fight as well as ever on empty stomachs; while, if things got too difficult, there were the riding camels to kill and eat; but the Indians, though Moslems, refused camel-flesh on principle.

I explained these delicacies of diet. Ali at once said that it would be enough for me to blow up the train, leaving him and the Arabs with him to do their best to carry its wreck without machine-gun support. As, in this unsuspecting district, we might well happen on a supply train, with civilians or only a small guard of reservists aboard, I agreed to risk it. The decision having been applauded, we sat down in a cloaked circle, to finish our remaining food in a very late and cold supper (the rain had sodden the fuel and made fire not possible), our hearts somewhat comforted by the chance of another effort.

At dawn with the unfit of the Arabs, the Indians moved away for Azrak, miserably. They had started up country with me in hope of a really military enterprise, and first had seen the muddled bridge, and now were losing this prospective train. It was hard on them; and to soften the blow with honour I asked Wood to accompany them. He agreed, after argument, for their sakes; but it proved a wise move for himself, as a sickness which had been troubling him began to show the early signs of pneumonia.

The balance of us, some sixty men, turned back towards the railway. None of them knew the country, so I led them to Minifir, where, with Zaal, we had made havoc in the spring.

The re-curved hill-top was an excellent observation post, camp, grazing ground and way of retreat, and we sat there in our old place till sunset, shivering and staring out over the immense plain which stretched map-like to the clouded peaks of Jebel Druse, with Um el Jemal and her sister-villages like ink-smudges on it through the rain.

In the first dusk we walked down to lay the mine. The rebuilt culvert of kilometre 172 seemed still the fittest place. While we stood by it there came a rumble, and through the gathering darkness and mist a train suddenly appeared round the northern curve, only two hundred yards away. We scurried under the long arch and heard it roll overhead. This was annoying; but when the course was clear again, we fell to burying the charge. The evening was bitterly cold, with drifts of rain blowing down the valley.

The arch was solid masonry, of four metres' span, and stood over a shingle water-bed which took its rise on our hill-top. The winter rains had cut this into a channel four feet deep, narrow and winding, which served us as an admirable approach till within three hundred yards of the line. There the gully widened out and ran straight towards the culvert, open to the sight of anyone upon the rails.

We hid the explosive carefully on the crown of the arch, deeper than usual, beneath a tie, so that the patrols could not feel its jelly softness under their feet. The wires were taken down the bank into the shingle bed of the watercourse, where concealment was quick; and up it as far as they could reach. Unfortunately, this was only sixty yards, for there had been difficulty in Egypt over insulated cable and no more had been available when our expedition started. Sixty yards was plenty for the bridge, but little for a train: however, the ends happened to coincide with a little bush about ten inches high, on the edge of the watercourse, and we buried them beside this very convenient mark. It was impossible to leave them joined up to the exploder in the proper way, since the spot was evident to the permanent way-patrols as they made their rounds.

Owing to the mud the job took longer than usual, and it was very nearly dawn before we finished. I waited under the draughty arch till day broke, wet and dismal, and then I went over the whole area of disturbance, spending another half-hour in effacing its every mark, scattering leaves and dead grass

201

over it, and watering down the broken mud from a shallow rain-pool near. Then they waved to me that the first patrol was coming, and I went up to join the others.

Before I had reached them they came tearing down into their prearranged places, lining the watercourse and spurs on each side. A train was coming from the north. Hamud, Feisal's long slave, had the exploder; but before he reached me a short train of closed box-waggons rushed by at speed. The rain-storms on the plain and the thick morning had hidden it from the eyes of our watchman until too late. This second failure saddened us further and Ali began to say that nothing would come right this trip. Such a statement held *rish* as prelude of the discovery of an evil eye present; so, to divert attention, I suggested new watching posts be sent far out, one to the ruins on the north, one to the great cairn of the southern crest.

The rest, having no breakfast, were to pretend not to be hungry. They all enjoyed doing this, and for a while we sat cheerfully in the rain, huddling against one another for warmth behind a breastwork of our steaming camels. The moisture made the animals' hair curl up like fleece, so that they looked queerly dishevelled. When the rain paused, which it did frequently, a cold moaning wind searched out the unprotected parts of us very thoroughly. After a time we found our wetted shirts clammy and comfortless things. We had nothing to eat, nothing to do and nowhere to sit except on wet rock, wet grass or mud. However, this persistent weather kept reminding me that it would delay Allenby's advance on Jerusalem, and rob him of his great possibility. So large a misfortune to our lion was a half-encouragement for the mice. We would be partners into next year.

In the best circumstances, waiting for action was hard. Today it was beastly. Even enemy patrols stumbled along without care, perfunctorily, against the rain. At last, near noon, in a snatch of fine weather, the watchmen on the south peak flagged their cloaks wildly in signal of a train. We reached our positions in an instant, for we had squatted the late hours on our heels in a steaming ditch near the line, so as not to miss another chance. The Arabs took cover properly. I looked back at their ambush from my firing point, and saw nothing but the grey hill-sides.

I could not hear the train coming, but trusted, and knelt

ready for perhaps half an hour, when the suspense became intolerable, and I signalled to know what was up. They sent down to say it was coming very slowly, and was an enormously long train. Our appetites stiffened. The longer it was the more would be the loot. Then came word that it had stopped. It moved again.

Finally, near one o'clock, I heard it panting. The locomotive was evidently defective (all these wood-fired trains were bad), and the heavy load on the up-gradient was proving too much for its capacity. I crouched behind my bush, while it crawled slowly into view past the south cutting, and along the bank above my head towards the culvert. The first ten trucks were open trucks, crowded with troops. However, once again it was too late to choose, so when the engine was squarely over the mine I pushed down the handle of the exploder. Nothing happened. I sawed it up and down four times.

Still nothing happened; and I realized that it had gone out of order, and that I was kneeling on a naked bank, with a Turkish troop train crawling past fifty yards away. The bush, which had seemed a foot high, shrank smaller than a fig-leaf; and I felt myself the most distinct object in the country-side. Behind me was an open valley for two hundred yards to the cover where my Arabs were waiting, and wondering what I was at. It was impossible to make a bolt for it, or the Turks would step off the train and finish us. If I sat still, there might be just a hope of my being ignored as a casual Bedouin.

So there I sat, counting for sheer life, while eighteen open trucks, three box-waggons, and three officers' coaches dragged by. The engine panted slower and slower, and I thought every moment that it would break down. The troops took no great notice of me, but the officers were interested, and came out to the little platforms at the ends of their carriages, pointing and staring. I waved back at them, grinning nervously, and feeling an improbable shepherd in my Meccan dress, with its twisted golden circlet about my head. Perhaps the mud-stains, the wet and their ignorance made me accepted. The end of the brake van slowly disappeared into the cutting on the north.

As it went, I jumped up, buried my wires, snatched hold of the wretched exploder, and went like a rabbit uphill into safety. There I took breath and looked back to see that the

203

train had finally stuck. It waited, about five hundred yards beyond the mine, for nearly an hour to get up a head of steam, while an officers' patrol came back and searched, very carefully, the ground where I had been seen sitting. However, the wires were properly hidden: they found nothing: the engine plucked up heart again, and away they went.

Mifleh was past tears, thinking I had intentionally let the train through; and when the Serahin had been told the real cause they said 'bad luck is with us.' Historically they were right; though they meant it for a prophecy, so I made sarcastic reference to their courage at the bridge the week before, hinting that it might be a tribal preference to sit on a camel-guard. At once there was uproar, the Serahin attacking me furiously, the Beni Sakhr defending. Ali heard the trouble, and came running.

When we had made it up the original despondency was half forgotten. Ali backed me nobly, though the wretched boy was blue with cold and shivering in an attack of fever. He gasped that their ancestor the Prophet had given to Sherifs the faculty of 'sight,' and by it he knew that our luck was turning. This was comfort for them: my first instalment of good fortune came when in the wet, without other tool than my dagger, I got the box of the exploder open and persuaded its electrical gear to work properly once more.

We returned to our vigil by the wires, but nothing happened, and evening drew down with more squalls and beastliness, everybody full of grumbles. There was no train; it was too wet to light a cooking fire; our only potential food was camel. Raw meat did not tempt anyone that night; and so our beasts survived to the morrow.

Ali lay down on his belly, which position lessened the hunger-ache, trying to sleep off his fever. Khazen, Ali's servant, lent him his cloak for extra covering. For a spell I took Khazen under mine, but soon found it becoming crowded. So I left it to him and went downhill to connect up the exploder. Afterwards I spent the night there alone by the singing telegraph wires, hardly wishing to sleep, so painful was the cold. Nothing came all the long hours, and dawn, which broke wet, looked even uglier than usual. We were sick to death of Minifir, of railways, of train watching and wrecking, by now. I climbed up to the main body while the early patrol searched the railway. Then the day cleared a little. Ali awoke, much refreshed, and his new spirit cheered us. Hamud, the slave, produced some sticks which he had kept under his clothes by his skin all night. They were nearly dry. We shaved down some blasting gelatine, and with its hot flame got a fire going, while the Sukhur hurriedly killed a mangy camel, the best spared of our riding-beasts, and began with entrenching tools to hack it into handy joints.

Just at that moment the watchman on the north cried "a train." We left the fire and made a breathless race of the six hundred yards downhill to our old position. Round the bend, whistling its loudest, came the train, a splendid two-engined thing of twelve passenger coaches, traveling at top speed on the favouring grade. I touched off under the first driving wheel of the first locomotive, and the explosion was terrific. The ground spouted blackly into my face, and I was sent spinning, to sit up with the shirt torn to my shoulder and the blood dripping from long, ragged scratches on my left arm. Between my knees lay the exploder, crushed under a twisted sheet of sooty iron. In front of me was the scalded and smoking upper half of a man. When I peered through the dust and steam of the explosion the whole boiler of the first engine seemed to be missing.

I dully felt that it was time to get away to support; but when I moved, learnt that there was a great pain in my right foot, because of which I could only limp along, with my head swinging from the shock. Movement began to clear away this confusion, as I hobbled towards the upper valley, whence the Arabs were now shooting fast into the crowded coaches. Dizzily, I cheered myself by repeating aloud in English, 'Oh, I wish this hadn't happened.'

When the enemy began to return our fire, I found myself much between the two. Ali saw me fall, and thinking that I was hard hit, ran out, with Turki and about twenty men of his servants and the Beni Sakhr, to help me. The Turks found their range and got seven of them in a few seconds. The others, in a rush, were about me—fit models, after their activity, for a sculptor. Their full white cotton drawers drawn in, bell-like, round their slender waists and ankles; their hairless brown bodies; and the love-locks plaited tightly over each temple in long horns, made them look like Russian dancers.

205

We scrambled back into cover together, and there, secretly, I felt myself over, to find I had not once been really hurt; though besides the bruises and cuts of the boiler-plate and a broken toe, I had five different bullet-grazes on me (some of them uncomfortably deep) and my clothes ripped to pieces.

From the watercourse we could look about. The explosion had destroyed the arched head of the culvert, and the frame of the first engine was lying beyond it, at the near foot of the embankment, down which it had rolled. The second locomotive had toppled into the gap, and was lying across the ruined tender of the first. Its bed was twisted. I judged them both beyond repair. The second tender had disappeared over the further side; and the first three waggons had telescoped and were smashed into pieces.

The rest of the train was badly derailed, with the listing coaches butted end to end at all angles, zigzagged along the track. One of them was a saloon, decorated with flags. In it had been Mehmed Jemal Pasha, commanding the Eighth Army Corps, hurrying down to defend Jerusalem against Allenby. His charges had been in the first waggon; his motor-car was on the end of the train, and we shot it up. Of his staff we noticed a fat ecclesiastic, whom we thought to be Assad Shukair, Imam to Ahmed Jemal Pasha, and a notorious pro-Turk pimp. So we blazed at him till he dropped.

It was all long bowls. We could see that our chance of carrying the wreck was slight. There had been some four hundred men on board, and the survivors, now recovered from the shock, were under shelter and shooting hard at us. At the first moment our party on the north spur had closed, and nearly won the game. Mifleh on his mare chased the officers from the saloon into the lower ditch. He was too excited to stop and shoot, and so they got away scathless. The Arabs following him had turned to pick up some of the rifles and medals littering the ground, and then to drag bags and boxes from the train. If we had a machine-gun posted to cover the far side, according to my mining practice, not a Turk would have escaped.

Mifleh and Adhub rejoined us on the hill, and asked after Fahad. One of the Serahin told how he had led the first rush, while I lay knocked out beside the exploder, and had been

206

killed near it. They showed his belt and rifle as proof that he was dead and that they had tried to save him. Adhub said not a word, but leaped out of the gully, and raced downhill. We caught our breaths till our lungs hurt us, watching him; but the Turks seemed not to see. A minute later he was dragging a body behind the left-hand bank.

Mifleh went back to his mare, mounted, and took her down behind a spur. Together they lifted the inert figure on to the pommel and returned. A bullet had passed through Fahad's face, knocking out four teeth, and gashing the tongue. He had fallen unconscious, but had revived just before Adhub reached him, and was trying on hands and knees, blinded with blood, to crawl away. He now recovered poise enough to cling to a saddle. So they changed him to the first camel they found and led him off at once.

The Turks, seeing us so quiet, began to advance up the slope. We let them come halfway, and then poured in volleys which killed some twenty and drove the others back. The ground about the train was strewn with dead, and the broken coaches had been crowded; but they were fighting under the eye of their Corps Commander, and undaunted began to work round the spurs to outflank us.

We were now only about forty left, and obviously could do no good against them. So we ran in batches up the little stream-bed, turning at each sheltered angle to delay them by pot-shots. Little Turki much distinguished himself by quick coolness, though his straight stocked Turkish cavalry carbine made him so expose his head that he got four bullets through his headcloth. Ali was angry with me for retiring slowly. In reality my raw hurts crippled me, but to hide from him this real reason I pretended to be easy, interested in and studying the Turks. Such successive rests while I gained courage for a new run kept him and Turki far behind the rest.

At last we reached the hill-top. Each man there jumped on the nearest camel, and made away at full speed eastward into the desert, for an hour. Then in safety we sorted our animals. The excellent Rahail, despite the ruling excitement, had brought off with him, tied to his saddle-girth, a huge haunch of the camel slaughtered just as the train arrived. He gave us the motive for a proper halt, five miles farther on, as a little party of four camels appeared marching in the same direction. It was our companion, Matar, coming back from his home village to Azrak with loads of raisins and peasant delicacies.

So we stopped at once, under a large rock in Wadi Dhuleil, where was a barren fig-tree, and cooked our first meal for three days. There, also, we bandaged up Fahad, who was sleepy with the lassitude of his severe hurt. Adhub, seeing this, took one of Matar's new carpets, and, doubling it across the camel-saddle, stitched the ends into great pockets. In one they laid Fahad, while Adhub crawled into the other as make-weight: and the camel was led off southward towards their tribal tents.

The other wounded men were seen to at the same time. Mifleh brought up the youngest lads of the party, and had them spray the wounds with their piss, as a rude antiseptic. Meanwhile we whole ones refreshed ourselves. I brought another mangy camel for extra meat, paid rewards, compensated the relatives of the killed, and gave prize-money, for the sixty or seventy rifles we had taken. It was small booty, but not to be despised. Some Serahin, who had gone into the action without rifles, able only to throw unavailing stones, had now two guns apiece. Next day we moved into Azrak, having a great welcome, and boasting—God forgive us—that we were victors.

Over the Top

by Arthur Guy Empey

Arthur Guy Empey was an American who fought
for the British in World War I. Born in Ogden, Utah,
Empey had spent most of his youth and early manhood knocking around the world, either as a sailor or
as a U.S. soldier. In 1916 he crossed the Atlantic to
join the British Army, volunteering for front-line duty
in France. This is his story of his first charge through
no-man's land.

On my second trip to the trenches our officer was making his rounds of inspection, and we received the cheerful news that at four in the morning we were to go over the top and take the German front-line trench. My heart turned to lead. Then the officer carried on with his instructions. To the best of my memory I recall them as follows: "At eleven a wiring party will go out in front and cut lanes through our barbed wire for the passage of troops in the morning. At two o'clock our artillery will open up with an intense bombardment which will last until four. Upon the lifting of the barrage, the first of the three waves will go over." Then he left. Some of the Tommies, first getting permission from the Sergeant, went into the machine-gunners' dugout, and wrote letters home, saying that in the morning they were going over the top, and also that if the letters reached their destination it would mean that the writer had been killed.

These letters were turned over to the captain with instructions to mail same in the event of the writer's being killed. Some of the men made out their wills in their pay book, under the caption, "will and last testament."

Then the nerve-racking wait commenced. Every now and then I would glance at the dial of my wrist-watch and was surprised to see how fast the minutes passed by. About five minutes to two I got nervous waiting for our guns to open up. I could not take my eyes from my watch. I crouched against the parapet and strained my muscles in a death-like grip upon my rifle. As the hands on my watch showed two o'clock, a blinding red flare lighted up the sky in our rear, then thunder, intermixed with a sharp, whistling sound in the air over our heads. The shells from our guns were speeding on their way toward the German lines. With one accord the men sprang up on the fire step and looked over the top in the direction of the German trenches. A line of bursting shells lighted up No Man's Land. The din was terrific and the ground trembled.

Then, high above our heads we could hear a sighing moan. Our big boys behind the line had opened up and 9.2's and 15-inch shells commenced dropping into the German lines. The flash of the guns behind the lines, the scream of the shells through the air, and the flare of them, bursting, was a spectacle that put Pain's greatest display into the shade. The constant *pup pup* of German machine guns and an occasional rattle of rifle firing gave me the impression of a huge audience applauding the work of the batteries.

Our eighteen-pounders were destroying the German barbed wire, while the heavier stuff was demolishing their trenches and bashing in dugouts or funk-holes.

Then Fritz got busy.

Their shells went screaming overhead, aimed in the direction of the flares from our batteries. Trench mortars started dropping "Minnies" in our front line. We clicked several casualties. Then they suddenly ceased. Our artillery had taped or silenced them.

During the bombardment you could almost read a newspaper in our trench. Sometimes in the flare of a shell-burst a man's body would be silhouetted against the parados of the trench and it appeared like a huge monster. You could hardly hear yourself think. When an order was to be passed down the trench, you had to yell it, using your hands as a funnel into the ear of the man sitting next to you on the fire step. In about twenty minutes a generous rum issue was doled out. After drinking the rum, which tasted like varnish and sent a shudder through your frame, you wondered why they made you wait until the lifting of the barrage before going over. At ten minutes to four, word was passed down, "Ten minutes to go!" Ten minutes to live! We were shivering all over. My legs felt as if they were asleep. Then word was passed down: "First wave get on and near the scaling ladders."

These were small wooden ladders which we had placed against the parapet to enable us to go over the top on the lifting of the barrage. "Ladders of Death" we called them, and veritably they were.

Before a charge Tommy is the politest of men. There is never any pushing or crowding to be first up these ladders. We crouched around the base of the ladders waiting for the word to go over. I was sick and faint, and was puffing away

211

at an unlighted fag. Then came the word, "Three minutes to go; upon the lifting of the barrage and on the blast of the whistles, 'Over the Top with the Best o' Luck and Give them Hell.'" The famous phrase of the Western Front. The Jonah phrase of the Western Front. To Tommy it means if you are lucky enough to come back, you will be minus an arm or a leg. Tommy hates to be wished the best of luck; so, when peace is declared, if it ever is, and you meet a Tommy on the street, just wish him the best of luck and duck the brick that follows.

I glanced again at my wrist-watch. We all wore them and you could hardly call us "sissies" for doing so. It was a minute to four. I could see the hand move to the twelve, then a dead silence. It hurt. Everyone looked up to see what had happened, but not for long. Sharp whistle blasts rang out along the trench, and with a cheer the men scrambled up the ladders. The bullets were cracking overhead, and occasionally a machine gun would rip and tear the top of the sandbag parapet. How I got up that ladder I will never know. The first ten feet out in front was agony. Then we passed through the lanes in our barbed wire. I knew I was running, but could feel no motion below the waist. Patches on the ground seemed to float to the rear as if I were on a treadmill and scenery was rushing past me. The Germans had put a barrage of shrapnel across No Man's Land, and you could hear the pieces slap the ground about you.

After I had passed our barbed wire and gotten into No Man's Land, a Tommy about fifteen feet to my right front turned around and looking in my direction, put his hand to his mouth and yelled something which I could not make out on account of the noise from the bursting shells. Then he coughed, stumbled, pitched forward, and lay still. His body seemed to float to the rear of me. I could hear sharp cracks in the air about me. These were caused by passing rifle bullets. Frequently, to my right and left, little spurts of dirt would rise into the air, and a ricochet bullet would whine on its way. If a Tommy should see one of these little spurts in front of him, he would tell the nurse about it later. The crossing of No Man's Land remains a blank to me.

Men on my right and left would stumble and fall. Some would try to get up, while others remained huddled and

212

motionless. Then smashed-up barbed wire came into view and seemed carried on a tide to the rear. Suddenly, in front of me loomed a bashed-in trench about four feet wide. Queer-looking forms like mud turtles were scrambling up its wall. One of these forms seemed to slip and then rolled to the bottom of the trench. I leaped across this intervening space. The man to my left seemed to pause in mid-air, then pitched head down into the German trench. I laughed out loud in my delirium. Upon alighting on the other side of the trench I came to with a sudden jolt. Right in front of me loomed a giant form with a rifle which looked about ten feet long, on the end of which seemed seven bayonets. These flashed in the air in front of me. Then through my mind flashed the admonition of our bayonet instructor back in Blighty. He had said, "Whenever you get in a charge and run your bayonet up to the hilt into a German, the Fritz will fall. Perhaps your rifle will be wrenched from your grasp. Do not waste time, if the bayonet is fouled in his equipment, by putting your foot on his stomach and tugging at the rifle to extricate the bayonet. Simply press the trigger and the bullet will free it." In my present situation this was fine logic, but for the life of me I could not remember how he had told me to get my bayonet into the German. To me, this was the paramount issue. I closed my eyes, and lunged forward. My rifle was torn from my hands. I must have gotten the German because he had disappeared. About twenty feet to my left front was a huge Prussian nearly six feet four inches in height, a fine specimen of physical manhood. The bayonet from his rifle was missing, but he clutched the barrel in both hands and was swinging the butt around his head. I could almost hear the swish of the butt passing through the air. Three little Tommies were engaged with him. They looked like pigmies alongside of the Prussian. The Tommy on the left was gradually circling to the rear of his opponent. It was a funny sight to see them duck the swinging butt and try to jab him at the same time. The Tommy nearest me received the butt of the German's rifle in a smashing blow below the right temple. It smashed his head like an eggshell. He pitched forward on his side and a convulsive shudder ran through his body. Meanwhile, the other Tommy had gained the rear of the Prussian. Suddenly about four inches of bayonet protruded from the throat of the Prussian soldier, who staggered forward and fell. I will never forget the look of blank astonishment that came over his face.

Then something hit me in the left shoulder and my left side went numb. It felt as if a hot poker was being driven through me. I felt no pain—just a sort of nervous shock. A bayonet had pierced me from the rear. I fell backward on the the ground, but was not unconscious, because I could see dim objects moving around me. Then a flash of light in front of my eyes and unconsciousness. Something had hit me on the head. I have never found out what it was.

I dreamed I was being tossed about in an open boat on a heaving sea and opened my eyes. The moon was shining. I was on a stretcher being carried down one of our communication trenches. At the advanced first-aid post my wounds were dressed, and then I was put into an ambulance and sent to one of the base hospitals. The wounds in my shoulder and head were not serious and in six weeks I had rejoined my company for service in the front line.

Shot Down

by Norman Archibald

In World War One the romantic figure of the mounted soldier rode out of history. But as the cavalry trooper disappeared, his place was taken by a new, perhaps more glamorous fighting man: the aviator. Nothing seemed more dashing than the young pilots of both sides who hunted and harried one another high above the earth, and the world thrilled to the exploits of the Captain Eddie Rickenbackers or Baron Manfred von Richthofens. In those days, to be an Ace, to have shot down five enemy planes, was indeed a high honor—and among those who fought for it was a young American flying officer named Norman Archibald. He tells of being shot down while flying with the 95th Aero Squadron, 1st Pursuit Group, A.E.F., over enemy territory.

The planes line up. We are ready. Fastening the safety belts I signal to my mechanics, take off, climb to a thousand feet and wait for the others. One by one they appear. In tight formation, each in his position, we follow our leader who heads for the Front.

Safe, free, winged on high, we are sailing along when the leader, with motor trouble, drops from the formation.

Now we are four.

One of the remaining four assumes the lead.

Another plane drops away.

Now we are three.

I know nothing of the etiquette in such a case but as the other remaining plane flies behind to the right of the leader, I fly behind to the left and, still rapidly climbing, we go on.

Over the Marne.

The altimeter registers twelve thousand feet and still we climb. Surely we are over the lines—where are the enemy planes?

WOOF! WOOF!

Anti-aircraft explosions pull my eyes to the right where puffs of smoke, black, hang in the air.

WOOF! WOOF!

More appear and more; closer now, above, to the right and the leader zigzags in his course to warn us that we are targets for these enemy shells.

The smoke puffs and muffled explosions hold my attention as a great spectacle, void of danger. They break again, still above, but to the left this time. So! we are being fired at! The thought thrills me, thrills me to thumb my nose at their vain attempts. At fifteen thousand feet the leader levels out, continuing into Germany.

Suddenly, ahead and one thousand feet below, planes are silhouetted against a large, white, cumulus cloud. Not in formation but playing, diving, zooming and cavorting around this dense ball of whiteness.

216

Enemy planes!

Now—for excitement!

Our leader turns and starts back. Why are we running away? Are they, perhaps, Allied planes?

The leader, turning again, starts after them. Following—maybe he planned an attack but first made certain there were no other planes about. Closer now . . . counting them. . . . One, two, three, four, five, six—seven! Seven Boches—seven, jet black against the white cloud.

Waggling his wings for close attention we follow our leader as he glides toward them. Their topsy-turvy maneuvers cease. A wonderful example of perfect team work as, instantly, they assume formation with four in one group and three in another. Nearer—white crosses on their black fuselages. Nearer —they invite us to dive on the smaller formation and so place ourselves in position for an attack from the other four.

Our leader opens fire.

Guns, from the Spad on my right, shoot out streams of smoke. This is my cue so I, too, aim, pull both triggers and smoking tracer bullets speed in the direction of the Huns. They break formation, instantly become disorganized and, like black water snakes, squirm in a sea of air.

Pulling up, we circle above them. They twist, turn, and their maneuvers to reach our level remind me of slimy animals, hideous and poisonous to touch. With such odds as seven to three our leader has no intention of seeking their level and keeps well above. Beneath, one black, evil body, with its nose pointed directly at me, leaps straight into the air.

Good God! Can these German planes climb straight up? If so, what chance have we? With my eyes glued on him he falls off into a dive. So! . . . he zoomed and took a pot shot at me. But he missed. . . . Pooh! did he think he could get me and my Spad that way? Again we circle—again we dive— this time I fire both guns at the mess in general. Down they go through a layer of clouds and one, in a deathlike spin, is lost to view.

The air is clear. Only our planes soar above the clouds and the leader starts for home. Crossing the lines more anti-aircraft welcomes us, warmly, as we zigzag a course to the Marne.

Why go home? Surely we could find more Germans! Is

217

it all over? Safe across the lines I take off my goggles and helmet. The fresh air streams through my hair and fans my hot face. Oh! for another whack at them! Never have I felt more rested, alive or with more energy but I settle down in the cockpit to enjoy the ride. Wonder if we got the plane—the one that went down in a spin?

My little Spad sails smoothly on, humming, humming with contentment and as docile as a thoroughbred jogging towards his stable after a race.

The ever-faithful mechanics are waiting, eagerly.

"Did you see any Germans?"

"Did you have a fight, Lieutenant?"

As it was my first experience I did not know if it was anything out of the ordinary or not but waited to read the leader's report.

It told of heavy anti-aircraft; sighting seven Fokkers; keeping altitude because of superior numbers; forcing them down through the clouds and of one plane falling in a spin. No confirmation was asked for the latter because we could not be sure. Whether we "got" the plane or not no one but the Germans ever knew.

The report, except for "heavy anti-aircraft" seemed perfect. Was that a great bombardment of the air? Thought it would be far worse. So! I had been in this terrific anti-aircraft! Pooh! Then it was my least concern.

We were about to leave for a patrol.

The wind, which usually blew across the field, blew towards the hangar. Therefore, the field's entire length was available for a take-off, a rare but satisfactory situation. At the far end of the aerodrome tall poplars formed a natural barrier. Ready to go, I pushed on the stick, opened the motor and, with the total length of the field ahead, purposely held the plane on the ground for a long, steady run, as, planning to zoom over the trees, I wanted all the speed possible. Three-quarters of the way down the field, going at full tilt, I eased up on the stick to take off. But it did not come back. Another slight pull. It was caught. A quick glance into the cockpit. Wires to the machine gun were wrapped around the stick. They held it in a vise and, taut, prevented it from coming back sufficiently to take off.

The trees were ahead. If the motor were "cut" I'd crash into them; if the stick were pushed forward to release the wires I'd nose over; I could not pull it back. A hell of a fix, but something must be done. Taking my left hand from the motor controls I frantically grabbed the wires, yanked them terrifically and at the same instant jerked the stick. The plane shot straight up. Both guns went off. A lurch. The landing gear grazed the tops of the trees, the plane fluttered but, as I pushed on the stick it dove, gained speed and leveled out. *WHEW!* My pulse slowed. Circling, to assure myself that everything was all right, I left the field.

My motor stopped.

The oil line had broken. Hot castor oil poured into the cockpit. Nosing over, barbed wire entanglement in front; oil in the cockpit at least three inches deep; and gliding over the wire with the plane held in a flat glide, I tried to get back to the field. Speed was lost. The ship fluttered. "Careful, don't break your neck the way Milham did," an inner voice whispered. "Land!—right now." So, pushing on the stick, at a good rate of speed I attempted to "pan-cake" on the wire entanglement. The landing gear caught; the plane whirled and, ducking into the cockpit—I waited. Terrific jerks. Then as the plane settled on its back, hot castor oil poured over me. As I crawled out, face, head and clothes were covered with the dirty lubricant. My plane was a total wreck.

"*Mon Dieu!*" . . . cried a high, shrill voice. "*Mon Dieu! Mon Dieu!*" A young girl, with black hair flying and her little petticoat flouncing behind, ran towards me. Arriving quite out of breath she waved her slender arms, gasping, "*Mon Dieu!* You . . . *Monsieur l'aviateur* . . . you will keel yourself."

It was hard to convince this highly strung little one of my wholeness. With hesitancy she believed me and then, with large brown eyes looking solemnly into mine, unclasped a fine gold chain from around her neck.

"*Voilà!*" she said, proudly holding up her little hand. "*Voilà!*"

In her palm was the replica of a lady bug, exquisitely made of cloisonné. Before I could remark about her tiny treasure she grabbed my hand and found my identification bracelet. After examining, with the puckered brow of a connoisseur, an ivory elephant, a monkey and other good luck

charms, she added her precious trinket. Then, abashed and
spinning on one heel, she announced, "You, *Monsieur l'aviateur
Americain* will never have the hurt when you wear theese."
I thanked her and started to leave when up she jumped, wound
her arms around my neck, kissed me and scampered off.

At the aerodrome Captain Peterson met me with a smile.
"Well, Archibald, did you do a job of cracking up?"

"Perfect, sir! A complete washout!"

"Fine! We need some spare parts," was his only comment.

"Lieutenant, that was some take-off," said my mechanic,
hinting for an explanation. None was offered, for my Spad—
my little Spad—was a complete wreck. I had fought in it, had
faith in it, knew its every characteristic, and felt it never, never
could be replaced, but the next day when Captain Peterson
assigned to me a brand-new ship, my spirits rose a bit.

August 11th, the day after, with Bill Russell flying rear
position on the right, I flew rear position on the left, and a
formation of five planes again sallied forth on its daily search
for Fokkers.

Two days previous, flying the same position, we were
well over Germany when the leader, banking left, headed
back towards the lines. In such a maneuver the pilot flying rear
must speed his motor and turn quickly in order to keep his
close position. Should he turn gradually he becomes separated,
lags in the rear and is easy prey for Boche planes hidden by
clouds or sun.

Bill lagged.

Far in the rear and above I saw him. The chances he took
were useless for ever-watchful enemy planes could easily shoot
him down before we would have the slightest chance of flying
to his aid.

Each moment I expected a group of Fokkers—they appeared and disappeared like magic—to swoop down on this
single, isolated ship which hung alone in that death-infested
space. A fearful anxiety gripped me until Bill finally resumed
his correct position.

Landing, the leader cautioned, "Don't take such risks,
Bill. Don't lag on the turns. If Huns are around they'll single
you out and you won't have a chance. Keep a tight formation."

Bill laughed. "All right," he said.

Utter nonsense, he thought. Bill had a positive contempt

for enemy tactics. He liked to be separated. To sit alone, above and where he could view the formation was his sheer delight.

This day we flew about four miles into Germany, were fifteen thousand feet up and with the identical movements of the previous day the leader swung left and started towards the lines.

Bill lagged.

I glanced back. There he sat, approximately five hundred feet behind and a relative distance above. With a strange premonition of danger I dove in front of the leader as a signal to turn and pick up Bill but, simultaneously, two Fokkers dove and poured streams of lead in Bill's direction. Trailing smoke. We all turned. The enemy planes pulled up, swerved and flying back to their hiding place behind a cloud were out of sight.

We were too late.

Bill's plane shot straight up. At the peak of a perpendicular ascent it sloped over and, dizzily whirling, dropped towards the earth.

"Pull up, Bill! . . . Pull up! . . . they're gone."

It was still possible that, in an attempt to draw his attackers beneath us, he was spinning purposely.

"Pull up, Bill! For God's sake, pull up!" and hoping against hope I strained my eyes to see him straighten out. Down—at a terrific rate—spinning—dropping—

"Bill!—surely he isn't hit. Bill!—he'll come out," but he fell in a terrible whirl. Down . . . Down . . . down . . . for thousands of feet I watched his plane until, below the horizon, the tiny speck of him melted into nothingness.

Bill was gone.

Instinctively we four functioned as one. With a sacred determination to avenge his death we cruised around looking for the Fokkers. They had vanished.

Flying back to the aerodrome—in the rear and on the left—I tagged along. Bill! To my right, where his little Spad should be, was a hazy, bluish space—white-flecked and empty.

A few days later a report confirmed what we already knew. The advancing Infantry had found a wrecked plane and the body of Lieutenant William H. Russell.

THE NEXT MORNING. September 8th. Sunday.

221

A glorious sunny day and, up early, I went first to the operations tent, then to the hangar.

"We're going on a patrol at eight-thirty," I told my mechanics.

"Lieutenant! . . . Say! . . . Gosh, it's good to see you." They grinned and bustled around a plane.

"Put a full belt of incendiary ammunition in the right-hand gun," I instructed them.

Hungry and needing a shave, I planned to have a snack of breakfast and clean up before we left but was so happy preparing for a flight, talking shop and examining the ship that time passed swiftly and, before I realized, it was nearly half-past eight.

The planes were wheeled out, the motors were started, whirred in the sunshine and, oblivious of everything but flying, I climbed into my ship.

"Everything all right?"

"Yes, Lieutenant. Good luck! and . . . be sure to come back."

"I'll be back all right," and thrilled with the day, the flight and unsolved problems ahead I took off with four others for a patrol over Watronville-St. Mihiel.

Two planes, with motor trouble, dropped out, leaving Avery, Heinricks and myself, who climbed and headed for the Front. The fever of flying suffused me and, in my element again, joy tingled to my very finger tips as we approached the lines at about six thousand feet altitude northwest of Watronville.

My motor, although running smoothly, was not turning up the required number of revolutions, so my ship did not climb as rapidly as usual and was gradually dropping behind and below Heinricks and Avery. But, thinking it would function normally as soon as it warmed up—I followed along. We continued into Germany about a mile, turned right and flew parallel to the front lines in the direction of St. Mihiel.

The air was still and, except for a speck of an observation plane at great altitude, too far away to attack, was void of enemy planes. We continued our course. By now—decidedly lagging—I was a considerable and dangerous distance in the rear and beneath the other two, but, confident that when the motor warmed up more I could catch up . . . trailed merrily along.

Avery and Heinricks leveled out, increased their speed and, flying swiftly far ahead, were rapidly disappearing. Gone. I was alone.

Crack! Crack! Crack! Ear-splitting explosions rent the air and puffs of black smoke, almost within reach, encircled my plane. Bewildered by the intense barrage, its suddenness and the accurate aim of German anti-aircraft, I could not believe I was trapped in a terrific bombardment. *Crack! Crack! Crack!* Instinct told me to dive but a split-second thought warned me that at low altitude, over the lines and harnessed with a weak motor I might be forced to land on enemy territory. Anything but that! Anything but that! *Crack! Crack! Crack! Crack!* Never had I witnessed such violent anti-aircraft; never such aim; never so close. What could I do? A light cloud bank above me. What a haven of refuge! I could climb—*Crack! Crack!*—hide in it and be safe from the Boche ground gunners.

I started up. *Crack! Crack! Crack!* Deafening explosions in rapid succession. Would I make it? Seconds seemed hours. *Crack! Crack! Crack! Crack!* Holding up the nose of the sluggish plane I tried to climb, but either the cloud was further away than I had reckoned or my plane was climbing unbelievably slowly. "One of these shells will break right under my seat in a minute," I thought. "That will be the end of me," but immediately assured myself with the contradiction, "Anti-aircraft has never hit me yet, they're damned close but they won't hit me now," so climbing toward the haze, but imbued with the latter thought, I felt secure from threatening destruction.

Crack! Crack! Crack! The smoke puffs were so close— could grab one if I wished; or two, or three, if I wanted, and let them sift through my fingers. Black, curling, thick gobs which hung, spread, and spiraled into grey. They fascinated me! They seemed to hypnotize and hold me! Making no effort to turn or dive out of the menacing mass I watched them, still pointing the ship's nose up, and struggled to reach the clouds of safety.

C-R-A-C-K! A thunderous explosion. My plane was tossed up.

C-R-A-C-K! A piece of aluminum cowling on the nose flew into space.

My motor stopped and I pushed on the stick.

W-H-A-M! Another shell burst and my plane, hurtled to

223

the right, flopped over and started down in a side slip. The right wing was low. Trying to right the ship I pushed the stick to the left but the control was useless, the plane did not respond and, still on my side, I continued to fall.

Luck had left me!

Shrapnel had struck my motor and hit my plane. Putting the stick to the right, I pulled it back and in this position my Spad, answering the controls, started to spiral. Frantic—I held my plane in this precarious tight turn, swiftly losing altitude. The anti-aircraft died away; no more shells exploded. What now? Were the gunners satisfied that they had fatally crippled me or was I falling too rapidly for them to aim their guns? Whatever the reason the bombardment stopped.

I was dropping—fast. In a last vain attempt to right the plane I cautiously and slowly moved the stick toward the center but, falling down again in a perilous side slip, quickly pulled back into another spiral, the only possible position in which the ship could be even partially controlled. A quick glance: a large hole torn in the upper right wing. This or an aileron, broken by shrapnel, was causing the trouble. Tossing . . . tumbling . . . feverishly endeavoring to control the shattered plane. . . . I lost my bearings. A crash was inevitable.

Dreading the result and dropping rapidly, I cautiously kept in a tight spiral, fearful of losing completely my thread-like hold on the doomed ship. Around and down . . . fighting Fate; down and around . . . combating Destiny. Confident and optimistic of the outcome I desperately looked below, praying to see a forest, for trees would break a dire collision with the earth. Trees, trees to lessen the certain and terrible blow, but in lieu of the longed-for blackish-green I saw, to my terror, a barren field, white as chalk and gutted with shell holes.

I was in the lap of the gods. In a minute—it would happen. In a second—it would be over. Every flying instinct was alive, and gripping the stick I held it well over and back to the right as down and around I dropped . . . dropped; down and around I spiraled . . . spiraled and—clinging to life—prepared to crash. "Judge your distance carefully," I admonished a stranger. "Kick the rudder just before you hit." The ground—rushing towards me. "Keep your head!" The earth . . . there it was . . . "Now or never!" and with a terrific blow I kicked right rudder. . . .

I Saw the Communist Revolution

by John Reed

The world movement known as communism had its visible birth on October 25, 1917, the day on which the Bolsheviks of V. I. Lenin seized power in the capital Russian city of Petrograd. In commemoration of that event, the city, though no longer the capital, is now called Leningrad, and the uprising has come to be known as the October Revolution, even though adoption of the Gregorian calendar has changed the date to November 7. Also, to understand what follows, remember that the October Revolution was itself subsequent to the revolt which had ousted Czar Nicholas II and placed Alexander Kerensky at the head of a shaky provisional government. It was against Kerensky that the Bolsheviks moved, and their success is described by one of their ardent admirers, the American socialist John Silas Reed, who was present that memorable day and whose ashes now rest beneath the Kremlin wall.

225

Early in the morning I went out to Smolny. Going up the long wooden sidewalk from the outer gate I saw the first thin, hesitating snow-flakes fluttering down from the grey, windless sky. "Snow!" cried the soldier at the door, grinning with delight. "Good for the health!" Inside, the long gloomy halls and bleak rooms seemed deserted. No one moved in all the enormous pile. A deep, uneasy sound came to my ears, and looking around, I noticed that everywhere on the floor, along the walls, men were sleeping. Rough, dirty men, workers and soldiers, spattered and caked with mud, sprawled alone or in heaps, in the careless attitudes of death. Some wore ragged bandages marked with blood. Guns and cartridge-belts were scattered about. . . . The victorious proletarian army!

In the upstairs buffet so thick they lay that one could hardly walk. The air was foul. Through the clouded windows a pale light streamed. A battered samovar, cold, stood on the counter, and many glasses holding dregs of tea. Beside them lay a copy of the Military Revolutionary Committee's last bulletin, upside down, scrawled with painful hand-writing. It was a memorial written by some soldier to his comrades fallen in the fight against Kerensky, just as he had set it down before falling on the floor to sleep. The writing was blurred with what looked like tears . . .

Alexei Vinogradov
D. Maskvin
S. Stolbikov
A. Voskresensky
D. Leonsky
D. Preobrazhensky
V. Laidansky
M. Berchikov

These men were drafted into the Army on November 15, 1916. Only three are left of the above.

Mikhail Berchikov, Alexei Voskresensky, Dmitri Leonsky

Sleep, warrior eagles, sleep with peaceful soul.
You have deserved, our own ones, happiness and
Eternal peace. Under the earth of the grave
You have straitly closed your ranks. Sleep, Citizens!

Only the Military Revolutionary Committee still functioned, unsleeping. Skrypnik, emerging from the inner room,
said that Gotz had been arrested, but had flatly denied signing
the proclamation of the Committee for Salvation, as had
Avksentiev; and the Committee for Salvation itself had re-
pudiated the Appeal to the garrison. There was still disaffec-
tion among the city regiments, Skrypnik reported; the Vol-
hynsky Regiment had refused to fight against Kerensky.

Several detachments of "neutral" troops, with Chernov
at their head, were at Gatchina, trying to persuade Kerensky
to halt his attack on Petrograd.

Skrypnik laughed. "There can be no 'neutrals' now," he
said. "We've won!" His sharp, bearded face glowed with an
almost religious exaltation. "More than sixty delegates have
arrived from the Front, with assurances of support by all the
armies except the troops on the Rumanian front, who have
not been heard from. The Army Committees have suppressed
all news from Petrograd, but we now have a regular system
of couriers. . . ."

Down in the front hall Kamenev was just entering, worn
out by the all-night session of the Conference to Form a New
Government, but happy. "Already the Socialist Revolution-
aries are inclined to admit us into the new Government," he
told me. "The right wing groups are frightened by the Revolutionary Tribunals; they demand, in a sort of panic, that we
dissolve them before going any further. . . . We have accepted the proposition of the *Vikzhel* to form a homogeneous
Socialist Ministry, and they're working on that now. You see,
it all springs from our victory. When we were down, they
wouldn't have us at any price; now everybody's in favor of
some agreement with the Soviets. . . . What we need is a
really decisive victory. Kerensky wants an armistice, but he'll
have to surrender. . . ."

That was the temper of the Bolshevik leaders. To a
foreign journalist who asked Trotsky what statement he had
to make to the world, Trotsky replied: "At this moment the

only statement possible is the one we are making through the mouths of our cannon!"

But there was an undercurrent of real anxiety in the tide of victory; the question of finances. Instead of opening the banks, as had been ordered by the Military Revolutionary Committee, the Union of Bank Employees had held a meeting and declared a formal strike. Smolny had demanded some thirty-five millions of rubles from the State Bank, and the cashier had locked the vaults, only paying out money to the representatives of the Provisional Government. The reactionaries were using the State Bank as a political weapon; for instance, when the *Vikzhel* demanded money to pay the salaries of the employees of the Government railroads, it was told to apply to Smolny. . . .

I went to the State Bank to see the new Commissar, a red-haired Ukrainian Bolshevik named Petrovich. He was trying to bring order out of the chaos in which affairs had been left by the striking clerks. In all the offices of the huge place, perspiring volunteer workers, soldiers and sailors, their tongues sticking out of their mouths in the intensity of their effort, were poring over the great ledgers with a bewildered air. . . .

The Duma building was crowded. There were still isolated cases of defiance toward the new Government, but they were rare. The Central Land Committee had appealed to the Peasants, ordering them not to recognize the Land Decree passed by the Congress of the Soviets, because it would cause confusion and civil war. Mayor Schreider announced that because of the Bolshevik insurrection, the elections to the Constituent Assembly would have to be indefinitely postponed.

Two questions seemed to be uppermost in all minds, shocked by the ferocity of the civil war; first, a truce to the bloodshed—second, the creation of a new Government. There was no longer any talk of "destroying the Bolsheviki"—and very little about excluding them from the Government, except from the Populist Socialists and the Peasants' Soviets. Even the Central Army Committee at the *Stavka*, the most determined enemy of Smolny, telephoned from Moghilev: "If, to constitute the new Ministry, it is necessary to come to an understanding with the Bolsheviki, we agree to admit them *in a minority* to the Cabinet."

Pravda, ironically calling attention to Kerensky's "humanitarian sentiments," published his dispatch to the Committee for Salvation:

> In accord with the proposals of the Committee for Salvation and all the democratic organizations united around it, I have halted all military action against the rebels. A delegate of the Committee has been sent to enter into negotiations. Take all measures to stop the useless shedding of blood.

The *Vikzhel* sent a telegram to all Russia:

> The Conference of the Union of Railway Workers with the representatives of both the belligerent parties, who admit the necessity of an agreement, protest energetically against the use of political terrorism in the civil war, especially when it is carried on between different factions of the revolutionary democracy, and declare that political terrorism, in whatever form, is in contradiction to the very idea of the negotiations for a new Government. . . .

Delegations from the Conference were sent to the Front, at Gatchina. In the Conference itself everything seemed on the point of final settlement. It had even been decided to elect a provisional People's Council, composed of about four hundred members—seventy-five representing Smolny, seventy-five the old *Tsay-ee-kah*, and the rest split up among the Town Dumas, the Trade Unions, Land Committees and political parties. Chernov was mentioned as the new Premier. Lenin and Trotsky, rumor said, were to be excluded. . . .

About noon I was again in front of Smolny, talking with the driver of an ambulance bound for the revolutionary front. Could I go with him? Certainly! He was a volunteer, a University student, and as we rolled down the street shouted over his shoulder to me phrases of execrable German: "*Also, gut! Wir nach die Kasernen zu essen gehen!*" I made out that there would be lunch at some barracks.

On the Kirochnaya we turned into an immense courtyard surrounded by military buildings, and mounted a dark stairway to a low room lit by one window. At a long wooden table

were seated some twenty soldiers, eating *shchi* [cabbage soup]
from a great tin washtub, with wooden spoons, and talking
loudly with much laughter.

"Welcome to the Battalion Committee of the Sixth Reserve Engineers' Battalion!" cried my friend, and introduced
me as an American Socialist. Whereat everyone rose to shake
my hand, and one old soldier put his arms around me and gave
me a hearty kiss. A wooden spoon was produced and I took
my place at the table. Another tub, full of *kasha*, was brought
in, a huge loaf of black bread, and of course the inevitable
tea-pots. At once everyone began asking me questions about
America: Was it true that people in a free country sold their
votes for *money?* If so, how did they get what they wanted?
How about this "Tammany"? Was it true that in a free
country a little group of people could control a whole city,
and exploited it for their personal benefit? Why did the people
stand it? Even under the Tsar such things could not happen
in Russia; true, here there was always graft, but to buy and
sell a whole city full of people! And in a free country! Had
the people no revolutionary feeling? I tried to explain that
in my country people tried to change things by law.

"Of course," nodded a young sergeant, named Baklanov,
who spoke French. "But you have a highly developed capitalist class? Then the capitalist class must control the legisla-
tures and the courts. How then can the people change things?
I am open to conviction, for I do not know your country; but
to me it is incredible. . . ."

I said that I was going to Tsarskoye Selo. "I, too," said
Baklanov, suddenly. "And I— and I—" The whole roomful
decided on the spot to go to Tsarskoye Selo.

Just then came a knock on the door. It opened, and in
it stood the figure of the Colonel. No one rose, but all shouted
a greeting. "May I come in?" asked the Colonel. *"Prosim!
Prosim!"* they answered heartily. He entered, smiling, a tall,
distinguished figure in a goat-skin cape embroidered with gold.
"I think I heard you say that you were going to Tsarskoye
Selo, comrades," he said. "Could I go with you?"

Baklanov considered. "I do not think there is anything
to be done here to-day," he answered. "Yes, comrade, we shall
be very glad to have you." The Colonel thanked him and sat
down, filling a glass with tea.

230

In a low voice, for fear of wounding the Colonel's pride, Baklanov explained to me. "You see, I am chairman of the Committee. We control the Battalion absolutely, except in action, when the Colonel is delegated by us to command. In action his orders must be obeyed, but he is strictly responsible to us. In barracks he must ask our permission before taking any action. . . . You might call him our Executive Officer. . . ."

Arms were distributed to us, revolvers and rifles—"we might meet some Cossacks, you know"—and we all piled into the ambulance, together with three great bundles of newspapers for the Front. Straight down the Liteiny we rattled, and along the Zagorodny Prospekt. Next to me sat a youth with the shoulder-straps of a Lieutenant, who seemed to speak all European languages with equal fluency. He was a member of the Battalion Committee.

"I am not a Bolshevik," he assured me, emphatically. "My family is a very ancient and noble one. I myself, am, you might say, a Cadet. . . ."

"But how—?" I began, bewildered.

"Oh, yes, I am a member of the Committee. I make no secret of my political opinions, but the others do not mind, because they know I do not believe in opposing the will of the majority. . . . I have refused to take any action in the present civil war, however, for I do not believe in taking up arms against my brother Russians. . . ."

"Provocator! Kornilovets!" the others cried at him gaily, slapping him on the shoulder. . . .

Passing under the huge grey stone archway of the Moskovsky Gate, covered with golden hieroglyphics, ponderous Imperial eagles and the names of Tsars, we sped out on the wide straight highway, grey with the first light fall of snow. It was thronged with Red Guards, stumbling along on foot toward the revolutionary front, shouting, singing; and others, grey-faced and muddy, coming back. Most of them seemed to be mere boys. Women with spades, some with rifles and bandoleers, others wearing the Red Cross on their arm-bands— the bowed, toil-worn women of the slums. Squads of soldiers marching out of step, with an affectionate jeer for the Red Guards; sailors, grim-looking; children with bundles of food for their fathers and mothers; all these, coming and going, trudged through the whitened mud that covered the cobbles of the highway inches deep. We passed cannon, jingling southward with their caissons; trucks bound both ways, bristling with armed men; ambulances full of wounded from the direction of the battle, and once a peasant cart, creaking along, in which sat a white-faced boy bent over his shattered stomach and screaming monotonously. In the fields on either side women and old men were digging trenches and stringing barbed-wire entanglements.

Back northward the clouds rolled away dramatically, and the pale sun came out. Across the flat, marshy plain Petrograd glittered. To the right, white and gilded and colored bulbs and pinnacles; to the left, tall chimneys, some pouring out black smoke; and beyond, a lowering sky over Finland. On each side of us were churches, monasteries. . . . Occasionally a monk was visible, silently watching the pulse of the proletarian army throbbing on the road.

At Pulkovo the road divided, and there we halted in the midst of a great crowd, where the human streams poured from three directions, friends meeting, excited and congratulatory, describing the battle to one another. A row of houses facing the cross-roads was marked with bullets, and the earth was trampled into mud half a mile around. The fighting had been furious here. . . . In the near distance riderless Cossack horses circled hungrily, for the grass of the plain had died long ago. Right in front of us an awkward Red Guard was trying to ride one, falling off again and again, to the childlike delight of a thousand rough men.

The left road, along which the remnants of the Cossacks had retreated, led up a little hill to a hamlet where there was a glorious view of the immense plain, grey as a windless sea, tumultuous clouds towering over, and the imperial city disgorging its thousands along all the roads. Far over to the left lay the little hill of Krasnoye Selo, the parade-ground of the Imperial Guards' summer camp, and the Imperial Dairy. In the middle distance nothing broke the monotony but a few walled monasteries and convents, some isolated factories, and several large buildings and unkempt grounds that were asylums and orphanages. . . .

"Here," said the driver, as we went on over a barren hill, "here was where Vera Slutskaya died. Yes, the Bolshevik member of the Duma. It happened early this morning. She was in an automobile, with Zalkind and another man. There was a truce, and they started for the front trenches. They were talking and laughing, when all of a sudden, from the armored train in which Kerensky himself was riding, somebody saw the automobile and fired a cannon. The shell struck Vera Slutskaya and killed her. . . .”

And so we came into Tsarskoye, all bustling with the swaggering heroes of the proletarian horde. Now the palace where the Soviet had met was a busy place. Red Guards and sailors filled the court-yard, sentries stood at the doors, and a stream of couriers and Commissars pushed in and out. In the Soviet room a samovar had been set up, and fifty or more workers, soldiers, sailors and officers stood around, drinking tea and talking at the top of their voices. In one corner two clumsy-handed workingmen were trying to make a multi-graphing machine go. At the center table, the huge Dybenko bent over a map, marking out positions for the troops with red and blue pencils. In his free hand he carried, as always, the enormous blue-steel revolver. Anon he sat himself down at a typewriter and pounded away with one finger; every little while he would pause, pick up the revolver, and lovingly spin the chamber.

A couch lay along the wall, and on this was stretched a young workman. Two Red Guards were bending over him, but the rest of the company did not pay any attention. In his breast was a hole; through his clothes fresh blood came welling up with every heart-beat. His eyes were closed, and his young, bearded face was greenish-white. Faintly and slowly he still breathed, with every breath sighing, *“Mir budit! Mir budit!* [Peace is coming! Peace is coming!]”

Dybenko looked up as we came in. “Ah” he said to Baklonov. “Comrade, will you go up to the Commandant’s headquarters and take charge? Wait; I will write you credentials.” He went to the typewriter and slowly picked out the letters.

The new Commandant of Tsarskoye Selo and I went toward the Ekaterina Palace, Baklanov very excited and important. In the same ornate, white room some Red Guards were rummaging curiously around, while my old friend, the Colonel, stood by the window biting his moustache. He greeted me like a long-lost brother. At a table near the door sat the French Bessarabian. The Bolsheviki had ordered him to remain, and continue his work.

"What could I do?" he muttered. "People like myself cannot fight on either side in such a war as this, no matter how much we may instinctively dislike the dictatorship of the mob . . . I only regret that I am so far from my mother in Bessarabia!"

Baklanov was formally taking over the office from the Commandant. "Here," said the Colonel nervously, "are the keys to the desk."

A Red Guard interrupted. "Where's the money?" he asked rudely. The Colonel seemed surprised. "Money? Money? Ah, you mean the chest. There it is," said the Colonel, "just as I found it when I took possession three days ago. Keys?" The Colonel shrugged. "I have no keys."

The Red Guard sneered knowingly. "Very convenient," he said.

"Let us open the chest," said Baklanov. "Bring an axe. Here is an American comrade. Let him smash the chest open, and write down what he finds there."

I swung the axe. The wooden chest was empty.

"Let's arrest him," said the Red Guard, venomously. "He is Kerensky's man. He has stolen the money and given it to Kerensky."

Baklanov did not want to. "Oh, no," he said. "It was the Kornilovets before him. He is not to blame."

"The devil!" cried the Red Guard. "He is Kerensky's man, I tell you. If *you* won't arrest him, then *we* will, and we'll take him to Petrograd and put him in Peter-Paul, where he belongs!" At this the other Red Guards growled assent. With a piteous glance at us the Colonel was led away. . . .

DOWN IN FRONT of the Soviet palace an auto-truck was going to the front. Half a dozen Red Guards, some sailors, and a soldier or two, under command of a huge workman, clambered in, and shouted to me to come along. Red Guards issued from headquarters, each of them staggering under an arm-load of small, corrugated-iron bundles, filled with *grubit* —which, they say, is ten times as strong, and five times as sensitive as dynamite; these they threw into the truck. A three-inch cannon was loaded and then tied onto the tail of the truck with bits of rope and wire.

We started away with a shout, at top speed of course; the heavy truck swaying from side to side. The cannon leaped from one wheel to the other, and the *grubit* bombs went rolling back and forth over our feet, fetching up against the sides of the car with a crash.

The big Red Guard, whose name was Vladimir Nicolaievich, plied me with questions about America. "Why did America come into the war? Are the American workers ready to throw over the capitalists? What is the situation in the Mooney case now? Will they extradite Berkman to San Francisco?" and others, very difficult to answer, all delivered in a shout above the roaring of the truck, while we held on to each other and danced amid the caroming bombs.

Occasionally a patrol tried to stop us. Soldiers ran out into the road before us, shouted "*Stoi!*" and threw up their guns.

We paid no attention. "The devil take you!" cried the Red Guards. "We don't stop for anybody! We're Red Guards!" And we thundered imperiously on, while Vladimir Nicolaievich bellowed to me about the internationalization of the Panama Canal, and such matters. . . .

About five miles out we saw a squad of sailors marching back, and slowed down.

"Where's the front, brothers?"

The foremost sailor halted and scratched his head. "This morning," he said, "it was about half a kilometer down the road. But the damn thing isn't anywhere now. We walked and walked and walked, but we couldn't find it."

They climbed into the truck, and we proceeded. It must have been about a mile further that Vladimir Nicolaievich cocked his ear and shouted to the chauffeur to stop.

"Firing!" he said. "Do you hear it?" For a moment dead silence, and then, a little ahead and to the left, three shots in rapid succession. Along here the side of the road was heavily wooded. Very much excited now, we crept along, speaking in whispers, until the truck was nearly opposite the place where the firing had come from. Descending, we spread out, and every man carrying his rifle, went stealthily into the forest.

Two comrades, meanwhile, detached the cannon and slewed it around until it aimed as nearly as possible at our backs.

It was silent in the woods. The leaves were gone, and the tree-trunks were a pale wan color in the low, sickly autumn sun. Not a thing moved, except the ice of a little woodland pool shivering under our feet. Was it an ambush?

We went uneventfully forward until the trees began to thin, and paused. Beyond, in a little clearing, three soldiers sat around a small fire, perfectly oblivious.

Vladimir Nicolaievich stepped forward. "*Zra'zvuitye*, comrades!" he greeted, while behind him one cannon, twenty rifles and a truck-load of *grubit* bombs hung by a hair. The soldiers scrambled to their feet.

"What was the shooting going on around here?"

One of the soldiers answered, looking relieved, "Why, we were just shooting a rabbit or two, comrade. . . ."

THE TRUCK HURTLED ON toward Romanov, through the bright, empty day. At the first cross-roads two soldiers ran out in front of us, waving their rifles. We slowed down, and stopped.

"Passes, comrades!"

The Red Guards raised a great clamor. "We are Red Guards. We don't need any passes. . . . Go on, never mind them!"

But a sailor objected. "This is wrong, comrades. We must have revolutionary discipline. Suppose some counter-revolutionaries came along in a truck and said: 'We don't need any passes'? The comrades don't know you."

At this there was a debate. One by one, however, the sailors and soldiers joined with the first. Grumbling, each Red Guard produced his dirty *bumaga* (paper). All were alike except mine, which had been issued by the Revolutionary Staff at Smolny. The sentries declared that I must go with them. The Red Guards objected strenuously, but the sailor who had spoken first insisted. "This comrade we know to be a true comrade," he said. "But there are orders of the Committee, and these orders must be obeyed. That is revolutionary discipline. . . ."

In order not to make any trouble, I got down from the truck, and watched it disappear careening down the road, all the company waving farewell. The soldiers consulted in low tones for a moment, and then led me to a wall, against which they placed me. It flashed upon me suddenly; they were going to shoot me!

In all three directions not a human being was in sight. The only sign of life was smoke from the chimney of a *dacha*, a rambling wooden house a quarter of a mile up the side road. The two soldiers were walking out into the road. Desperately I ran after them.

"But comrades! See! Here is the seal of the Military Revolutionary Committee!"

They stared stupidly at my pass, then at each other.

"It is different from the others," said one, sullenly. "We cannot read, brother."

I took him by the arm. "Come!" I said. "Let's go to that house. Some one there can surely read." They hesitated. "No," said one. The other looked me over. "Why not?" he muttered. "After all, it is a serious crime to kill an innocent man."

We walked up to the front door of the house and knocked. A short, stout woman opened it, and shrank back in alarm, babbling, "I don't know anything about them! I don't know anything about them!" One of my guards held out the pass. She screamed. "Just to read it, comrade." Hesitatingly she took the paper and read aloud, swiftly:

The bearer of this pass, John Reed, is a representative of the American Social-Democracy, an internationalist. . . .

Out on the road again the two soldiers held another consultation. "We must take you to the Regimental Committee," they said. In the fast-deepening twilight we trudged along the muddy road. Occasionally we met squads of soldiers, who stopped and surrounded me with looks of menace, handing my pass around and arguing violently as to whether or not I should be killed. . . .

It was dark when we came to the barracks of the Second Tsarskoye Selo Rifles, low sprawling buildings huddled along the post-road. A number of soldiers slouching at the entrance asked eager questions. A spy? A provocator? We mounted a winding stair and emerged into a great, bare room with a huge stove in the center, and rows of cots on the floor, where about a thousand soldiers were playing cards, talking, singing, and asleep. In the roof was a jagged hole made by Kerensky's cannon. . . .

237

I stood in the doorway, and a sudden silence ran among the groups, who turned and stared at me. Of a sudden they began to move, slowly and then with a rush, thundering, with faces full of hate. "Comrades! Comrades!" yelled one of my guards. "Committee! Committee!" The throng halted, banked around me, muttering. Out of them shouldered a lean youth, wearing a red arm-band.

"Who is this?" he asked roughly. The guards explained. "Give me the paper!" He read it carefully, glancing at me with keen eyes. Then he smiled and handed me the pass. "Comrades, this is an American comrade. I am Chairman of the Committee, and I welcome you to the Regiment. . . ." A sudden general buzz grew into a roar of greeting and they pressed forward to shake my hand.

"You have not dined? Here we have had our dinner. You shall go to the Officers' Club, where there are some who speak your language. . . ."

He led me across the court-yard to the door of another building. An aristocratic-looking youth, with the shoulder-straps of a Lieutenant, was entering. The Chairman presented me, and shaking hands, went back.

"I am Stepan Georgevich Morovsky, at your service," said the Lieutenant, in perfect French. From the ornate entrance-hall a ceremonial staircase led upward, lighted by glittering lusters. On the second floor billiard-rooms, card-rooms, a library opened from the hall. We entered the dining-room, at a long table in the center of which sat about twenty officers in full uniform, wearing their gold- and silver-handled swords, the ribbons and crosses of Imperial decorations. All rose politely as I entered, and made a place for me beside the Colonel, a large, impressive man with a grizzled beard. Orderlies were deftly serving dinner. The atmosphere was that of any officers' mess in Europe. Where was the Revolution?

"You are not Bolsheviki?" I asked Morovsky.

A smile went around the table, but I caught one or two glancing furtively at the orderly.

"No," answered my friend. "There is only one Bolshevik officer in this regiment. He is in Petrograd to-night. The Colonel is a Menshevik. Captain Kherlov there is a Cadet. I myself am a Socialist Revolutionary of the right wing. . . . I should say that most of the officers in the Army are not Bolshevik, but like me they believe in democracy; they believe that they must follow the soldier-masses. . . ."

Dinner over, maps were brought, and the Colonel spread them out on the table. The rest crowded around to see.

"Here," said the Colonel, pointing to pencil marks, "were our positions this morning. Vladimir Kyrilovich, where is your company?"

Captain Kherlov pointed. "According to orders, we occupied the position along this road. Karsavin relieved me at five o'clock."

Just then the door of the room opened, and there entered the Chairman of the Regimental Committee, with another soldier. They joined the group behind the Colonel, peering at the map.

"Good," said the Colonel. "Now the Cossacks have fallen back ten kilometers in our sector. I do not think it necessary to take up advanced positions. Gentlemen, for tonight you will hold the present line, strengthening the positions by—"

"If you please," interrupted the Chairman of the Regimental Committee. "The orders are to advance with all speed, and prepare to engage the Cossacks north of Gatchina in the morning. A crushing defeat is necessary. Kindly make the proper dispositions."

There was a short silence. The Colonel again turned to the map. "Very well," he said, in a different voice. "Stepan Georgevich, you will please ——" Rapidly tracing lines with a blue pencil, he gave his orders, while a sergeant made shorthand notes. The sergeant then withdrew, and ten minutes later returned with the orders typewritten, and one carbon copy. The Chairman of the Committee studied the map with a copy of the orders before him.

"All right," he said, rising. Folding the carbon copy, he put it in his pocket. Then he signed the other, stamped it with a round seal taken from his pocket, and presented it to the Colonel. . . .

Here was the Revolution!

I RETURNED to the Soviet palace in Tsarskoye in the Regimental Staff automobile. Still the crowds of workers, soldiers and sailors pouring in and out, still the choking press of trucks, armored cars, cannon before the door, and the shouting, the laughter of unwonted victory. Half a dozen Red Guards forced their way through, a priest in the middle. This was Father Ivan, they said, who had blessed the Cossacks when they entered the town. I heard afterward that he was shot. . . .

Dybenko was just coming out, giving rapid orders right and left. In his hand he carried the big revolver. An automobile stood with racing engine at the curb. Alone, he climbed in the rear seat, and was off—off to Gatchina, to conquer Kerensky.

Toward nightfall he arrived at the outskirts of the town, and went on afoot. What Dybenko told the Cossacks nobody knows, but the fact is that General Krasnov and his staff and several thousand Cossacks surrendered, and advised Kerensky to do the same.

As for Kerensky—I reprint here the deposition made by General Krasnov on the morning of November 14th:

> Gatchina, November 14, 1917. To-day, about three o'clock [A.M.], I was summoned by the Supreme Commander [Kerensky]. He was very agitated, and very nervous.
>
> "General," he said to me, "you have betrayed me. Your Cossacks declare categorically that they will arrest me and deliver me to the sailors."
>
> "Yes," I answered, "there is talk of it, and I know that you have no sympathy anywhere."
>
> "But the officers say the same thing."
>
> "Yes, most of all it is the officers who are discontented with you."
>
> "What shall I do? I ought to commit suicide!"
>
> "If you are an honorable man, you will go immediately to Petrograd with a white flag, you will present yourself to the Military Revolutionary Committee, and enter into negotiations as Chief of the Provisional Government."
>
> "All right. I will do that, General."
>
> "I will give you a guard and ask that a sailor go with you."
>
> "No, no, not a sailor. Do you know whether it is true that Dybenko is here?"
>
> "I don't know who Dybenko is."
>
> "He is my enemy."

"There is nothing to do. If you play for high stakes you must know how to take a chance."

"Yes. I'll leave to-night!"

"Why? That would be a flight. Leave calmly and openly, so that everyone can see that you are not running away."

"Very well. But you must give me a guard on which I can count."

"Good."

I went out and called the Cossack Russkov, of the Tenth Regiment at the Don, and ordered him to pick out ten Cossacks to accompany the Supreme Commander. Half an hour later the Cossacks came to tell me that Kerensky was not in his quarters, that he had run away.

I gave the alarm and ordered that he be searched for, supposing that he could not have left Gatchina, but he could not be found. . . .

And so Kerensky fled, alone, disguised in the uniform of a sailor and by that act lost whatever popularity he had retained among the Russian masses. . . .

I WENT BACK TO Petrograd riding on the front seat of an auto truck, driven by a workman and filled with Red Guards. We had no kerosene, so our lights were not burning. The road was crowded with the proletarian army going home, and new reserves pouring out to take their places. Immense trucks like ours, columns of artillery, wagons, loomed up in the night, without lights, as we were. We hurtled furiously on, wrenched right and left to avoid collisions that seemed inevitable, scraping wheels, followed by the epithets of pedestrians.

Across the horizon spread the glittering lights of the capital, immeasurably more splendid by night than by day, like a dike of jewels heaped on the barren plain.

The old workman who drove held the wheel in one hand, while with the other he swept the far-gleaming capital in an exultant gesture.

"Mine!" he cried, his face all alight. "All mine now! My Petrograd!"

241

A Million-in-One Wound

by George Orwell

George Orwell was that rare thing: a writer who practiced what he preached. During the Spanish Civil War of 1936–39, his sympathy was with the Loyalists against the revolt led by General Francisco Franco, and he went to fight for them early in the war. The events narrated in this selection occurred in June 1937, before Orwell became disillusioned by the Communist takeover of the Loyalist cause, and it tells of his astonishing recovery from a wound that would ordinarily have been fatal.

W_e were still at Huesca, but they had placed us further to the right, opposite the Fascist redoubt which we had temporarily captured a few weeks earlier. I was now acting as "teniente"—corresponding to second-lieutenant in the British Army, I suppose—in command of about thirty men, English and Spanish. They had sent my name in for a regular commission; whether I should get it was uncertain. Previously the militia officers had refused to accept regular commissions, which meant extra pay and conflicted with the equalitarian ideas of the militia, but they were now obliged to do so. Benjamin had already been gazetted captain and Kopp was in process of being gazetted major. The Government could not, of course, dispense with the militia officers, but it was not confirming any of them in a higher rank than major, presumably in order to keep the higher commands for Regular Army officers and the new officers from the School of War. As a result, in our division, the 29th, and no doubt in many others, you had the queer temporary situation of the divisional commander, the brigade commanders and the battalion commanders all being majors.

T_{HERE WAS NOT} much happening at the front. The battle round the Jaca road had died away and did not begin again till mid-June. In our position the chief trouble was the snipers. The Fascist trenches were more than a hundred and fifty yards away, but they were on higher ground and were on two sides of us, our line forming a right-angle salient. The corner of the salient was a dangerous spot; there had always been a toll of sniper casualties there. From time to time the Fascists let fly at us with a rifle-grenade or some similar weapon. It made a ghastly crash—unnerving, because you could not hear it coming in time to dodge—but was not really dangerous; the hole it blew in the ground was no bigger than a wash-tub. The nights were pleasantly warm, the days blazing hot, the mos-

244

quitoes were becoming a nuisance, and in spite of the clean clothes we had brought from Barcelona we were almost immediately lousy. Out in the deserted orchards in no man's land the cherries were whitening on the trees. For two days there were torrential rains, the dugouts flooded and the parapet sank a foot; after that there were more days of digging out the sticky clay with the wretched Spanish spades which have no handles and bend like tin spoons.

THEY HAD PROMISED us a trench-mortar for the company; I was looking forward to it greatly. At nights we patrolled as usual—more dangerous than it used to be, because the Fascist trenches were better manned and they had grown more alert; they had scattered tin cans just outside their wire and used to open up with the machine-guns when they heard a clank. In the daytime we sniped from no man's land. By crawling a hundred yards you could get to a ditch, hidden by tall grasses, which commanded a gap in the Fascist parapet. We had set up a rifle-rest in the ditch. If you waited long enough you generally saw a khaki-clad figure slip hurriedly across the gap. I had several shots. I don't know whether I hit anyone—it is most unlikely; I am a very poor shot with a rifle. But it was rather fun, the Fascists did not know where the shots were coming from, and I made sure I could get one of them sooner or later. However, the dog it was that died—a Fascist sniper got me instead. I had been about ten days at the front when it happened. The whole experience of being hit by a bullet is very interesting and I think it is worth describing in detail.

It was at the corner of the parapet, at five o'clock in the morning. This was always a dangerous time, because we had the dawn at our backs, and if you stuck your head above the parapet it was clearly outlined against the sky. I was talking to the sentries preparatory to changing the guard. Suddenly, in the very middle of saying something, I felt—it was very hard to describe what I felt, though I remember it with utmost vividness.

Roughly speaking it was the sensation of being "at the centre" of an explosion. There seemed to be a loud bang and a blinding flash of light all round me, and I felt a tremendous shock—no pain, only a violent shock, such as you get from an electric terminal; with it a sense of utter weakness, a feeling of being stricken and shrivelled up to nothing. The sand bags in front of me receded into immense distance. I fancy you would feel much the same if you were struck by lightning. I knew immediately that I was hit, but because of the seeming bang and flash I thought it was a rifle nearby that had gone off accidentally and shot me. All this happened in a space of time much less than a second. The next moment my knees crumpled up and I was falling, my head hitting the ground with a violent bang which, to my relief, did not hurt. I had a numb, dazed feeling, a consciousness of being very badly hurt, but no pain in the ordinary sense.

The American sentry I had been talking to had started forward. "Gosh! Are you hit?" People gathered round. There was the usual fuss—"Lift him up! Where's he hit? Get his shirt open!" etc., etc. The American called for a knife to cut my shirt open. I knew that there was one in my pocket and tried to get it out, but discovered that my right arm was paralyzed. Not being in pain, I felt a vague satisfaction. This ought to please my wife, I thought; she had always wanted me to be wounded, which would save me from being killed when the great battle came. It was only now that it occurred to me to wonder where I was hit, and how badly; I could feel nothing, but was conscious that the bullet had struck me somewhere in the front of the body. When I tried to speak I found that I had no voice, only a faint squeak, but at the second attempt I managed to ask where I was hit. In the throat, they said. Harry Webb, our stretcher-bearer, had brought a bandage and one of the little bottles of alcohol they gave us for field-dressings. As they lifted me up a lot of blood poured out of my mouth, and I heard a Spaniard behind me say that the bullet had gone clean through my neck. I felt the alcohol, which at ordinary times would sting like the devil, splash on to the wound as a pleasant coolness.

They laid me down again while somebody fetched a stretcher. As soon as I knew that the bullet had gone clean through my neck I took it for granted that I was done for. I had never heard of a man or an animal getting a bullet through the middle of the neck and surviving it. The blood was dribbling out of the corner of my mouth. "The artery's gone," I thought. I wondered how long you last when your carotid artery is cut; not many minutes, presumably. Everything was very blurry. There must have been about two minutes during which I assumed that I was killed. And that too was interesting—I mean it is interesting to know what your thought would be at such a time. My first thought, conventionally enough, was for my wife. My second was a violent resentment at having to leave this world which, when all is said and done, suits me so well. I had time to feel this very vividly. The stupid mischance infuriated me. The meaninglessness of it! To be bumped off, not even in battle, but in this stale corner of the trenches, thanks to a moment's carelessness! I thought, too, of the man who had shot me—wondered what he was like, whether he was a Spaniard or a foreigner, whether he knew he had got me, and so forth. I could not feel any resentment against him. I reflected that as he was a Fascist I would have killed him if I could, but that if he had been taken prisoner and brought before me at this moment I would merely have congratulated him on his good shooting. It may be, though, that if you were really dying your thoughts would be quite different.

They had just got me on to the stretcher when my paralyzed right arm came to life and began hurting damnably. At the time I imagined that I must have broken it in falling; but the pain reassured me, for I knew that your sensations do not become more acute when you are dying. I began to feel more normal and to be sorry for the four poor devils who were sweating and slithering with the stretcher on their shoulders. It was a mile and a half to the ambulance, and vile going, over lumpy, slippery tracks. I knew what a sweat it was, having helped to carry a wounded man down a day or two earlier. The leaves of the silver poplars which, in places, fringed our trenches brushed against my face; I thought what a good thing it was to be alive in a world where silver poplars grow. But all the while the pain in my arm was diabolical, making me swear and then try not to swear, because every time I breathed too hard the blood bubbled out of my mouth.

The doctor re-bandaged the wound, gave me a shot of morphia, and sent me off to Sietamo. The hospitals at Sietamo were hurriedly constructed wooden huts where the wounded were, as a rule, only kept for a few hours before being sent on to Barbastro or Lerida. I was dopey from morphia but still in great pain, practically unable to move and swallowing blood constantly. It was typical of Spanish hospital methods that while I was in this state the untrained nurse tried to force the regulation hospital meal—a huge meal of soup, eggs, greasy stew and so forth—down my throat and seemed surprised when I would not take it. I asked for a cigarette, but this was one of the periods of tobacco famine and there was not a cigarette in the place. Presently two comrades who had got permission to leave the line for a few hours appeared at my bedside.

"Hullo! You're alive, are you? Good. We want your watch and your revolver and your electric torch. And your knife, if you've got one."

They made off with all my portable possessions. This always happened when a man was wounded—everything he possessed was promptly divided up; quite rightly, for watches, revolvers and so forth were precious at the front and if they went down the line in a wounded man's kit they were certain to be stolen somewhere on the way.

By the evening enough sick and wounded had trickled in to make up a few ambulance-loads, and they sent us on to Barbastro. What a journey! It used to be said that in this war you got well if you were wounded in the extremities, but always died of a wound in the abdomen. I now realized why. No one who was liable to bleed internally could have survived those miles of jolting over metal roads that had been smashed to pieces by heavy lorries and never repaired since the war began. Bang, bump, wallop! It took me back to my early childhood and a dreadful thing called the Wiggle-Woggle at the White City Exhibition. They had forgotten to tie us into the stretchers. I had enough strength in my left arm to hang on, but one poor wretch was spilt on to the floor and suffered God knows what agonies. Another, a walking case who was sitting in the corner of the ambulance, vomited all over the place. The hospital in Barbastro was very crowded, the beds so close together that they were almost touching. Next morning they loaded a number of us on to the hospital train and sent us down to Lerida.

I was five or six days in Lerida. It was a big hospital, with sick, wounded, and ordinary civilian patients more or less jumbled up together. Some of the men in my ward had frightful wounds. In the next bed to me there was a youth with

248

black hair who was suffering from some disease or other and was being given medicine that made his urine as green as emerald. His bed-bottle was one of the sights of the ward. An English-speaking Dutch Communist, having heard that there was an Englishman in the hospital, befriended me and brought me English newspapers. He had been terribly wounded in the October fighting, and had somehow managed to settle down at Lerida hospital and had married one of the nurses. Thanks to his wound, one of his legs had shrivelled till it was no thicker than my arm. Two militiamen on leave, whom I had met my first week at the front, came in to see a wounded friend and recognized me. They were kids of about eighteen. They stood awkwardly beside my bed, trying to think of something to say, and then, as a way of demonstrating that they were sorry I was wounded, suddenly took all the tobacco out of their pockets, gave it to me, and fled before I could give it back. How typically Spanish! I discovered afterwards that you could not buy tobacco anywhere in the town and what they had given me was a week's ration.

After a few days I was able to get up and walk about with my arm in a sling. For some reason it hurt much more when it hung down. I also had, for the time being, a good deal of internal pain from the damage I had done myself in falling, and my voice had disappeared almost completely, but I never had a moment's pain from the bullet wound itself. It seems this is usually the case. The tremendous shock of a bullet prevents sensation locally; a splinter of shell or bomb, which is jagged and usually hits you less hard, would probably hurt like the devil. There was a pleasant garden in the hospital grounds, and in it was a pool with gold-fishes and some small dark grey fish—bleak, I think. I used to sit watching them for hours. The way things were done at Lerida gave me an insight into the hospital system on the Aragon front—whether it was the same on other fronts I do not know. In some ways the hospitals were very good. The doctors were able men and there seemed to be no shortage of drugs and equipment. But there were two bad faults on account of which, I have no doubt, hundreds or thousands of men have died who might have been saved.

One was the fact that all the hospitals anywhere near the front line were used more or less as casualty clearing-stations.

The result was that you got no treatment there unless you were too badly wounded to be moved. In theory most of the wounded were sent straight to Barcelona or Tarragona, but owing to the lack of transport they were often a week or ten days in getting there. They were kept hanging about at Sietamo, Barbastro, Monzon, Lerida, and other places, and meanwhile they were getting no treatment except an occasional clean bandage, sometimes not even that. Men with dreadful shell wounds, smashed bones and so forth, were swathed in a sort of casing made of bandages and plaster of Paris; a description of the wound was written in pencil on the outside, and as a rule, the casing was not removed till the man reached Barcelona or Tarragona ten days later. It was almost impossible to get one's wound examined on the way; the few doctors could not cope with the work, and they simply walked hurriedly past your bed saying: "Yes, yes, they'll attend to you at Barcelona." There were always rumours that the hospital train was leaving for Barcelona "mañana." The other fault was the lack of competent nurses. Apparently there was no supply of trained nurses in Spain, perhaps because before the war this work was done chiefly by nuns. I have no complaint against the Spanish nurses, they always treated me with the greatest kindness, but there is no doubt that they were terribly ignorant. All of them knew how to take a temperature, and some of them knew how to tie a bandage, but that was about all. The result was that men who were too ill to fend for themselves were often shamefully neglected. The nurses would let a man remain constipated for a week on end, and they seldom washed those who were too weak to wash themselves. I remember one poor devil with a smashed arm telling me that he had been three weeks without having his face washed. Even beds were left unmade for days together. The food in all the hospitals was very good—too good, indeed. Even more in Spain than elsewhere it seemed to be the tradition to stuff sick people with heavy food. At Lerida the meals were terrific. Breakfast, at about six in the morning, consisted of soup, an omelette, stew, bread, white wine, and coffee, and lunch was even larger—this at a time when most of the civil population was seriously underfed. Spaniards seem not to recognize such a thing as a light diet. They give the same food to sick people as to well

250

ones—always the same rich, greasy cookery, with everything sodden in olive oil.

One morning it was announced that the men in my ward were to be sent down to Barcelona today. I managed to send a wire to my wife, telling her that I was coming, and presently they packed us into buses and took us down to the station. It was only when the train was actually starting that the hospital orderly who travelled with us casually let fall that we were not going to Barcelona after all, but to Tarragona. I suppose the engine-driver had changed his mind. "Just like Spain!" I thought. But it was very Spanish, too, that they agreed to hold up the train while I sent another wire, and more Spanish still that the wire never got there.

They had put us into ordinary third-class carriages with wooden seats, and many of the men were badly wounded and had only got out of bed for the first time that morning. Before long, what with the heat and the jolting, half of them were in a state of collapse and several vomited on the floor. The hospital orderly threaded his way among the corpselike forms that sprawled everywhere, carrying a large goat-skin bottle full of water which he squirted into this mouth or that. It was beastly water; I remember the taste of it still. We got into Tarragona as the sun was getting low. The line runs along the shore a stone's throw from the sea. As our train drew into the station a troop-train full of men from the International Column was drawing out, and a knot of people on the bridge were waving to them. It was a very long train, packed to bursting-point with men, with field-guns lashed on the open trucks and more men clustering round the guns. I remember with peculiar vividness the spectacle of that train passing in the yellow evening light; window after window full of dark, smiling faces, the long tilted barrels of the guns, the scarlet scarves fluttering—all this gliding slowly past us against a turquoise-coloured sea.

"*Estranjeros*—foreigners," said someone. "They're Italians."

Obviously they were Italians. No other people could have grouped themselves so picturesquely or returned the salutes of the crowd with so much grace—a grace that was none the less because about half the men on the train were drinking out of up-ended wine bottles. We heard afterwards

251

that these were some of the troops who won the great victory at Guadalajara in March; they had been on leave and were being transferred to the Aragon front. Most of them, I am afraid, were killed at Huesca only a few weeks later. The men who were well enough to stand had moved across the carriage to cheer the Italians as they went past. A crutch waved out of the window; bandaged forearms made the Red Salute. It was like an allegorical picture of war; the trainload of fresh men gliding proudly up the line, the maimed men sliding slowly down, and all the while the guns on the open trucks making one's heart leap as guns always do, and reviving that pernicious feeling, so difficult to get rid of, that war is glorious after all.

The hospital at Tarragona was a very big one and full of wounded from all fronts. What wounds one saw there! They had a way of treating certain wounds which I suppose was in accordance with the latest medical practice, but which was peculiarly horrible to look at. This was to leave the wound completely open and unbandaged, but protected from flies by a net of butter-muslin, stretched over wires. Under the muslin you would see the red jelly of a half-healed wound. There was one man wounded in the face and throat who had his head inside a sort of spherical helmet of butter-muslin; his mouth was closed up and he breathed through a little tube that was fixed between his lips. Poor devil, he looked so lonely, wandering to and fro, looking at you through his muslin cage and unable to speak. I was three or four days at Tarragona. My strength was coming back, and one day, by going slowly, I managed to walk down as far as the beach. It was queer to see the seaside life going on almost as usual; the smart cafés along the promenade and the plump local bourgeoisie bathing and sunning themselves in deck-chairs as though there had not been a war within a thousand miles. Nevertheless, as it happened, I saw a bather drowned, which one would have thought impossible in that shallow and tepid sea.

Finally, eight or nine days after leaving the front, I had my wound examined. In the surgery where newly arrived cases were examined, doctors with huge pairs of shears were hacking away the breast-plates of plaster in which men with smashed ribs, collar-bones and so forth had been cased at the dressing-stations behind the line; out of the neck-hole of the huge clumsy breast-plate you would see protruding an anxious, dirty face, scrubby with a week's beard. The doctor, a brisk, handsome man of about thirty, sat me down in a chair, grasped my tongue with a piece of rough gauze, pulled it out as far as it would go, thrust a dentist's mirror down my throat and told me to say 'Eh!' After doing this till my tongue was bleeding and my eyes running with water, he told me that one vocal cord was paralyzed.

"When shall I get my voice back?" I said.

"Your voice? Oh, you'll never get your voice back," he said cheerfully.

However, he was wrong, as it turned out. For about two months I could not speak much above a whisper, but after that my voice became normal rather suddenly, the other vocal cord having "compensated." The pain in my arm was due to the bullet having pierced a bunch of nerves at the back of the neck. It was a shooting pain like neuralgia, and it went on hurting continuously for about a month, especially at night, so that I did not get much sleep. The fingers of my right hand were also semi-paralyzed. Even now, five months afterwards, my forefinger is still numb—a queer effect for a neck wound to have.

The wound was a curiosity in a small way and various doctors examined it with much clicking of tongues and "*Que suerte. Que suerte!*" One of them told me with an air of authority that the bullet had missed the artery by "about a millimetre." I don't know how he knew. No one I met at this time—doctors, nurses, Practicantes, or fellow-patients—failed to assure me that a man who is hit through the neck and survives it is the luckiest creature alive. I could not help thinking that it would be even luckier not to be hit at all.

"Somehow, You Must Get to Paris . . ."

by René de Chambrun

René de Chambrun is French on the side of his father, General René de Chambrun, and American on the side of his mother, the former Clara Longworth. At the outbreak of World War II he was, at thirty-three, a successful international lawyer. But he was also a captain in the French reserves and in the critical days of 1939 he was among the first reservists ordered to active duty. The following May, with the German armies poised for the dash that would bring about the collapse of France and make necessary the famous British evacuation at Dunkirk, Captain Chambrun was ordered to make his escape to Paris with vital documents for General Weygand, the French commander-in-chief.

On May 26 we were completely surrounded. The German advanced mechanized units, which had reached the Channel coast at Abbeville, were pushing detachments northward from the line which they held running through Bethune, Saint-Omer, and just south of Calais. It was impossible for us to discover exactly where the enemy was as our communications were cut off. Enemy tanks and armored cars which had penetrated deeply into the pocket from Sedan to the sea and then spread out in a fanlike formation would suddenly appear in the most unexpected spots.

The headquarters of the corps of liaison officers were situated at that time just outside of Hazebrouck. I arrived there early in the afternoon to report to Colonel de Cardes, and found his headquarters in a small red brick house surrounded by a garden of flowers. Three weeks before when I had seen him at Arras he prophesied the beginning of the blitzkrieg. The colonel was one of those rare officers of our army whose mind was constantly living in the future and not looking into the past. He believed, as did the German staff, General Weygand and a very few other French generals, that the war of 1940 would be fought with 1940 methods and not with those which had won the war for us in 1918. Just as it is a handicap for an old champion to bear upon his shoulders the prestige of a world title when he meets an aggressive and tough challenger, so one of France's weaknesses during this war seemed to have been the memory of her victory in 1918.

As I walked into Colonel de Cardes' room he did not even say "I told you so," because that belonged to the past, but began to talk about his plans of establishing another base for training liaison officers south of the Somme in case the war were to continue for a long time. Then he told me what he wanted me for.

"You are to try and get to Paris as quickly as you can," he ordered. "I know it will not be an easy job but these documents must not fall into enemy hands and I want them to be at our headquarters as soon as possible. The only way to get to Paris now that we are surrounded is to try and reach Dunkerque. From there you can probably cross the Channel. In England you will easily find a plane to take you over to France." He hastily scribbled a line to his wife and gave it to me with the bulky pile of documents, repeating again that I was to do as best I could and for God's sake not to lose any time.

I left immediately and motored to General Blanchard's headquarters which were only a few miles away. I walked down into a little wood near the château where I found the cars which were at the disposal of the officers of the staff. They were camouflaged under the trees with leaves, branches and nets. I asked the small group of chauffeurs if any one of them was ready to try to get me to the coast. Every single one volunteered for the job, so I picked out the youngest who was not married.

After bidding farewell to General Blanchard's Chief of Staff and throwing a few of my belongings into my bag, I hopped in next to the chauffeur in one of the small Renaults. I wanted to be where I could read the map and direct the way.

By that time I had acquired the technique for protecting myself against the bombs or machine-gun bullets from the Stukas. As soon as I heard the roaring of one of them or saw it approaching from a distance I stopped the car and jumped into the ditch on one side of the road while the chauffeur would do the same on the other side. We had to hunt cover several times on our way to Cassel, while I kept watching the road as far ahead as possible on the lookout for enemy tanks. You never knew when you were going to run into a German tank. As we neared Cassel I began to hear more and more distinctly intense machine-gun fire. I lowered the dusty windshield and noticed that the refugees some distance down the road, instead of forming a long column, were scattering in every direction. I decided to reconnoiter, so I stopped the car and ran up to the top of a small bank a few yards away. With my field glasses I discovered a column of German tanks pushing its way along the road and across the fields, spraying light artillery shells and machine-gun bullets in every direction, apparently firing on soldiers, women, children, and horses—everyone in sight except the dead lying upon the ground.

I rushed back to the car and shouted at the chauffeur to turn around and drive back as fast as he could. The car wasn't any use to me now. With my bag, the heavy parcel of documents and my revolver, I crouched down for a second behind a tree by the roadside to figure things out.

I realized immediately, of course, what had happened. The enemy's detachments which, as I said before, had broken through to the Channel coast to the south of us, were now filtering northwards through the pitifully thin line of defenses that had been hastily thrown up by General Curtis' division on the Lys Canal. It seemed as though my only chance of escape was to work northward as quickly as possible, but for this my only shelter was a long hedgerow three or four hundred yards ahead and between me and the Germans. It bordered a path running in a northerly direction from the road to a large wood.

My heart was hammering through my chest as I ran along the line of trees toward the hedge in the midst of stray machine-gun bullets and shells. For a few seconds I dropped down behind the hedge and peered through the leaves. The tanks were coming along the road in my direction and in addition a light detachment of German infantry had just poured out of armored buses and was spreading northward to attack a few British soldiers who had been hurriedly rushed to the spot. Between the village and my hiding place I saw a few soldiers and refugees fall dead while the others ran desperately in every direction.

The rough path along the hedge, to which I shall always feel indebted for my escape, led to a wood about a mile away. I ran towards this shelter as quickly as I could with my heavy load, stooping down now and then when the whistling of bullets came too near my ears. By the time I reached the edge of the wood I was completely exhausted, so I dropped down among the trees and tried to figure out what to do next. It was obvious that I would never reach Dunkerque unless I was able to strike just the right balance between speed and prudence. I got out my map. It did not take more than a few seconds to memorize what seemed to me the best itinerary. I lightened my bag, regretfully throwing away my new uniform, my field glasses, which were too heavy, and everything else that I could discard. In their place I piled up the documents entrusted to me on top of a small framed picture of my wife, and started off. At a jog trot I cut through the woods and away from the danger zone with roughly forty kilometers to go that night if I was to reach the coast by morning.

Luckily dusk was falling as I began the longest walk I had ever taken. When it became too dark to read the road signs I discovered that I had forgotten my flashlight but fortunately found a box of matches in my pocket, so whenever I came to a road junction I climbed up the iron posts and struck a match in order to make sure that I was on my route. I became more and more tired and lonely tramping along the monotonous road among the unknown Belgian soldiers and refugees lying heavily on the wayside, but the appearance of each kilometer stone gave me a feeling of relief and comfort. Indeed those little square white stones sticking out of the ground in the darkness seemed to be my only companions.

Sometime toward the middle of the night I came to a bridge guarded by a British military policeman. He could have been a brother of the one I saw standing in front of the ruined station at Alost; as a matter of fact, all British military police look alike. My muscles were aching and I felt too exhausted to go further without rest, so I asked the sentry if he would lend me his coat, which was lying on the bridge parapet, to serve as a blanket, and let me have an hour's rest. He promised to wake me in exactly one hour, and as I looked up at him from where I lay it seemed that I had acquired a guardian angel. I could hear the bombing of Dunkerque and the heavy shelling which seemed to be going on south of the city probably along the seashore. I guessed that the loudest guns which pierced the night from time to time were probably the heavy guns from battleships firing upon the German columns which I knew were advancing on the road from Boulogne to Dunkerque. Just before I fell asleep I thought of Paris. By this time the twisting banks of the Seine and the towers of Notre Dame, which had suddenly sprung up before my mind when Colonel de Cardes gave me my orders, seemed terribly far away from the banks of the little Flanders river where I was resting. I remember the stars were very bright that night.

An hour later the sentry tapped me on the shoulder. I do not believe that I can ever again feel as stiff and weary as on that most laborious awakening near the Yser. When I was able to assemble a few words I thanked the sentry and walked three hours more before night began slowly to fade away. Each time I felt too stiff and tired to continue my walk I sat down for a while on the roadside. Then, having resolved to carry my bag so many hundred paces further, I would limp on. And all the while the noise of the war thunderstorm around Dunkerque seemed to become more and more violent.

Just as he apparently had done for the Polish campaign, Hitler again commanded the most extraordinary spell of fine weather for his blitzkrieg. We had not seen a cloud in the sky since the tenth of May, although whenever we had time to think about it we prayed for rain or fog. As I approached the suburbs of Dunkerque I realized that this was going to be another of those damnably beautiful days. The battle in the air was going on and I observed a few columns of smoke slowly mounting from the city. At last I reached the first houses of Dunkerque. As I walked by the *octroi* scales for weighing loads of produce entering the town, the policeman on duty shouted to me from the trench to go under a shelter or to join him in his hole.

"How long do these raids last?" I demanded.

"They practically never end," he replied philosophically. "When one squadron of bombers leaves, another one comes along. But," he added rather cheerfully, "we are bringing them down one after the other so the day will come when there'll be no more left." He pronounced the "we" as if he, personally, took an important share of responsibility in the combats.

I couldn't have got much farther without a rest anyway, so I accepted the policeman's invitation and dropped heavily into the trench with my valise. I propped myself against the side of the hole and at first did not even make the effort to lift my head and watch the fights which were going on in the air, but things got so active above us that I finally looked up despite my stiff neck. My policeman had learned all the technique of aerial encounters in the last few days. Dunkerque was a ringside seat.

"You see," he explained, pointing into the air, "when

a big one falls you can be sure it is a German bomber. The little ones that zoom up and down like silver fish in a huge aquarium, *ce sont les Anglais.*"

And one . . . two . . . three . . . big ones wavered and fell as we were watching. The crashes which shook the town were terrible and my guide told me that it was because the Heinkels had not had time to unload their bombs.

A few seconds later two "little ones" were fighting against one another and I saw one of them fall like a stone in a trail of smoke. A swift burst of machine-gun firing had won this miniature war far up in the sky. I asked the policeman whether it was a French, a British, or a German plane, and he replied, "That's anybody's guess. I like to watch these fights. It looks so easy." For a few seconds he watched the loser fall like a burning arrow and added, "You see, *mon Capitaine*, those planes die much quicker than we do—*c'est une belle mort.*" The other Heinkels of the squadron by that time decided to move on and try an easier job, and a lull set in.

A decrepit old man could have come out of that hole quicker than I did that day. Here I was at my destination, Dunkerque, with only eight or nine hundred yards to go, but I had no strength left to finish the final stretch with a sprint. The Navy Yard was very near and still it seemed like the end of the world. I was worn out, rusty, broken down and dizzy when I passed between the heavy steel and concrete bastions with their doors made of the plates of battleships. Beside the door, at attention, stood the impressive *fusiliers marins* with their blue caps, red pompons, white spats. Each man proudly held a small musket with a short glittering bayonet.

There was extraordinary animation in the yard. A few British officers, French gunners, land, naval officers and messengers were rushing madly around. It looked as though some complicated project was under way, a colossal preparation for something that had never been done before; and indeed Admiral Abrial, hidden in one of the alcoves of a bastion, was working night and day getting ready to carry out the heroic evacuation that will go down in history as one of the great military miracles of modern times.

Dunkerque had been built centuries ago as a naval base to protect France against an English attack by sea; in a few days the city was to be turned into an entrenched camp to

261

stop the Germans coming by land. The town created as a
defense against England, our foe, was to cover the retreat
and embarkation of England, our ally. As I dragged into the
bastion where Admiral Abrial had his headquarters, my uniform dusty and worn, I felt like a tramp and forgot for a
few moments that I was an officer. I was surprised to see the
guard present arms to me, while another sailor on duty took
me to the Admiral's Chief of Staff.

"You have just time enough to reach the port where two
speedboats will leave shortly for Dover," the officer told me.
And he continued, "You'll have to take a chance if you really
want to go this morning as our defense at sea by cruisers and
destroyers will only be well organized tomorrow. This afternoon we are embarking only a few thousand men. The real
job begins tonight."

He sent for his car to take me to the harbor. By that
time seven or eight bombers had appeared in the sky and my
driver raced through the streets of the city as though the devil
were after him. I will never forget coming to the waterside.
Around the quadrangular piers with stones tumbling down
every minute into the sea rose what was left of the walls of
the ancient houses which had withstood the long-range artillery shelling of the World War. The shattered, burned
walls could not conceal the chaos which lay behind the broken
windows. Between four walls there was always a mound of
ashes and stones, and it was only if one examined the wreck-
age closely that blood and pieces of clothing could be discovered. In some houses four or five bombs had fallen, boring
holes deep into the cellars; still parts of the walls stood proudly
on the ocean façade as if attempting to conceal from the sea
the grisly sights within. A few burnt ships leaning on their
keels seemed to have been abandoned forever in the muddy,
oily water of the harbor.

As we drove across the square surrounded by piers, zig-
zagging in order to avoid bomb holes, I noticed a small boat
coming slowly into the harbor. Two bombers, pursued by a
fighter, like vultures swooping down on a victim, dived for a
crack at the defenseless ship. The vessel was only bringing
back dead bodies from the beach of Malo a few miles away.
Of course the German pilots couldn't know it, yet when I saw
one of the bombers spiral down into the water under the fire

of a Hurricane, it seemed as though it was the vengeance of Death for this audacious attempt to violate the bodies of those few dead soldiers who already belonged to him.

My chauffeur and I climbed out of the bomb craters where we had taken cover, and came to a trench where twelve or thirteen officers, mostly British, were waiting to take their chance on the embarkation. When I arrived a petty officer was explaining to the group that as soon as the motorboats arrived at the pier we were to form two groups and dash on board as quickly as possible. I did not know which boat to choose and I had a strong instinctive conviction that the decision was important. When I was a child in Washington before the World War, my American mother taught me how to make up my mind by reciting "Eenie, meenie, minie, moe: Catch a nigger by the toe...." Why not try that? I did and that old game put me aboard the second speedboat: the first was lost somewhere between Dunkerque and Dover.

When the petty officer's whistle blew, we rushed for our boats, dumped our luggage and jumped down from the dock. We could see bombers out over the Channel, circling around. "What are they doing?" I inquired of the pilot as our craft slipped away from the pier which was already in ruins.

"Dropping small mines out there for us. They have been doing that for several days," was his grim answer.

As we were speeding out of the harbor, two of the Heinkels whirled around and swept in to attack and the guns of our small craft answered defiantly as the bombers raked our decks with their machine guns.

And then, just as we were leaving the shores of France, three squadrons of Heinkels, twenty-seven planes in all, converged upon the city from three different directions, and, as if they had had some secret rendezvous with the Germans, six small British planes appeared almost at the same moment, flying at a very high altitude. The Germans began to pour their bombs just as the British fighters swooped down upon them. The sound of the British engines was unlike any plane I knew, and their guns sounded strange too, but they did the most deadly job of dogfighting I have seen. I counted within a few minutes nineteen trails of smoke as Heinkel after Heinkel dropped and the six little fighters took control of the sky. It was only when I arrived in Dover that I was told that the

first Defiants with revolving turrets had been sent over to
Dunkerque by the R.A.F. that morning.

During the whole crossing I sat next to the pilot, wondering about those mines which had been falling from the sky
for days. Where were they? I didn't mind the Stukas so much,
as the terrific noise they made revealed where the danger was
coming from, but I dreaded the idea of a hidden mine which
could hit us without warning and against which there was no
protection. We soon lost sight of the motorboat which had
preceded us, and I will never know whether it was sunk by a
bomb, a mine, or a torpedo. The crossing lasted three hours,
during which our machine-gunners repelled two more attacks from enemy planes, but the consciousness of those mines
dragged three hours out into an eternity.

Save for the presence of a few warships in the harbor,
Dover looked much as it did before the war. Not a bomb had
fallen on this side of the Channel during the continuous attacks on the French side. Germany was fighting France before
declaring real war on Great Britain and Great Britain, long
asleep, was slowly preparing for her turn to come.

The fact that the British coast had not been bombed sub-
stantiated my growing conviction that the German bombing
force was taking a lot of punishment. Goering's men were
concentrating all their efforts over Dunkerque and their losses
were terrific. I have never been able to believe that the Germans had the air power to bottle up the seaports of Great
Britain, for, during five days and five nights, in spite of continuous air raids, French and British ships came into Dunkerque with food and ammunition and left with 335,000 men.

An hour after our arrival I was seated beside a British
R.A.F. officer in the compartment of a train speeding from
Dover to London. I put to him the same question that I asked
of the officers of the R.A.F. whom I met during the Battle
of Flanders: "Why were the British keeping seventy-five per
cent of their pursuit planes in England while Germany was
concentrating all her air force on bombing France?"

I got the same answer I had heard before: Their indus-
trial towns had to be protected; the civil population needed
assurance of protection; above all, the English ports had to
be guarded at all costs.

"But now there is no actual danger. England isn't being

attacked. If those Spitfires and Hurricanes were in France destroying German bombers, wouldn't they actually be defending Britain better than by being idle over here?" I pointed out.

He shrugged.

As we passed through one town I noticed crowds standing around watching young and husky men playing football, and it was hard for me to believe that I was in a country fighting a battle on the outcome of which its very life depended. England seemed to me then to be just as I had always seen her before, a leisurely country enjoying life and peace.

I went to the Savoy Hotel and talked to our ambassador on the telephone. He said that nothing could be done that night, but if I phoned the Air Attaché the next morning he would arrange to have me flown over to France without delay. Then I rushed to a bath, a meal and a bed, and while Great Britain was getting ready for war I plunged into a profound slumber.

I SAW THE FRENCH ATTACHÉ in the morning and told him that I had with me urgent documents for General Weygand. He said he could arrange to have me leave for Paris that night in a bomber of the Royal Air Force—or still better, as I was in such a hurry, in a small plane which was at that time engaged on special duty. I asked the Air Attaché what "special duty" might mean, and was told that a young sub-lieutenant who had been accustomed to piloting a small private plane before the war had volunteered to engage in perilous missions in taking officers to inaccessible locations, such as those surrounded by enemy forces, or where ordinary military planes could not land. The pilot's name was Robaud and I was told that if he succeeded in returning safe from Dunkerque, where he had just taken a high-ranking officer, the Air Attaché would let me know.

An hour later I received a telephone call announcing that Lieutenant Robaud had returned and was already on his way to pick me up at my hotel. A few minutes later he arrived, and I immediately realized that Robaud was one of those typical characters that the French Army produces in times of necessity. To paraphrase the tile of a recent American book, *Danger Was His Business*; and as with so many of

the pilots of the French air force, I could see that it was a
business he thoroughly enjoyed.

I asked him at what airport his plane had landed and he
replied in a very casual way that he had left it in a little field
just outside the London suburbs. With the help of his road
map he thought we would be able to find it if we took a taxicab. We drove across Piccadilly Circus and through the east
suburbs of London. Then Robaud began to guide the taxi-
driver with his map.

I must confess that I was a bit dismayed when I saw
what my pilot called an airplane, but what to me appeared
more like a large grasshopper crouching in the grass. It looked
like one of those joy-ride airplanes one sees at county fairs;
and with the skies filled with enemy Stukas, I wondered how
in the devil we would ever reach Paris without being shot
down. My guide and pilot told me that the real virtue of this
plane, his own invention, was its miniature size: it was so
small and looked so inoffensive that it didn't seem worth attacking. He added that it was also the best-camouflaged plane
in France. He had painted the small wings green and sky-blue
himself.

As we were walking toward the machine, he explained
how by flying it a few feet above the ground level, too low
to leave a shadow visible from above, it was difficult for the
enemy planes lying at high altitudes to detect his presence.
Then he asked if I had good eyesight. I told him that unfortunately I was slightly nearsighted and had lost my spectacles
in the Flanders ordeal.

"Well," he observed philosophically, "that doesn't matter. The only thing I'll ask you to do, while I'm watching
ahead, is to keep an eye on what is happening behind. If you
see an enemy plane coming down for us, just yell out and
I'll try to land somewhere; in which case, don't lose a second
but jump out of the plane and throw yourself into the nearest ditch or any hole that's handy. That's the way I've already
avoided several rounds from their machine guns." He added
that the trip might seem a little long to me, the cruising speed
of his plane being only about seventy miles an hour.

More and more dubious, I climbed into the plane, where
I had the feeling of sitting in a small bathtub which had suddenly sprouted wings. We took off and began to hedgehop

266

over the trees of southern England, a method of flying which was ideal for our purpose but by no means to be recommended for pleasure. One minute the plane would be skimming over a freshly plowed field—then suddenly my head would be snapped back as the little craft bounced upwards to avoid the branches of a large tree or the roof of a house. I remembered my first impression of the plane and my instinctive thoughts comparing it to a large green grasshopper, now I was learning that its grasshopper characteristics went deeper than its mere appearance. I kept staring into the sky, saw a few friendly and enemy reconnaissance planes, and began to have the comforting feeling that after all I was probably in the hands of France's best pilot.

After about an hour's flight we came to the Channel and landed on a beach. My companion piled out and walked calmly over to the edge of a field where he broke off a small branch from a tree. I watched him as he wandered back, stripping the twigs from his branch, and wondered what in the world he wanted with that stick. He opened his gas tank and I realized he was measuring his fuel! I felt a bit nervous when, after examining the stick, he announced that he didn't have quite enough to go down to Havre, and that we would have to take a chance of cutting across and hitting the coast near Abbeville. That was about where the Germans were.

We took off again and began skimming the sea until the French coast lay there before us. As we approached, I noticed two or three anti-aircraft guns spitting fire. The pilot, who had seen them too, pushed our nose up, but when we were about two or three thousand feet up, he decided that the guns firing at us were French. He gave the plane an extraordinary wiggle, the effect of which, he told me, was to show the French markings on the wings. The little machine-gun flashes ceased, and we pointed southward toward Paris.

It was at this point that we saw two squadrons of Heinkel bombers flying right over us, apparently heading toward Havre. Possibly they did not see us; but I thought more likely that they took us for some honeymoon couple in an amateur plane and didn't think it worth while wasting precious rounds of cartridges on us. However, a few minutes later the keen eyes of my friend discovered three German pursuit planes at a great distance and a great height, but apparently coming in our direction. Luckily the ground was flat under us and we shot down into a field. I leaped out of the plane and hugged the ground under a tree. The fighters came down toward us at great speed, but then went zooming away. An hour later we were flying over the smoky suburbs of Paris and landed at Le Bourget.

I thanked my audacious pilot and told him that he deserved a better plane than the one he was flying, even if it had brought me safely home. He replied that for months he had been attempting to get hold of a regular army pursuit plane. "But you see, that's the trouble," he added. "We went to sleep for several years; and today, while in Germany they have too many planes for their number of pilots, over here we possess the pilots but not the planes."

I jumped into a taxicab and after picking up a few refugees who were trudging along the roadside toward Paris I reached the gates of the city. There I deposited the refugees and told my driver to get me to Vincennes as quickly as he could, where I left the documents I was carrying with an officer of General Weygand's staff. Then I hurried in to the Place du Palais Bourbon.

Every time I had felt myself to be in real danger in Belgium, in northern France, or on the Channel, I had thought of my wife and wondered if I would see her and my peaceful Paris home again. I found her there when I arrived. She had received not one of the letters I gave to Belgian refugees, and had been without news from me since the attack began. For all she knew, I had been killed, wounded, or was a prisoner. I believe that my unexpected return to Paris was the happiest moment in our lives.

Up the Republic!

by Brendan Behan

Napoleon once said: "Poverty, privation and misery are the school of the good soldier." Judging from the following selection, such adversity has also been the education of Irish wit and humor. The time is early World War II and the place a British prison. The characters are a guard and a number of his charges, among them the Irish writer Brendan Behan, who was caught coming into Liverpool in possession of explosives, with which, under orders of the Irish Republican Army, he hoped to blow up a British warship. Another prisoner is a comical fellow named Callan, who seems to be able to roar orders under his breath.

I got paper for the purpose of preparing my defence and wrote on it:

> My lord and gentlemen, it is my privilege and honor today, to stand, as so many of my countrymen have done, in an English court, to testify to the unyielding determination of the Irish people to regain every inch of our national territory and to give expression to the noble aspirations for which so much Irish blood has been shed, so many brave and manly hearts have been broken, and for which so many of my comrades are now lying in your jails.

Outside the doctor's one morning I met another Irishman. He was from Monaghan and I am ashamed to say that he might have been from the moon as from Monaghan for all I had in common with him, outside of being for Ireland, against England. By God he was that, all right. Callan was his name and he was a mad Republican. Not that he was in over the I.R.A. but was in over his own business, which was stealing an overcoat from Sir Harry Lauder's car outside the Maghull Alhambra. He gave out to me from between set lips about the two men that were under sentence of death in Birmingham.

But in two months Walton Jail had made me very anxious for a truce with the British. I had come to the conclusion, not only that everything I had ever read or heard in history about them was true, but that they were bigger and crueler bastards than I had taken them for, lately. Because with tyrants all over Europe, I had begun to think that maybe they weren't the worst after all but, by Jesus, now I knew they were, and I was not defiant of them but frightened.

> Pay them back, blow for blow, give them back woe for woe,
> Out and make way for the Bold Fenian Men.

Yes, but for Christ's sake not here. Not here where they could get you kicked to death for a Woodbine, or an extra bit of bread, if they didn't want the trouble of doing you in more officially.

This goddamned Callan though nearly seemed to like the idea of being a martyr. He had been to the great annual procession to Wolfel Tone's grave at Bodenstown, County Kildare. I had marched there myself, first as a Fianna boy, since I was able to walk, and later in the I.R.A., and more often than Callan, but I had to admit that he had the order of the parade and the drill off all right. Except that he gave a whole impression of the procession while we were walking round the exercise yard, I'd have enjoyed it.

He was able to roar in a whisper. When we'd go on the exercise yard, he'd start: "First Cork Brigade, fall in, by the left! Belfast Number One Brigade! Quick march Third Tipperary Brigade, by the left! Third Battalion, Dublin Brigade, South County Battalion, Dublin Number Two, dress by the right, eyes left Clan na Gael contingent Camp Number One, New York City. . . ." By the time the screw was standing on the steps and scratching his head and wondering where the muttered roars were coming from, Callan had finished drilling the entire Irish Republican movement from the thirty-two counties of Ireland, Boston, New York, Liverpool, and London and had them on the march to Tone's grave, to the stirring scream of the warpipes, proceeding from the side of his mouth.

He did it so well that the others started marching round the exercise yard in step to his piping, even despite themselves.

> Proudly the note of the trumpet is sounding,
> Loudly the war cry arise on the gale,
> Swiftly the steed by Lough Swilly is bounding.
> To join the thick squadrons by Saimear's green Vale,
> On! every mountaineer, stranger to fright and fear!
> Rush to the standard of dauntless Red Hugh!
> Bonnoght and gallowglass, rush from your mountain
>   pass,
> On for old Erin, O'Donnell abu!

He didn't sing the words of course but made a noise like the pipes playing them that went like this:

> Burp burp buh burp burp bee burp burp beh burp
>   burp, ur ur uh hur hur deh dur dur duh dur,
> Birp birp bih birp birp bir birp birp bih birp birp

271

which went just to a steady sensible marching noise, till he got
to a frenzied screech of the pipes at the end:

> ... Miaow aow aow aow aow aow, miaow yaow yaow
>   aow, haow yaow,
> Yaow aow aow aow aow, yaow aow haow yaow yaow!

For a time the screw stood on the steps in amazement
looking round and straining his ears to catch the faint but
rhythmic and persistent drone of Callan's piping. Then he
screwed up his eyes and spoke through his teeth.

" 'Oo's making that bleedin' noise, eh?"

We all looked around to show him our mouths and to
show it wasn't us. Callan did too, and I was the only one to
know that it was him was making the noise, and I wouldn't
have known it but I'd already heard his preliminary drilling
and ordering of the troops.

The other prisoners were terrified of getting into trouble
over the noise and would have stopped whoever was doing
it double quick, and Callan or me quicker than anyone, but
his mouth never moved. It's ventriloquism Callan should have
gone in for, in place of patriotism and overcoat-robbing.

The others did not know in the name of God where the
noise was coming from, and were getting as worried about
it as the screw.

He was doing his nut, standing up there on the steps. He
stared at each face in turn, in a quiet frenzy, but still the piping went on. He came down off his steps and stood on the
edge of the ring as we passed him, and looked into each face.

Callan came up in his turn and just stared quietly and
passed on after the others. I was following and opened my
mouth so that at least he'd be certain it wasn't me. . . . The
piping had ceased, and the screw went back on his steps, and
the piping started again, resolute, though quiet. The screw
stared about him, and cocked his ears to see if he was imagin-
ing the noise, and then nodded his head slowly and looked
about him in horror. We looked at him in horror, Callan looking at him in horror, even while he went on with the march.

Then the screw fixed his eyes on one of us. I hoped to
the dear Christ it wasn't me. He took a run down the steps,
and Callan stopped his music. The screw came forward and
I ducked with the rest. He made a dive on a boy from Glas-

272

gow that had hardly ever been heard to open his mouth in the place, even to ask you to pass the wax-end at labour.

"Aaarh, you Scotch bastard. Want to play your bleedin' bagpipes, do you?"

He caught a hold of poor Jock and beat him up the steps, to the gate, where he shouted through the bars for the screw on duty inside in the wing to come and take control of Jock.

"Play the bleedin' bagpipes through 'is bleedin' teeth, 'e was."

The other screw gave the usual reproachful look one screw gave when you were accused of having talked or broken any rule while in charge of another screw. As much as to ask how could you find it in your heart to do anything that would make life difficult for such a good kind man. Then he gave Jock a routine blow into the face and took him by the scruff of the neck, and nodded reassuringly to the exercise screw as much as to say that he wouldn't let these bastards take advantage of his good nature.

When Jock had been dragged off to his cell to await the Governor, the screw came from the gate and stood on the steps, shaking his head with satisfaction, while we all, myself included, more shame to me, breathed easier, and plodded round in our less martial and more resigned gait.

And then, in despair, because we couldn't help it, our steps tramped in unison and our backs straightened and our heads went up. Callan was at it again. This time it was drums and trumpets that blared discreetly out the side of his mouth, as he crashed into the old Republican march with a warning roll of the drums:

> Burump de dumpiddy dum, burump de dumpiddy dum,
> Step together, boldly tread, firm each foot, erect each head,
> Fixed in front be every glance, forward! at the word advance!
> Noise befits neither hall nor camp,
> Eagles soar on silent feather,
> Proud sight, left! right! steady boys, steady boys! and step together!
> Steady boys! and step together!
> Bardiddly bardiddly bar bar bar bar!

The screw looked down at us and said the exercise was over and all inside, and up to our cells. While we passed him on the steps into the wing, he kept his ears cocked to each prisoner's face. But Callan was not as green as he was Irish and we broke off and went into our cells without his musical accompaniment, though I thought when we halted in the Y.P. ring before falling out that he was going to shout in a whisper, "Irish Republican Army, dismiss!"

Safely in the cell I was pleased with Callan's performance. I had never seen anyone get the better of the screws before. It was hard luck on poor Jock, though. If it had been one of the English bastards I wouldn't have cared a God's curse . . . (except for Charlie or Ginger, of course.)

On Tuesday I heard that Callan had nearly started a riot in the carpenter's shop. They'd started at him over the executions on the next morning, and he'd gone for someone with a wood chisel, and when we were going to our cells that evening, I noticed that his cell which was on the ground floor and under me was locked, so that he must have been there before the others. Going up to my cell I hoped that he would keep easy till morning, and then in my cell and I drinking my cocoa, I was ashamed of myself for hoping that, but it didn't change me from hoping that Callan would keep quiet. It only made me ashamed as well as being afraid.

There were two innocent men and one of them was arrested in London within half an hour of the explosion which happened in Coventry.

They were brave men. One of them before he was sentenced to death said that he would walk out smiling, thinking of all the other men that had died for Ireland.

And when he was sentenced to death, he'd said as good a thing.

The judge said, "May the Lord have mercy on your soul," and he replied, "You too."

The humour of that would be appreciated in his part of Ireland, where it was a reply to such commonplace greetings as "Hello," or "Good health."

Still and all, I was here, on my own in this place, thinking of them, and even thinking of them having to face the rope in the morning didn't inspire me. It would inspire the crowds at home and in Madison Square Garden where they

274

would burn Union Jacks and curse the British Empire into hell and out of it back into it and think with pride and the blood surging through their veins of these brave men. The song of the Manchester Martyrs to the air of the American Civil War song, "Tramp, tramp, tramp, the boys are marching," would roar from ten thousand throats:

"God save Ireland," cried the heroes,
"God save Ireland," cry we all,
"Whether on the scaffold high or the battlefield we die,
Sure, no matter when for Ireland dear we fall."

It didn't inspire me. I thought it better to survive the night. I sat with my legs in my mailbag sewing my cell task, and thinking of sadness and sorrow and shame, and hoping that my demeanour was a peaceable one, and that the book I was going to read was a very meek one. Not that that would count with the screws. Most of them couldn't read anyway. Well, not books. My book was *Cranford* by Mrs. Gaskell.

I got into bed when the bell rang, thankful that Callan had let the night go past without starting a heave, and comfortable and warm opened my book.

It was a very comfortable class of a book. I'd never heard of it before, and when I saw it lying on my table with my other library book, I didn't think much of the look of it. It was in a heavy old cover, from the times of Queen Victoria, and I only knew of one class of book like that that was worth a God's curse, and they were by Charles Dickens. When I didn't see his name on it, I thought it wouldn't be worth opening and when I saw it was written by "Mrs." Someone, I said goodnight, Joe Doyle, this is a dead loss.

All that class of book was about little sweeps' boys that saved up money to buy their mothers cloaks or little girls going out to put on the light in the lighthouse when their fathers were not able to do it. They were probably lying someplace pissed drunk, I thought to myself, but that wasn't in those books of course.

So I took no heed of this *Cranford* other than to read it in bits, for a throwaway, like in the middle of the day, after dinner, when I would be going out again out of the cell and only wanted to look at something besides the bare whitewashed walls of the cell for a while. I reserved any good or readable books for the night, when I would want something to read at my real read in bed. I could read when I was four years old, well in a kind of a way, and was always very fond of reading, but every one of the prisoners was the same with regard to their books, which were the principal and only thing we enjoyed, well the only thing we enjoyed with official permission. They could hardly stop us dreaming or thinking bad thoughts. We all kept our best book for the night, and read or looked at the worst rubbish at dinner-time.

I started this *Cranford* at dinner-time, but after I got into it a bit, I promoted it to the night time, and even had to ration myself to twenty pages a night, which would leave forty each for Saturday and Sunday.

This night, I decided, I could lawfully allow myself a few pages extra, as a matter of that, and as much as I could read before I went asleep, and forgot everything.

> For Miss Barker had ordered (nay, I doubt not, prepared, although she did say, "Why, Peggy, what hev you brought us?" and looked pleasantly surprised at the unexpected pleasure) all sorts of good things, for supper—scalloped oysters, potted lobsters, jelly, a dish called "little Cupids" (which was in great favour with the Cranford ladies, although too expensive to be given except on solemn and state occasions—macaroons sopped in brandy, I should have called it, if I had not known its more refined and classical name). In short we were to be feasted with all that was sweetest and best; and we thought it better to submit graciously, even at the cost of our gentility—which never ate suppers in general, but which, like most non-supper-eaters, was particularly hungry on all special occasions.
>
> Miss Barker, in her former sphere, had, I dare say, been made acquainted with the beverage they call cherry-brandy. We none of us had ever seen such a thing, and rather shrank back when she proffered it us: "Just a leetle, leetle glass, ladies; after the oysters and lobsters, you know." We all shook our heads like female mandarins; but at last, Mrs. Jamieson suffered to be persuaded, and——

There was an unmerciful roar from a cell beneath me: "U—u—u—u-up the Rep—u-u-u-u-u-ub—lic!" roared Callan.

That the devil may choke you and the Republic, I snarled to myself, and why the fughing hell isn't he satisfied with his own exclusive martyrdom without dragging me into it. You're not much good alone and unarmed, are you? I said to myself and answered, No, by Jesus, I am not, not worth a light. But maybe with the help of the Holy Mother of God, he'll carry on his Plan of Campaign by himself, all honour to him, of course, I'll never deny it to him, but tell them at home how all alone he stood and shouted for the cause all on his own. If he only leaves me out of it.

"Bee—eee—han. Bren—daaaaaaaaan Be—ee—haaan!"

You lousebound bastard, said I to myself, putting down *Cranford*.

"Uu—uuuuu—up the Rep—uuuuuuub—lic!"

Answer you better, you whore's melt, to give the man back his overcoat and leave the Republic to look after itself.

"Breeeeeeeeeennnnnn—daaaaaaaaaannn Beeeeeeeee—hann! Get up and give a shout—a sh—oooooouuuuuuut!"

A kick up in the ballocks is what I'd like to give you, said I resentfully, getting out of the bed. I stood for a moment in my shirt, wondering what to do. May God direct me, said I to myself.

"Uuuuu—uuu—uup the Rep—uuuub—lic, Beeee—haaaaan."

All right, all right. I gave a discreet shout down the ventilator of "Up the Republic."

"I caaaaaaaa—n't heeeeeeeer youuuuuuu riiiiiightly," answered Callan.

"I'm shouting," I said in a low tone down the ventilator, "the walls here are three feet thick."

"All right. Goooooood maaaaaaan. Up the Reeeeee—puuuub—liiic!"

"Up the Republic," I said, but in a lower tone down the ventilator. "We defy you. To hell with the British Empire," I added in a hurried whisper, for I'd heard voices down below, and the noise of keys at Callan's door.

I jumped back into bed. Callan was getting done. They'd burst open his door and were on top of him. They'd be round to my door in a few seconds, for a look in the spy-hole. And where was I, when they did come round? In bed reading *Cranford*.

277

"What are you doing there, Behan?" they shouted in from the spy-hole.

I put down my book and looked up at the door. "I'm reading, sir."

He snuffled something of a threatening nature, and went off. I heard Callan's door being opened and heard moaning. They were after finishing with him, and were carrying him down to the chockey cells.

I went back to *Cranford*.

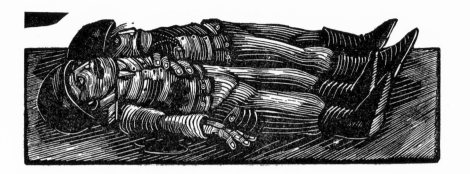

The Death of Captain Waskow

by Ernie Pyle

During World War II, whenever a little man with tired eyes and wispy white hair drove his jeep past a line of marching soldiers, the chances were good that one of the GIs would glance up and shout, "There goes Ernie Pyle! Hey, Ernie, how's about writing a story on our outfit?" And the chances were also good that Ernie Pyle would write it, for no correspondent ever loved or understood the ordinary footsoldier as he did. In the end, having shared GI Joe's portion of mud and misery, fatigue and fear, Ernie Pyle shared his fate. He was killed on Ie Shima off Okinawa during the last battle of the war. In "The Death of Captain Waskow" Ernie Pyle is at his poignant best.

I n this war I have known a lot of officers who were loved and respected by the soldiers under them. But never have I crossed the trail of any man as beloved as Captain Henry T. Waskow, of Belton, Texas.

Captain Waskow was a company commander in the Thirty-sixth Division. He had led his company since long before it left the States. He was very young, only in his middle twenties, but he carried in him a sincerity and a gentleness that made people want to be guided by him.

"After my father, he came next," a sergeant told me.

"He always looked after us," a soldier said. "He'd go to bat for us every time."

"I've never known him to do anything unfair," another said.

I was at the foot of the mule trail the night they brought Captain Waskow down. The moon was nearly full, and you could see far up the trail, and even partway across the valley below.

Dead men had been coming down the mountain all evening, lashed onto the backs of mules. They came lying belly-down across the wooden packsaddles, their heads hanging down on one side, their stiffened legs sticking out awkwardly from the other, bobbing up and down as the mules walked.

The Italian muleskinners were afraid to walk beside dead men, so Americans had to lead the mules down that night. Even the Americans were reluctant to unlash and lift off the bodies when they got to the bottom, so an officer had to do it himself and ask others to help.

I don't know who that first one was. You feel small in the presence of dead men, and you don't ask silly questions.

They slid him down from the mule, and stood him on his feet for a moment. In the half-light he might have been merely a sick man standing there leaning on the others. Then they laid him on the ground in the shadow of the stone wall alongside the road. We left him there beside the road, that first one, and we all went back into the cowshed and sat on water cans or lay on the straw, waiting for the next batch of mules.

Somebody said the dead soldier had been dead for four days, and then nobody said anything more about it. We talked soldier talk for an hour or more; the dead man lay all alone, outside in the shadow of the wall.

Then a soldier came into the cowshed and said there were some more bodies outside. We went out into the road. Four mules stood there in the moonlight, in the road where the trail came down off the mountain. The soldiers who led them stood there waiting.

"This one is Captain Waskow," one of them said quietly.

Two men unlashed his body from the mule and lifted it off and laid it in the shadow beside the stone wall. Other men took the other bodies off. Finally, there were five lying end to end in a long row. You don't cover up dead men in the combat zones. They just lie there in the shadows until somebody comes after them.

The unburdened mules moved off to their olive grove. The men in the road seemed reluctant to leave. They stood around, and gradually I could sense them moving, one by one, close to Captain Waskow's body. Not so much to look, I think, as to say something in finality to him and to themselves. I stood close by and I could hear.

One soldier came and looked down, and he said out loud, "God damn it!"

That's all he said, and then he walked away.

Another one came, and he said, "God damn it to hell anyway!" He looked down for a few last moments and then turned and left.

Another man came. I think he was an officer. It was hard to tell officers from men in the dim light, for everybody was bearded and grimy. The man looked down into the dead captain's face and then spoke directly to him, as though he were alive, "I'm sorry, old man."

Then a soldier came and stood beside the officer and bent over, and he too spoke to his dead captain, not in a whisper but awfully tenderly, and he said, "I sure am sorry, sir."

Then the first man squatted down, and he reached down and took the captain's hand, and he sat there for a full five minutes holding the dead hand in his own and looking intently into the dead face. And he never uttered a sound all the time he sat there.

Finally he put the hand down. He reached over and gently straightened the points of the captain's shirt collar, and then he sort of rearranged the tattered edges of the uniform around the wound, and then he got up and walked away down the road in the moonlight, all alone.

The rest of us went back into the cowshed, leaving the five dead men lying in a line end to end in the shadow of the low stone wall. We lay down on the straw in the cowshed, and pretty soon we were all asleep.

Brig-Rat

by Robert Leckie

In the modern Navy and Marine Corps a *brig* is not a sailing ship; it is the place where enlisted men are confined for such violations as going AWOL or looking too long upon the wine when it is red. In Marine brigs the prisoners have their heads shaved, for which ratty look they are called *brig-rats*. The author of this narrative was a brig-rat in Melbourne, Australia, to which the First Marine Division had come in 1943 following its great victory at Guadalcanal, and where many Marines had such exuberant fun that they landed in the brig.

I have heard it said that General Smedley Butler was fond of observing: "Give me a regiment of brig-rats, and I'll lick the world."

It may be that Old Gimlet Eye never said this. But it is exactly the sort of thing he might have said, or, if not he, then many another Marine commander. For it is most especially a Marine sentiment, and when analyzed, it turns out to be not shameless or shocking, but merely this: a man who lands in the brig is apt to be a man of bold spirit and independent mind, who must occasionally rebel against the harsh and unrelenting discipline of the camp.

I am not attempting to exalt what should be condemned. I am not suggesting that because of their boldness or independence the brig-rats be forgiven and escape punishment. Brigged they must be, and brigged they were. Nor am I speaking of the habitual brig-rat, the steady malingerer, the good-for-nothing who is more often in the brig than out of it and who seeks to avoid every consequence of his uniform, even fighting. I speak of the young, high-hearted soldier whose very nature is bound to bring him into conflict with military discipline and to land him—unless he is exceptionally lucky—in the brig.

I speak of Chuckler and Chicken and Oakstump and a dozen others—and, of course, of myself.

George Washington's birthday was the day on which Chuckler and I smudged the purity of our record books. The division was to parade in Melbourne that way. We were to march up Swanston Street, hardly a month after our arrival in Australia, to accept the plaudits of a city and nation still mindful of the Jap threat that had existed on Guadalcanal.

But Chuckler and I did not want to march. We wanted to see the parade, and this, you will understand, is quite impossible to the person who marches in it, rifle glued to his shoulder, eyes straight ahead and unswervingly focused on the nape of the forward fellow's neck.

By some subterfuge we evaded this odious duty, and so it was that we were firmly entrenched outside the City Club, drinks in hand, when the First Marine Division marched in Melbourne on the afternoon of February 22, 1943. Around us rose the cheerful and delighted calls of the Australians, as our comrades swung past.

"Good on you, Yank!" "Ah, a bonzer bunch, indeed!" "Good-o, lads!" "Hurrah for the Yankee lads!"

The men wore field uniforms, combat packs and full combat dress. Rifles were slung and bayonets fixed; each man wore or carried the weapon which was his in battle. So they were impressive; lean, hard, tanned—clean-limbed and capable-looking. I swallowed frequently, and my eyes were moist as they passed by. Even the Australians—who have inherited the British fondness for heel-clicking, arm-swinging, strutting troops—even they finally fell silent at the noiseless passage of the First Marine Division, walking in that effortless yet wary way that marks the American fighting man moving to the front.

Soon, Chuckler sighted the waving red-and-gold banner of our regiment. We ducked out of sight, moving from our front-row position back to the third or fourth. The First Battalion swung by. Then came ours, and our hearts beat faster. E Company, F Company—now, at last, H Company. There they were! There were Hoosier and Runner, Lieutenant Ivy-League and the Gentleman and Amish—all of them! Oh, what a proud sight! It was exhilarating, it was heady, it was as good as reading your own obituary or hearing your own funeral oration—to see them move so confidently and so proudly along, and to mark the admiration in the eyes of the Australians around us. Great day, indeed! We hoped it would never end, but it did, and there was nothing left to do but to substitute for this rare and genuine exhilaration that other artificial sort which is kept, corked and capped, in inexhaustible supply within bottles. So we turned around and re-entered the City Club.

And of course we drank too much.

By nightfall, we had had it. But Chuckler was due to stand guard at the slop chute that night. He took his leave, wavering slightly. But by the time he arrived at the Cricket Grounds, I was sure, the waver would be gone. Chuckler had that faculty.

285

After a time, I too returned to camp, arriving there only by luck or the intercession of my guardian angel. I ran for a tram speeding up Wellington Parade, leapt for the platform, missed it, grabbed the handrail and was dragged for two blocks until a pair of strong-armed Diggers were able to pull me aboard, like a drowning man.

Wavering, I came erect and thrust out my chest: "Tha's nothin'," I said. "Las' night—I got hit by one!" There was laughter until I reached my stop and got off.

I found Chuckler standing glumly outside the slop chute entrance. He had hoped for interior guard, where he might sneak a beer or two.

"I'll get you one," I promised.

I returned with a big glass seidel, out of which Chuckler might take a surreptitious sip. There were more seidels, until Chuckler said, "I've got to go to the head. Here, cover for me." He gave me his pistol belt and helmet, and made off.

For a sentry to be drunk, and then to desert his post and surrender his weapon, is to combine cardinal sin with unforgivable offense. I was anxiously hoping that he would hurry back. But then an unfortunate thing happened.

Lieutenant Ivy-League came striding down the corridor.

I say it was unfortunate because Ivy-League was the officer of the day. More than that, he was still the man who had filched my cigars—the enlisted men's cigars, if you will. My anger was nourished by the alcohol within me and I drew Chuckler's pistol and pointed it at him and said, "Stop where you are, you lousy cigar-stealing son of a bitch—or I'll blow your gentleman's ass off." Or words to that effect.

Whatever the phraseology, the pistol made the point. Lieutenant Ivy-League retreated, returning reinforced by the corporal of the guard (Smoothface . . .) and the sergeant of the guard. While Ivy-League engaged me in conversation, Smoothface and the sergeant were infiltrating. Suddenly they sprang. I had been outwitted—now I was overpowered.

"Get that pistol and pistol belt," ordered Ivy-League, white with rage. "Now, find that damn fool Chuckler!"

There was no need. He came hurrying up, too late, alas! Ivy-League ordered him imprisoned. Quivering with fury, his hands clenching and unclenching, his lantern jaw so tautly set one could almost hear the molars grinding, Ivy-League surveyed us. Then—

"Brig 'em!"

Smoothface led us away. Unaccountably, as we neared the forbidding steel-cage façade of the brig, we were given a reprieve. The sergeant said something and Smoothface halted.

"G'wan up to youah sacks," he said. "Ivy-League'll see yawl in the mawnin'." He shook his head sadly, especially sorrowful as his gaze fell upon me. "Ah dunno what the damn hell's got into yawl, Licky. Tryin' to shoot the O.D.! Ah know a guy got ten years, just for sockin' 'n officer."

Someone awakened me roughly in the morning. It was the sergeant of the night before.

"C'mon, get your clothes on. Full greens. You're going to see the man."

He stood bleakly by as I hastily covered my long under-wear with battle jacket and trousers. The sergeant might be bleak exteriorly, but I was positively frozen interiorly. What I had done the preceding night was now upon me: twenty years at hard labor would not be too severe punishment for assaulting the officer of the day!

Frostier than either of us, the battalion sergeant major awaited us outside the colonel's door. Tall, sharp-featured, his sandy hair thinning and the hairs of his military mustache bristling like bayonets, he seemed more a sergeant of Scots Guards than American Marines.

"The prisoner," he said, looking through me, heedless of my horror upon hearing myself so described—"the prisoner will enter the colonel's office when I give the order. Upon the command to halt he will come to attention before the colonel and remain there until dismissed. Tenn-shun! Forrr-rrd harch. Prisoner halt!"

My eyes fell upon the pink bald pate of Mr. Five-by-Five, our battalion commander.

Mr. Five-by-Five got his nickname from his build—a few inches over five feet in height and almost that much in breadth. It was an affectionate nickname, and we were really fond of him, or at least had been on Guadalcanal, when not a day passed that did not bring Mr. Five-by-Five toiling up and down those mountain ridges to look over his lines and his men.

Now the sergeant major was reading the charges, the crispness of his military style occasionally defeated by a diffi-culty with words. Then he had finished and the colonel

287

looked up and through me, as though my stomach were transparent.

"Lieutenant, let's hear your version of what happened."

Ivy-League's voice came floating over my shoulder. I felt Mr. Five-by-Five's eyes upon me while Ivy-League, talking in a strained voice—as though either he, too, were abashed by the colonel, or else he were reluctant to do what he had to do—related the night's events. He told the truth, including the most important piece of evidence, the fact that I had been drinking; for drunkenness goes a long way toward mitigating an offense in the Marine Corps.

The colonel studied me sternly. I stared ahead, trying not to swallow, trying to put steel into my stature, trying to keep from blinking, trying to keep my tongue moist so that I might answer quickly and clearly when spoken to—trying in every way to raise a false strength upon the sinking sands of my craven stomach. The colonel's manner was stern. I could learn nothing from his face, while he studied my record book, leafing the pages slowly, seeming to weigh these against the words of the sergeant major and of Ivy-League. Would he be cruel or kind? I could not tell. But, I knew this, as every soldier knows in war: my future, my life even, was his to dispose of. It is a most unsettling thought.

"How d'ya plead?"

Against my will, I cleared my throat and swallowed. "Guilty, sir."

He studied the book again. He raised his gaze and held my eyes.

"I'm not going to ruin your life," he said, and my stomach that had been fleeing seemed to pause, and turn. "I could put you away for a long time for what you've done. Being drunk is no excuse—a Marine is supposed to be able to handle his liquor. You've got a good war record, though"—he went on, leafing the pages of my record book again—"and you seem to have a good background. So I'm not going to ship you back to Portsmouth, where the book says I should ship you—but I'm not going to let you get away with it either." His face hardened. "Five days bread-and-water. Reduced to private."

The sergeant major's commands snapped out. I obeyed mechanically, so happy I almost missed the look of chagrin on Ivy-League's face, the look of the hunter whose prey has eluded him. Ivy-League did not want to ruin me either, but he would have appreciated a stiffer sentence. Five days bread-and-water! I could have got five years! I was elated and could have hugged the prison chaser when he appeared outside the colonel's office, rifle at port arms, and escorted me away.

Going to the brig in the Marine Corps—especially to the bread-and-water cell—is like going abroad.

First you must go to sick bay for a physical examination to determine if you are strong enough to stand such a diet and confinement; then you must visit the company office, to have the black marks entered in your record, and more important, to be sure you are docked in pay for the time you spend imprisoned; next you must revisit your company area to surrender your weapon and your gear to your property sergeant —and then, clad only in baggy, faded dungarees, the livery of the brig, you are ready for the door to clang shut behind you.

Back in your company, you are a dead man for five days. Even your bunk is denuded of pad and blankets. You are a cipher—the scapegrace whose picture is turned to the wall.

Every foot of the way in these progressions made at an odd, doglike pace, there follows your prison chaser, trotting grimly behind, his rifle at high port, like a canoeist with paddle poised—your shadow and your shame. The large black circles adorning front and back of your costume are almost endowed with weight, you feel them so poignantly; for you know that these are there for the prison chaser to aim at, should you break for freedom.

The brig receives you, and you are nothing; even the clothes you wear belong to the brig and bear its mark; your very belt and razor blades have been entrusted to the brig warden—you have nothing—you are nothing. The steel cage door clangs behind you, 0 cipher, and there is the brig warden standing there, suggestively flexing a length of rubber hose, and you realize that he has been chosen for his cruelty. Suddenly, things have become serious. There is no one to appreciate the humor of the situation. A chill rises from the cement floor and the heart within you freezes, gazing upon the brig warden with the cruelty shining from his black eyes.

It is cold and you are alone, and there against you stands the brig warden in his neatly pressed uniform, and behind him the United States Marines, and behind them the United States of America—and behind the brig warden, again in all reality, a door is opening and a voice commands, "Forrr-ward, harch!" and you walk in on stilts to greet your companions in the bread-and-water cell.

I had entered a shadowy world. I had entered a place that seemed a cavern hollowed out of the submarine rock of a subterranean river. But then I heard the murmur of voices, and the shadows seemed to take on substance and I heard a laugh— and then even this foul place seemed to brighten with that great flaming thing, the human spirit, and I realized, of course, that I was not in hell at all, but only in the brig for five days.

My eyes having adjusted to the gloom, I found myself in a room about twenty feet by fifteen, into which a murky light sneaked through a rectangle of thick glass set high in one wall. The floor was of bare cement, as were the walls, and it sloped inward toward a drain set in the center. In the middle of the right-hand wall was a water tap, on which hung two or three metal canteen cups. The bread-and-water cell was a converted shower room. I noticed, now, that my shadows were leaning against the walls, regarding me with curiosity and expectation. A voice questioned from the murk.

"What're you in for?"

I swallowed and answered. There was an awesome silence. Then—

"What're you—crazy, man? What d'ya want to try to shoot the O.D. for?"

"He stole my cigars on Guadalcanal."

Somebody growled, "To bad you didn't kill the bastard," and another asked, "What'd they give you?"

"Five days bread-and-water," I answered.

This time there was a general ejaculation of disbelief.

"How'd you get away with it? Hell! I got thirty days P-and-P just for going over the hill a couple days. And you get only five! For what you did—they should've shipped you back to Portsmouth and brigged your ass forever!"

"Hell, yes! Tryin' t'shoot the O.D. Who do you know, fellah? Yer old man a general or sump'n?"

Suddenly a rifle butt smacked sharply on the door.

"Quiet in there!"

There was a low grumbling, and gradually silence fell upon the bread-and-water cell. My eyes were now fully accustomed to the bad light and I studied my fellow brig-rats. There was no one from my company, although I saw other men, from the battalion, whom I knew by sight. Every face seemed disfigured by that look of peevish dejection common to victims of petty persecution or to city youth or to disenchanted dilettantes; but not one but was mitigated by the suggestion that, let the prison gates fly open, and every trace of rancor or resentment would vanish. Apart from that look, aside from vain grumbling against the officers or N.C.O.'s who had landed them here, or direful but empty threats of vengeance, there was nothing to distinguish the brig-rats from the men on the outside; they were merely Marines who had got into trouble.

The shadows still stood, no one sat, and I asked a man close to me why. He pointed to the floor and said, "They wet the deck. You can't sit down, unless you want a wet behind."

The floor was wet, and just then, the door flew open and a private began sloshing buckets full of water on the floor. Behind him stood another private, with rifle at high port. I felt myself go hot with anger. "Take it easy," said the shadow beside me. "You'll get used to it. The brig ain't no country club, you know. They wet the deck whenever they catch somebody smoking in here."

"Smoking?"

He nodded and I followed his eyes.

Hardly had the door closed on the bucket-wielding private, before two shades huddled opposite us lighted a blackened cigarette butt. They concealed the match flare by taking off both of their dungaree coats, and placing them, like a tent, over the head of one of them. They smoked by inhaling little bursts, expelling them quickly downward, and then dissipating the telltale clouds by quick, fanlike movements of the hands. It was a caricature, but no one thought it funny.

There were fierce whispers of displeasure, but the smokers ignored them, continuing to jeopardize the entire room for a pleasure that could only derive from the knowledge that they were breaking a rule. Certainly, the way they smoked could not be pleasant.

"They're long-termers," the shade beside me explained. "They've each got about twenty, twenty-five days more to do. They don't care if they get caught, now—a few more

291

days don't mean anything to them. That's how they get the cigarettes," he went on, "long-termers get a full meal every fourth day. When they march them down to chow with the regular straight-time prisoners, somebody slips them a cigarette. They smuggle it in by sticking it in their hair or between their fingers—or even in their mouth. They wait until it dries out."

The door flew open again, and I cringed—expecting more water. But it was mealtime.

"Rookie, rookie, rookie—come and get your chow," one of the guards chanted in a mock falsetto. Then he slid a big wooden box into the middle of the room and slammed the door.

They fell upon it like ravening wolves! They leapt upon that box and tore at the loaves of bread within it with the fury of a mob plucking at the flesh of a fallen tyrant. With a single soundless bound they pounced upon it and wrestled and shoved and pulled until, each with a handful of bread crammed against his lips, they fell back against the wall, there to crouch like caged animals, munching wordlessly on their fodder, their eyes angry and suspicious, their shoulders hunched and their very bodies suggestive of a snarl. Occasionally, a shade would rise to his feet and draw a cup of water from the tap, or take a pinch of salt from the grains spilled carelessly in the bottom of the box.

This was bread-and-water.

It was repeated, noon and night; and I, who had stood off in horror when the first shattering leap had come, I found only a crust or so to reward my revulsion. Thereafter, I learned to leap upon the first syllable of the guard's mocking chant.

Night falls in the brig with the swift silent plunge of dark dropping on the jungle. There is no dusk. A last feeble ray of light dies in the air about you, and suddenly it is pitch dark. Suddenly, too, you are tired. The evening bread box has been and gone; there is nothing to expect but the passage of a day and the approach of freedom. Better to sleep, to forget it, to pass the night in soft blissful oblivion and to awake one day nearer release.

The guards appear with the blankets, two to a man; one to place between body and the still-damp concrete, the other for a cover. Like Robin Hood's men, we throw ourselves upon this rude couch and go to sleep. We, the prisoners, are more fortunate than our jailers; for while we sleep, a guard must stand among us. We repose in the hollow of the hand of God, even we prisoners do this, and our guard must stand sleepless and erect, wary and fretful even, that some prisoner may outwit him and escape. But we sleep.

Morning brings the melancholy. We stand or crouch, faceless and formless; waiting for the bread box; longing for the night and dreading the dawn; counting the days and cursing the explosion of time, the eruption of minutes into hours and hours into days and four little days into an era; hating the officers and inventing impossible means of vengeance; sinking, sinking, sinking so deep into the abyss of self-pity that soon the very world is thrown out of balance, and blankets and bread box become magnified beyond proportion, occupying a man's whole mind, usurping the dwelling place of the world by a process of inverse mysticism that destroys time in reverse, that is the very black and evil heart of despair.

But there is a morning that brings freedom. The prison chaser trots behind again, there are the visits to the sick bay and the company office, and then, release. The steel cage door clangs behind; behind are the melancholy inmates of the bread-and-water cell, ciphers once again, their faces featureless and irretrievable.

The thing has left its mark. Five little days, even, and there is a scar. There is the memory of a debasing thing to be shared with all birds whose wings have been clipped, and with all caged beasts and imprisoned vagrants, with the lowest and the highest in the history of time.

Yet, a man who is getting out of the brig in which he has been imprisoned for the first time—if such a man has spirit and the sense to profit by misfortune—a man like this will turn and gaze upon the place and smile. Then he will laugh. Because who can hurt him now? He's had bread-and-water!

Chuckler was awaiting summary court-martial when I got out, and his counsel called me as a defense witness. Runner, too, was to appear, as a character witness.

All three of us were filled with fear when the day of the trial came—Chuckler because of the gravity of his offense and the possibility that he might be remanded to the far graver trial of a general court-martial, Runner because his loyalty to

Chuckler might lead him to an inadvertent disclosure of his own sins; myself for the same reason, fortified by the fact that I had already tasted the brig.

We were fearful too, because at first glance, the court seemed such a travesty of justice.

I say at first glance, for from its make-up and its conduct, such it would seem to have been; yet it was no such thing at all, for it ended in a finding that was as just as it was practical.

A lawyer might still insist that Chuckler's court was a travesty. A lawyer might be convulsed with mirth by Chuckler's counsel, a brand-new second lieutenant, younger, even, than we, fresh from an uncompleted prelaw course in a New York City college, most obviously destined to be a politician rather than a pleader. A lawyer would sneer at the prosecution and the judges, all chosen from the ranks of lieutenants and captains who had but two years ago been college boys with no more pressing judgments to make than to decide whether or not to spend the weekly allowance on beer or books. Such was Chuckler's court. But it ended by reducing him from corporal to private and giving him ten days in the straight-time brig. No one, least of all Chuckler, could dispute such a wise and merciful sentence.

It is unfortunate that my memory is so miserably unproductive here; I wish I could recall more of that trial.

Once, I remember, the prosecution halted Chuckler's counsel as he questioned me on my friendship for the defendant. "That's a leading question," the prosecutor snapped, whereupon the defense counsel—at first startled that this typical courtroom phrase should be turned against him, the only man in the room with legal training—gathered his facial muscles together in a crushing look of contempt and continued his interrogation.

The judges, all too aware of the defense counsel's legal talent, uncrossed and recrossed their legs, fluttered their hands —and let the objection die.

So Chuckler lost his chevrons and drew ten days in the comparative comfort of the straight-time brig, and his only complaint when he finally emerged was that, unlike me, he had been incarcerated under a brig officer who delighted in shaving the heads of his brig-rats as clean as a rat's tooth. Poor Chuckler was a skin-head when he came out, and he displayed a heretofore unsuspected vanity by wearing an overseas cap pulled down over his shining skull until the beautiful blond hair grew back.

MILITARY POLICE were more numerous. The hated black brassard with its block white lettering—*MP*—was becoming a roving wet blanket.

When we boarded the Australian ship, HMS *Manoora*, preparatory to maneuvers in Melbourne Bay, the MPs came down to guard the gate. They became the hair shirts of our existence. Only a clever man indeed might slip past them.

We were all eager to go ashore, hating the *Manoora* as we did—finding the ship's very name coarsely expressive of our dislike—hating the tedium of just waiting there for maneuvers to begin, eating, meanwhile, such barbaric food as tripe and boiled potatoes for breakfast, sleeping in hammocks below decks and spending our waking hours polishing the *Manoora*'s endless expanses of lacquered wood.

But one night came the news that the MPs had been withdrawn from the gate. Only civilian guards remained. Within an hour, the ship was emptied of Marines. They clambered over the wire fence between docks and road, or even sauntered boldly through the gate, rightly anticipating no restraining hands being laid upon them by the aged civilian guards.

Chuckler and Runner and I and another Louisville lad, a cousin of the Gentleman's, called the Chicken for his tender years—now, not quite nineteen—came with us. We slipped ashore the bold way, the grapevine having informed us that the civilians didn't care.

We stopped at the first restaurant we found, one lying on the coastal road. The *Manoora*'s tasteless cuisine had so impoverished our palates that we were ravening for our favorite Australian dish: steak and eggs, with wine or beer, or sometimes even with pitchers of thick, creamy milk and plates of Australian bread—milky white and of the texture of cake, sliced thin and overspread with butter as thick as cheese.

The restaurant was a great barn of a place, with what seemed a gallery or mezzanine running around the single spacious room. This was reached by a stairway to the right. At the end of the room were swinging doors leading to the kitchen. To the left of these was a smaller private dining room, in which I noticed a round table with some stiff-backed chairs.

We ate our dinner, and began to drink. Chuckler had telephoned his girl, who was coming out by train to meet him; but this would be in another hour. So we drank, as did half a dozen other parties of dungaree-clad Marines. Among them was a dark handsome slender fellow from E Company—their company barber in fact, the man who would cut hair for a few bob. He was quite noticeably drunk.

Some of the Marines had girls and were dancing with them to the music of a juke box. Through the open front door one could see the pavement of the street glistening darkly in the light thrown from our room. It had been drizzling all day.

A jeep pulled up outside the door—appearing there so suddenly as to seem placed there—and a quartet of MPs burst into the room on the run. We scattered like frightened sheep, the effect of panic heightened by the sound of scraping chairs and overturning tables—but there was no sound of a human voice, not even a scream from the girls.

I darted up the gallery stairs, the MPs pelting madly after me. Light gleamed through an open door, as I ran swiftly down the corridor. I slanted in and slipped the door shut behind me, bolting it. I ran through a room as a hammering started at the door, and came into a bathroom. There stood an Australian, half clad in trousers and underwear shirt, his face white with lather and a razor in his hand. His whole body asked the question: "What's up, Yank?" Breathing hard, my eyes casting about for exit, I said: "The MPs are after me."

"Oh, the bloody provos, eh? Well, 'ere's a go, Yank—over here, now, out the window with you. Out on the roof, see? They'll never follow you out there. There's a good lad, now. I'll take care of the bloody provos!"

I slipped out on the roof as the hammering continued. I crawled to the ledge and let myself down, hanging there by my hands. In a moment, I could hear the MPs talking to the Australian, but I could not distinguish their words. There was the sound of the window going up and flashlight beams slicing eerily into the oozing darkness overhead, then only the darkness, silence and the window going down again. The ledge was cutting into my fingers and the flesh strained so beneath my arms I feared it would part and leave only my arms hanging there. But I had to hang on. To haul myself back up on the roof again would have been a superhuman achievement. I could not let myself fall, for the sound would bring the MPs down on me, and I was afraid to move my head to look for them. I had to hang on, intolerable as the pain might seem, until I heard the jeep cough into voice and roll away.

Then I let go. It was not much of a drop, and I landed on pavement—for the Australian's room had fronted on the street. In fact, I might have been visible to the MPs, had they cared to glance my way. I held the darkness until I was sure they were out of sight, and then, swinging my arms to set the blood running freely again, I made for the shaft of light that came through the open doorway and slipped back into the restaurant.

I began to drink again, waiting for Chuckler and Runner and the Chicken to reappear. But they did not. Other Marines came drifting back, laughing, boisterously rehearsing their escape from the MPs, but no comrade of mine was among them.

"Hey, E Company," I asked of the group which included the handsome now-drunk barber, "you seen anything of my buddies from H Company? The MPs get 'em?"

"Nope." Then they laughed. "MPs didn't get nobody. They all went up them stairs after you, you simple tool! How the hell'd you get away from them?"

"I told them I was from E Company, so they took pity on me," I replied.

"They'd know that was a crock o' crap," someone replied. "You don't see nobody from E Company hauling ass. They'd know it was H Company right away from the view."

We exchanged insults, and there might have been a fight, had not the barber slipped in stupor from his chair. They bent to aid him and, as they did, the MPs came charging into the room again. They pounced so quickly there was no escape. I had moved toward the private dining room, but an MP intercepted me.

"Where you think you're going?"

"After my hat."

"Hat hell! C'mon with me, buddy."

The other MPs had the barber propped between them. His head lolled foolishly. His buddies apparently had escaped, sacrificing the barber and myself to their retreat. One of our captors jammed the barber's hat on his head and began to propel him out the door. I turned to the MPs who held me.

"How about my hat?"

"Whaddya mean—hat?"

"It's in that room there. I've got to get it. You're not going to make me leave it behind, are you?"

"Okay. But I'm coming with you."

I approached the other door with the MP crowding behind me. I opened it. Then I kicked sharply behind me, slammed it shut, crossed the room, yanked open the other door, darted through, pounded past the swinging doors, and ran into the kitchen, shouting: "Quick, which way out?" I followed the eyes of a waitress to the rear and lunged through another door. Here a courtyard confronted me, and beyond this a high stone wall topped with barbed wire. But the sound of the pursuing MPs impelled me across that couryard like a cannon shot. Up against the wall I flung myself, grasping the ledge with clutching fingers, legs up, up, up, strain and over—and there I was, arching through the dark and moist night.

A shot.

The son of a bitch shot at me!

The force of my fall sank me to my knees. I felt my hands bleeding from flesh torn by the barbed wire. My coat was likewise torn. But I could think only of the shots and I felt a hot rush of anger.

But now I must defend myself against a pack of dogs that had gathered silently about me after I landed in their alley. Now they were snapping and yapping—making my progress through this dark lane impossible of stealth. Lights were coming on in the tumble-down houses which stood back to back on the alley.

I crept along, feeling my way, fending off the dogs, stumbling against fences.

A light came on in a house to my left. A door swung open and light flowed into the black. I crouched to avoid it. A woman's voice called out: "Who's out there?" It would have been foolish to pretend there was no one there. The dogs were growing more ferocious, growling deep in their throats, ringing me round now that they could see as well as smell me.

"It's an American," I said. "I'm a Marine. The MPs are chasing me."

"The bloody provos," she growled, advancing to a back gate, her flashlight in her hand.

"Here, come over here. Go, you pack of mongrels, get away from here! G'wan! Scat!" She menaced the dogs with the flashlight, as I slipped through the gate. Her light fell on my hands.

"You're hurt," she said quickly. "Come, I'll fix you up. I used to be a sister. A nurse, you'd call it."

I followed her into the house. She cleaned the cuts, put mercurochrome on them, and bandaged them. I watched her. She was a plain, strong-faced woman in her early fifties. She was alone in the house, but it did not occur to her that she should be afraid.

"What are you running from the provos for?" she asked, bandaging me with precision.

"They're after me. They've been after me all night. We're aboard the *Manoora* and a lot of us went ashore tonight. But we're not supposed to be on liberty—we're never supposed to be in work clothes like this."

"I thought so," she said. "I wondered to see you sloppy like that. Your lads are always so neat—all shined and creased like you'd just stepped out of the clothespress."

I followed her through a narrow and dark hall. She made it seem casual, as though she might be doing this night after night. I shrank behind a curtain separating her hall from her kitchen.

She opened the door.

Two shots rang out!

She slammed the door.

"Oops," she said, "they've just shot one of your mates!"

It might have been that it had stopped raining, so calm was her voice. "Oops," she said, reporting a fact somewhat more than commonplace—that the MPs had shot poor Barber through the thigh, and with a .45 bullet at that, as I learned later.

"He was running down the street, and just as I opened the door I heard the shots and saw him fall. Sshh, now—I hear them coming."

I shrank back further into the dark and saw to my amazement that she was cautiously reopening the door.

"Ahhh," she sighed, closing the door softly, "they're

going now." She raised a hand; I listened. There was the noise of a jeep in movement away from us. "Your cobber's all right, I guess," she continued. "He's alive, anyway. They're taking him away in their auto." I came forward, and she said, "Do they always do that?"

"No," I growled. "I never heard of it before. Did they really shoot him?"

"Oh, yes. I saw him fall."

"They'll be sorry," I said.

"What do you mean?"

"I wouldn't like to be that MP—not when that fellow's buddies find out who shot him."

"Well, I hope they give him a beating he'll never forget. Bloody provos!"

I thanked her and slipped out into the street.

To my left I could see the shore road and light breaking through the clouds above the water. I walked toward the bay, determined to find Chuckler or Runner and to slip back aboard the *Manoora*. I had had enough of playing hide-and-seek with MPs who turned the game into a pig-sticking excursion. I peered cautiously around a building, once I had gained the shore road, and saw the restaurant marked by the beam of light slanting out the front door. There were no MPs in sight. I crossed the road and descended wooden steps onto the beach.

Chuckler would be here somewhere with his girl. He had no other place to go, not clad as he was. The sand swallowed the sound of my footsteps so I whistled loudly lest I come upon them without warning and cause embarrassment. Thus whistling, I sat alongside a boat drawn up on the beach. Within ten minutes, Chuckler was by my side, appearing suddenly and silently out of the mist.

"Where's Hope?" I asked.

"Gone home. She took a cab to the railroad station. C'mon. We'd better get moving."

En route to the dock, our path crossed that of the Chicken. He grinned when he saw us.

"Damn, Lucky! I would've swore the MPs had your ass. I nearly split a gut when I saw you tear ass up them stairs. I was runnin' myself—but I couldn't keep from laughing. They got Runner, you know."

"Runner!"

"Sure. He was the first one they grabbed. I seen it just as I took off."

Chuckler shouted with laughter. "Well, whaddya know? They finally caught up with old cautious. Runner in the brig at last!"

"Sure enough, Chuck," said the Chicken. "Ol' Runner's a member of the club now."

We all fell silent approaching the gatehouse. An ancient Australian, attired in the uniform of the civilian guards, was coming off duty. He motioned us to him, and whispered: "Don't try it. The officer of the day is watching the gatehouse. He's arresting your lads as they come in."

We thanked him profusely and fell back to take counsel. We decided to climb the fence. We were over it in moments. But then, we found that the wharf was some feet offshore, and could be reached only by entering one of the small boats moored there, casting off and paddling with our hands.

In the lee of the wharf, I held fast to one of the pilings while first Chicken and then Chuckler shinned up. They did it so well and so silently one could hear the lapping of the water against the pilings above the sound of their going. I called up to them, softly, but got no answer. Fearing to raise the sentry, I did not call again, but secured the boat and shimmied up the piling.

A strange tableau was presented to my eyes the moment my head came above the level of the wharf. Chuckler and Chicken stood side by side, bodies poised for flight—but their hands held high above their heads while a helmeted sentry menaced them with his rifle. I sought to duck but the sentry had seen me. He motioned with his rifle, and I ranged my person and my hands in the desired attitude. From the sentry's very bearing we could tell that he was a recruit just in from the States. Almost no veteran would have detained any of his comrades so, nor would a veteran have been less than horrified at the thought of confronting one of his comrades with a rifle. Chuckler spoke softly to him.

"That rifle loaded?"

"Yeah," said the sentry, carefully watching his interrogator.

"Cartridge in the chamber?"

"Uh-uh. Nope."

301

We breathed more easily, and I, who had inched toward him during the conversation, suddenly broke for the dark hulk of the ship. I counted upon the sentry either not firing or else swinging to cover me, and thus giving Chuckler and Chicken the chance to bowl him over, knock him off the wharf into the water, or to scatter themselves in such a way as to make it difficult for him to aim.

But the sentry was both quicker and smarter than the three of us.

He sprang back to forestall Chuckler and Chicken and brought his rifle to his shoulder to cover me. He slammed the bolt home. When I heard that deadly snick of cartridge into breech, I froze. We all froze. We contemplated the sentry in incredulity and consternation.

"You stupid, chicken boot!" Chuckler hissed. "What the hell do you think we are—Japs? Put that damned rifle down!"

The sentry surveyed us open-mouthed, as though Chuckler's angry words had fallen upon some heretofore unsuspected ground of loyalty. His eyes seemed to see us again as different persons, not the abstract transgressors of a moment ago, whom his general orders commanded him to detain—but now flesh-and-blood Marines from his own battalion, and he seemed to realize that he was menacing us with a loaded rifle that could kill. He began to lower it.

But it was too late.

Across the wharf and out of the great shadow cast by the ship came loping the officer of the day.

Involuntarily, I hardened the muscles of my stomach, as though bracing them for a bullet, when I saw it was Lieutenant Racehorse. For Racehorse was the most feared, the most respected and the most bloodthirsty leader in the battalion. As I stood there with my hands raised, watching his approach, seeing him draw his pistol as he ran, bawling for the corporal of the guard, I saw him dimly in the past—walking along the Guadalcanal hills and practicing drawing his pistol from behind his back, practicing quick drawing and shooting, practicing, perhaps, with that very pistol he now drew and pressed into my belly as he came up.

He looked out at me from beneath his helmet, but I could read no emotion in that lean confident face with the flaring nostrils and the small wide-set eyes.

302

"Search them," he said, pressing the pistol deeper into my belly.

"What do you want to search me for?" I asked him. "You know me, Lieutenant. I'm no fifth columnist."

"Search them," Lieutenant Racehorse repeated, and the sentry obliged. He was blushing now.

"Give us a break," Chuckler said, and I was surprised to hear it. But then I remembered that Racehorse had come up through the ranks, and presumed that perhaps Chuckler was appealing to this.

"No breaks tonight," said Racehorse. His voice was high. "You should have thought of that before you jumped ship and went ashore without leave. And out of uniform, too." He looked us over coolly. "Sentry, get behind these men and cover them."

"C'mon, Lieutenant," Chuckler pleaded. "Give us a break. We didn't do any worse than any of the other fellows. Hell! The whole Second Battalion was ashore tonight. We're just the unlucky ones who got caught."

"No, you're not. I caught dozens of them coming through the gate. And I let them all off. But not you. I watched that whole business from across the wharf. You guys are too smart —and if I had been that sentry, you'd all be dead."

He marched us to the *Manoora* and up the gangplank and up to the forward part of the ship and down a ladder and into a whitewashed hole lighted by a single glaring electric bulb. This was the *Manoora*'s brig. It was not a room at all, rather a seagoing Little-Ease, a vacancy occurring as port and starboard of the *Manoora* joined to point the prow. The ribs of the ship's sides were visible. One man could barely turn around, three not at all. We had been stuffed into the place, literally—and when the hatch clanged shut, we discovered a plate fastened to the bulkhead which bore this inscription: "This brig certified fit to contain one able-bodied seaman." We looked at each other, counted each other— and guffawed.

Then we fell asleep—Chuckler, being the heaviest, lying on the deck, I on top of him, and Chicken on top of me.

We awoke to the realization that we had put to sea. The prow rose and fell steadily, and we, stuck away in our hole up high, rose and fell in the exaggeration of our height. Our

303

brig, like a rabbit hutch quivering beneath the hunter's foot-fall, shuddered and shivered with the *Manoora's* motions and the throbbing of her motors. We rose and fell, sometimes dizzily, sometimes rushingly, sometimes with that long gliding rise, that fateful pause and dead bottomless drop that is the worst of all. But we were not sick, or even unhappy. The motion of the ship meant that the maneuver had begun, and this, we concluded, would mean that our commanders would be too busy to try us for our misdeeds.

But they weren't.

THE BREAD-AND-WATER CELL blazed with good cheer. I entered with Chicken. There had been a deck court-martial before the Battalion Executive Officer. He had removed the Pfc. stripe I had only recently regained, fined me, and withal sentenced me to ten days bread-and-water. Chicken fared as badly, though Chuckler had escaped the brig by forfeiting his second pair of corporal's chevrons.

When we entered, there were delighted cries of wel-come—"Look who's back!" and "Welcome aboard, mate!" It was like a class reunion. Almost everyone had been in before, and everyone knew everyone else. Even the guards were alumni.

Our appearance interrupted an election. This was a regular occurrence, the election of a mayor of the brig—and it was the most fairly conducted contest in my memory. Only two things qualified a candidate: frequent incarceration and length of service. Elections had to be held as often as the present mayor's time expired and he happily vacated his office.

One of the candidates was concluding a windy oration, dark with dire promises of vengeance upon the officers, bright with pledges of innumerable blossoms for the incarcerated lotus-eaters. Our own Oakstump was his rival. His speech was solid.

"He's a bloody short-termer," Oakstump said of his opponent. "It's only his second time in." He thumped his massive chest. "I've got another fifteen days to do—and it's my fourth visit."

Oakstump was elected by acclamation.

"Congratulations, Mr. Mayor," I said to him, but his beaming reply was cut short by the arrival of the bread box.

Everybody leapt—I lunging with them—so easily do men accustom themselves to privation.

Oakstump drew a canteen of water from the faucet. He tore a huge length of bread in two, surveying the halves thoughtfully. "Guess I'll make a sandwich," he said.

I snorted, "What the hell with—air?"

"Salt," he said. "I always make a salt sandwich."

He stopped, grabbed a handful of salt from the box, and deposited it on one half of bread, smoothing it carefully. He patted it and placed the second half upon it.

"Just right," he said dreamily. "Just enough salt for this sandwich."

He began to munch, pausing to sip the water, so satisfied it seemed sinful. Had I not recalled Guadalcanal, mixing his wormy rice with the contents of a stray can of peanut butter and smacking his lips over the mess, I might have pronounced him mad. But this was Oakstump of the oxen back and matching brain and unconquerable palate—and I ask you, how can such men be defeated?

That night, our own H Company took over the guard. Runner was the bread-and-water sentry. Though he had been caught by the MPs during the *Manoora* episode, his luck had held—they had let him go.

When darkness fell and we had thrown ourselves down on our blankets, Runner slung his rifle, dug out a cigarette and lighted it for me. Soon, other cigarettes glowed in the dark.

"How about some food?" I whispered.

"Where? The galley's closed."

"Out at the kiosk by the main gate. You can get hot dogs."

"Okay—as soon as I get off guard. Keep it to yourselves, though, or the whole damn brig'll want hot dogs."

I fell asleep, happily anticipating a reawakening by Runner. It was close to midnight when Runner awoke me. He had a brown bag filled with kiosk food. I awoke Chicken. Runner slipped out of the cell.

We devoured the food. What a banquet! Here was the lowly hot dog, but it was spiced with risk, flavored with prohibition, and washed down with the nectar of a watering mouth.

He feasted us again the following night, and would have

done it the next night, too, had H Company not relinquished the guard.

But the fourth night there came a stranger awakening.

A flashlight played impudently on my face.

"That's him," a voice said, and I was commanded to arise. So was Chicken.

We were taken outside, fearing, of course, the worst. But we were being freed. We were placed in the custody of a tall, gaunt newcomer to the battalion known as Eloquent, both for his passion for the polysyllable and for his expressive hands.

He marched us down the corridor toward the battalion sergeant major's, and we were startled to see men still going out on liberty. It was only nine o'clock, but we had been asleep two hours already.

"What's the catch?" I asked Eloquent.

"You were improperly confined," he replied.

"How come?"

"The Exec was a bit too enthusiastic. He wanted to throw the book at you, but he threw too big a book. On a deck court-martial you may reduce a man in rank or fine him or confine him. But you can't do all three, as he did to you."

"You mean I get my rank and money back?"

Eloquent gave me a pitying look. "Don't be a dreamer. The sergeant major has a nice new court-martial all written up for you two."

"What's the punishment?"

"Loss of rank and fifty-dollar fine, same as before."

"But what about the four days of bread-and-water we just did?"

"You never did them."

Chicken and I stopped dead, rooted by impotent anger.

"The new court-martial merely says that you have been punished by loss of rank and the fine, and when it's entered in your record book that's how it will be. There won't be any mention of the brig."

"Yes there will," I said, fighting a losing battle against my temper. "Because I'm not signing. Take me back to the brig and I'll finish the ten days." I turned to Chicken. "What about it—are you going back with me?" Chicken look at me sheepishly. "I dunno, Lucky. I dunno as we can git back. Whut're we gonna do if the sergeant major says we got to sign? Yuh cain't fight City Hall, Lucky."

"There speaks a sensible man," Eloquent said grandly.

"You call that sensible?" I blazed at him. "That rotten major makes a mistake and we're supposed to pay for it! We serve four days we weren't supposed to serve, and we're supposed to forget it. Forget it in writing—make the lie official! That's sensible! Well, I say the hell with you and the sergeant major. You can tell the sergeant major to take his court-martial and your sensibility between thumb and forefinger and at the count of three, he can stuff it smartly up his official ———."

"Whoa, now, take it easy," Eloquent interrupted. "You can't take on the whole United States Marines. You're absolutely right, and the major's absolutely wrong. But unfortunately you're a right private and he's a wrong major."

There was nothing to do but glower at him. He had put it well: a right private has no chance against a wrong major.

"Don't think I don't admire your spirit," Eloquent was saying. "It probably would have been appreciated more in the Middle Ages. But I would advise you to conform and sign the court-martial."

"C'mon, Lucky," said Chicken, "sign the silly thing, so's we can go out and get somethin' to eat. Yuh cain't fight City Hall."

I signed the court-martial, while the sergeant major sat wordlessly behind his desk. I signed it stiffly, detesting the very letters that formed my name.

I was relieved to get out of the office and to find that Eloquent could spare a pound until payday. We took it and slipped off to Richmond to devour steak and eggs, to drink beer and to curse the major.

As far as the U.S. Marines are concerned, Chicken and I never served those four days. Nor were we ever reimbursed for the four-days' pay we were docked while imprisoned.

"Let's face it, Lucky," said Chicken, chewing his steak with audible relish. "They got us on a one-way street."

OUR DAYS IN MELBOURNE were drawing to a close. "When are you leaving?" the girls asked. "They say you lads will be leaving soon," said the people who invited us into their homes. They knew. They always seemed to know before we did.

Now we could not get enough pleasure; there were not enough girls; we could not drink enough. It was going to end soon. Drought would soon dessicate this torrent of delights, and we would be back on a desert. It was as though we were trying to store it up.

Then, one day in late September, 1943, they marched us from the Cricket Grounds to the docks and onto the ships and back to the war.

Crowds of women had gathered dockside. There may have been men among all that vast and waving throng, but our eyes could see only the girls, squealing their good-bys as they had squealed and hugged themselves in greeting nine months before.

"Look at them, Lucky," said Hoosier. "Don't kid yerself, they're out just to say good-by. They ain't only wavin', they're waitin'—they're waitin' fer the first boatload of doggies comin' into the harbor."

"So?" shrugged Chuckler. "You'd do the same if you was them. You're just jealous."

"Hell, yes, Chuckler," Hoosier said, replying with eagerness. "Ah'm jus' beefin' because Ah'm on the wrong boat."

Just then, as though to fit the Hoosier's estimate of the farewell scenes, as though to summarize the Great Debauch now lying behind us, that period receding ever faster with the ever-widening water between the docks and our stern, the men aboard the ship took to a farewell gesture of their own.

They dug from their pockets and wallets those rubber balloon-like contraptions for which they had no longer any use, and they inflated them. These they set adrift on the currents of wind whipping about the fantail. Soon the space between the docks and our departing transport was filled with these white and sausage-shaped balloons—dozens, then hundreds, then thousands of them—dancing in the breeze, bouncing up and down, seeming to flutter even on the wind of noise raised between the ever-separating camps, the hoarse and vulgar hooting of the Marines and the shrill and pseudo-shocked shrieking of the girls—answering one another like rutting beasts in the forest, counterpointing one another like the coarsest concerto grosso.

In the diminishing distance we could still see the balloons.

Hail and farewell, women of the West. We who are about to die insult you.

The Bloody Ridges

by Russell Davis

The Marine assault on Peleliu in the fall of 1944 touched off one of the most vicious battles of the island war against Japan, and the fight on Bloody Nose Ridge was the fiercest fought on Peleliu. Here the Japanese had stationed the bulk of ten thousand fanatic soldiers sworn to fight to the death—as they did—from hundreds of armored coral caves. Some of these holes were big enough to hold a battalion, others small enough for a single soldier; still others were constructed four and five layers beneath the coral. All spat fire as the Marines groped blindly forward in 120-degree heat, seeking to find the invisible foe before they could dig him out. Such was Bloody Nose Ridge, described by Russell Davis, who fought there as a scout and then as a rifleman.

Old Marines talk of Bloody Nose Ridge as though it were one, but I remember it as a series of crags, ripped bare of all standing vegetation, peeled down to the rotted coral, rolling in smoke, crackling with heat and stinking of wounds and death. In my memory it was always dark up there, even though it must have blazed under the afternoon sun, because the temperature went up over 115°, and men cracked wide open from the heat. It must have been the color of the ridge that made me remember it as always dark—the coral was stained and black, like bad teeth. Or perhaps it was because there was almost always smoke and dust and flying coral in the air. I spent four days and nights up on the ridges and it is difficult to untangle that time and to remember when specific things happened.

We went against the first ridge on the morning after John was killed. I went up with the assault company, across a clearing littered with stumps and coral and the scrap of war, up and down low hillocks and through a draw, and then onto the foot of the ridge. We got part way up the ridge and then the hills opened and fire poured down on our heads. Two riflemen and I were plastered down into a hole and there we lay while the world heaved up all around us. We could do nothing but huddle together in terror. We couldn't go back. We were witless and helpless, with nothing to do but lie and take it. We couldn't run and we couldn't fight. Not one of the three of us bothered to fire a shot while we lay there through the morning.

We lay in it. Artillery shrieked. Men shrieked. And small arms whined. Mortars, defective in flight, whimpered overhead, and men whimpered. Every living thing on that hill cried out for something.

"Help, for God's sake, help us!"

"Corpsman! Here! Corpsman! Doc, I'm hurt bad."

"Plasma."

"Water."

"Artillery! Get it onto them. Stop them from hitting us like this."

"Air! Air strike! Come over with the air strike."

"Support!"

"Help!"

"God!"

In the afternoon Buck and I went out with Lieutenant Mac. He had specifically requested Buck because he enjoyed irritating him. We managed to get almost to the top of the ridge without coming under too much fire. There, Mac spread his map, dry-washed his hands, called his radioman to him and said: "My message is this: At J—that's Jane—and at five o'clock on Jane Space, we will try one round on for size."

The radioman began to chant:

"Hello, Dancer Charlie Peter. Hello, Dancer Charlie Peter."

"This is Falcon Oboe Peter. This is Falcon Oboe Peter."

"Come in, Dancer Charlie Peter. Come in, Dancer Charlie Peter."

"Over."

The radioman was silent as he received the answering call. Then he said:

> "Dancer Charlie Peter.
> Dancer Charlie Peter.
> I hear you five by five.
> I hear you five by five.
> How do you hear me?
> How do you hear me?
> Over."

The radioman listened and then said:

> "Dancer, here's a target.
> Dancer, here's a target.
> Jane at five o'clock.
> Jane at five o'clock.
> Fire one. Fire one.
> Over."

Mac and I edged up to the ridge line and waited for the first great bird to come howling over. The radioman yelled up to us: "On the way!"

The shell came shrieking over and made a vast flame against a distant hill, beyond a deep draw.

"Lovely," Mac breathed. "Lovely." He called down to his radioman: "Pour it onto Janie."

Shells swished by in a steady stream and the hillside flamed and writhed under the barrage. Mac searched for new targets. "Is that a gun that just stuck its tongue out at Item Three? I do believe it is. We'll get to you, my friend, in due course." He called down the new target and then rubbed his hands together with satisfaction. "Oh, the beauty of high ground! I will never run out of targets."

We ducked down as mortar fire came in over the lip of the ridge.

"Insolence will get you nowhere," Mac chortled. "The Falcon will strike again."

We went on spotting targets and Buck was very good at it. The war went on around us, but we scarcely noticed it. On that hill we were the big guns and the other action was beneath our notice.

We spotted targets all through the afternoon. All around us the riflemen stayed low in their holes, but there was something about calling down the thunder of sixteen-inch guns that made us contemptuous of return fire. We felt no fear and we did not bother to get down when the puny return fire of mortars came in.

The heat was terrible. One big, redheaded man, horribly burned and cracked around the face and lips, suddenly roared out of his hole like a wild horse. "I can't go the heat," he bellowed. "I can take the war but not the heat!"

He shook his fist up at the blazing sun above. Two of his mates pounced on him and rode him down to earth, but he was big and strong, and he thrashed away from them. There was something bad for everybody on that hillside.

Mac kept spotting targets until it got too dark to see and then he tried to talk Buck into staying out on the line that night. "I want to be here bright and early," Mac said. "Nothing like a few hot sixteen-inch shells right on the breakfast table. Starts the day right for them."

Buck agreed to stay if we would move down to the foot of the ridge behind the company command post. Mac hated to be that far away from the action but he agreed and we dug in just behind the company command post. We had scooped our holes in the coral, spread our ponchos and arranged our

312

weapons for the night when the Japanese counterattacked over the hill. We had to go back to the ridges with Mac.

The first night on the ridge was a night of terror. Mac pulled fire right in on top of us. He even fired behind us. To control the fire of ships miles away and to fire into the dark on the word of an observer who couldn't see the man in the next hole was a job which required complete confidence and courage. Mac had both. There would be a whispered word from the nervous radioman: "Under way, sir."

"All rightee," Mac would say. "Let's see where this one lands."

Buck and I, our knees pressing together and our hands on our heads, would wait, while the big bird came screeching up out of the darkness behind us. Orange flamed out in a star with a hundred points and the smash of the hit was like a blow from a dark fist, as all the ground shook. There was a terrible silence while we waited for the cry for corpsmen to come from our riflemen. But no cry came. Instead a flare popped overhead. In the ghastly light Mac grinned at us. He seemed some terrible Irish ha'nt as he said: "Sure, the man who had my job before, poor lad, tried this blessed same thing one night. For the life of me I can't remember what he did wrong exactly. Well, we need not worry at all. It will come to me."

Buck had little sense of humor at best, and no sense of humor at night. He muttered, loud enough for Mac to hear: "That miserable, crazy Mick will kill us all."

Insults, even from enlisted men, never bothered Mac.

"Now, now, Sergeant," he cautioned Buck. "I've been on this job almost three days and I've never lost an observer team." To the radioman, he said: "Let's bring that fire in a bit. Where are we?"

Late that night we went back to our holes and Buck was close to collapse. He lay down behind his shallow barricade of splintered wood and coral, got his body down as far as he could get it into the shallow depression we had made in the coral, muttered a few curses on Mac, began to mutter his prayers, and fell dead asleep. It was the first time, that I knew of, that Buck had slept since the landing.

The fourth day got lost in a blaze of heat. Men let the camouflage covers of their helmets down to shade their necks from the sun and to protect them from the sting of the rock dust that was everywhere. The riflemen looked like desert soldiers. Dark men grew darker, and light-complexioned men suffered the tortures of broiled faces, cracked lips, and almost sightless eyes. Many men threw away their helmets and wore only the old, soft, floppy fatigue caps of the Army. The round hat was a favorite in the First Division. It could be bent into any shape and serve against the rain or the sun.

There seemed to be no morning to that fourth day. While the sun blazed, we swung to the right of the first ridge, crossed a road that led nowhere, and came up against a sheer cliff. Down from this cliff, steep and studded with caves and holes, came Japanese fire. Only by hugging the base of it could we move. Machine-gunners were set up across the road, and the riflemen were assembled at the base of the cliff. The orders were to take the cliff. It was a stupid order.

While the riflemen were being assembled, the fire landed on E Company machine guns, and their screams came to our ears and racked our nerves. Buck, who had been hugging the cliff in terror, reacted as he usually did when there was something to be done. He walked out across the road and stood up on a rock while mortars poured down around him. Buck and a sergeant from E Company organized a team of riflemen snipers and they began to pick off the mortar observers who were up on the forward slope of the ridge. They also got a bazooka man to fire into a nest of mortars. Then they called in the company and battalion mortars and the Japanese fire dried up and died. When it did, Buck ambled back to the protection of the ridge, and, once he was there, he showed fear again. Our companies started up the cliff.

We had lost heavily, ever since the beach, but I had not realized how bad the losses were until our companies moved out on the cliff. Clawing and crawling up the cliff went platoons that were no more than squads, and companies that were no more than large platoons. I counted one platoon. It mustered eighteen men on that push. But they went up.

From the base of the cliff, we could pick out each man and follow him until he got hit, went to ground, or climbed to the top. Not many made the top. As they toiled, caves and gulleys and holes opened up and Japanese dashed out to roll grenades down on them, and sometimes to lock, body to body, in desperate wrestling matches. Knives and bayonets flashed on the hillside. I saw one man bend, straighten, and club and kick at something that attacked his legs like a mad dog. He reached and heaved, and a Japanese soldier came end-over-end down the hill. The machine-gunners yelled encouragement.

As the riflemen climbed higher they grew fewer, until only a handful of men still climbed in the lead squads. These were the pick of the bunch—the few men who would go forward, no matter what was ahead. There were only a few. Of the thousands who land with a division and the hundreds who go up with a company of the line, there are only a few who manage to live and have enough courage to go through anything. They are the bone structure of a fighting outfit. All the rest is so much weight and sometimes merely flab. There aren't more than a few dozen in every thousand men, even in the Marines. They clawed and clubbed and stabbed their way up. The rest of us watched.

Watching them go up, Buck, the old rifleman, said: "Take a look at that sight and remember it. Those are riflemen, boy, and there ain't many like them. I was one once."

I looked up the cliff, but everything had changed. There was no longer anyone in sight. Our men who had gone up were either in holes near the top, dead, or lying out wounded and cooking in the sun. Another wave of riflemen got ready to go up, but before they could move out, heavy fire fell again, tearing apart the command posts and scattering machine-gunners and even dropping in behind the low ridge beyond the road, on the company mortar men. Once more, Buck moved out in it and called targets. This time I went with him, out of shame.

We could see Japanese observers, scurrying around near the top of the ridge line. We put everything we had in on them and Buck even yelled: "I wish that crazy officer was here with his big guns."

Before I could answer, a mortar whooshed in and blasted us both from the rock on which we stood. I landed on my feet and ran head-down for the base of the ridge. There, safe under an overhanging ledge, I sat, sobbing with an effort to get my breath. I saw Buck pick himself up, dust himself off, and climb back onto the rock. I sat for ten minutes, and then, ashamed of myself, I went out and relieved Buck. If he knew that I had run, he said nothing about it.

In the afternoon we went out on a long patrol, swinging around the nose of the cliff in a sweep to our right. We still had a few men up on the cliff, but we had learned something. Beyond that cliff was a deep gorge. After fighting up to it, we found ourselves isolated, with no chance to go ahead. So we went around. I went out with Larry and a platoon leader and a dozen men and we got a long way out until we were pinned into a blockhouse by heavy fire from the hills ahead. The lieutenant decided that somebody had to go back and report, and the job fell to Larry and me.

We moved to the steps of the dugout and stood there while the fire thundered down overhead. It was a very tough blockhouse. The roof creaked and mortar and sand sifted down on us, but it didn't breach. We took off out of the blockhouse, running. On the way in, everything happened. We hit a Japanese patrol and were pinned down and chased. Then we were spotted from the ridge and pinned down with mortars. Then our own naval guns made a wall of fire which blocked us off. Probably, Mac was calling those shots. When we hit the naval guns, Larry said: "We best run for it. Good luck to you!"

We ran for it. I got in but I don't remember arriving or reporting. I remember Buck dumping pineapple juice into my mouth from his canteen cup. The fruit juice had been sent in from the ships of the line, and never was there a more welcome gift. Men were dropping from dehydration and sun. Larry and I drew two cans each and I drank myself sick, but after the sun went down I could walk again. I even helped Buck prepare our position for the night.

The next morning I got up and joined the line, which was already moving off to our right along the route we had taken the day before. We got all the way to the bunker before we were stopped by fire from ridges which lay beyond a road and a causeway. The colonel took over the bunker as the battalion command post. Later, the regimental command post moved in. It was the best cover in the area. For me, it was like home. When I ran in from the causeway or the swamps, which were off to our right, the bunker was a welcome sight. Once inside, no matter what was coming in overhead, I felt secure. I knew every chink and crack in that foul and damp tomb, but it was home. It was a domed-roof pillbox, two steps down into the

316

ground, concrete on top, steel reinforced, and concrete inside. It took direct hits until the mortar was all shaken out of the chinks between the clocks. But it held.

We were moved over toward a narrow causeway that ran through the swamp toward the road and the ridges. "Hold here," the lieutenant said.

Up on the causeway a memorable thing happened. A Marine came dashing out along it, moving toward the ridge. He was hit and knocked flat. I remember his muddy fingers stretched toward where we lay. He was clenching and un-clenching his hand, either from pain or through some death reflex beyond his control. A second man, unable to stand the pitiful sight of that hand, clambered up onto the causeway and drove toward the wounded man. The second man was shot to a skidding stop. He lay on his back, without a twitch. A corpsman, who had seen it, said, "Shove this, I'm gonna get those guys." He rolled up onto the bank, got to his knees and never did stand up. The sniper shot him as he still knelt.

A fourth man, a squat and burly ape of a man with extra-long arms, reached up over the edge of the causeway and began to pull the men in. He exposed no more than his long, thick arm, and he must have had phenomenal strength to drag the weight he pulled with one arm. I could see him straining and sweating as he began to bug the first of the wounded men over the edge of the bank. The sniper poured fire in at that thick, heavy arm that seemed to reach up out of the swamp like the tentacle of some hidden monster. Mortars harrumphed and clopped into the mud but the man pulled all three wounded men to safety.

Late in the afternoon, they began to patch the line companies with every able-bodied man they could send up from the rear. In came men from the war-dog platoons, the military police, the division band, the division laundry platoon, regimental headquarters men and battalion clerks. I was assigned to take these men, each of them carrying a load of ammunition, out through the swamp and into the lines. Most of them were quiet and good men who were scared but not too scared to do what they were told. But a few of them had never visited the front lines and had no intention of going out there. They felt that the riflemen were a special breed, created to do all the suffering and dying for the division.

A fat clerk complained to me: "I haven't been trained for this. What good will I do?"

I had neither pity nor sympathy for him. "You'll do fine, Fatty," I told him. "You will probably stop two bullets and save two good men."

That fat clerk hated me long before we got into the swamp. Twice I caught him lagging back and looking for a chance to duck. Both times he had dumped his ammunition so he could run better. He finally did bolt when we got into the high grass, and I never saw him again.

At the time I was watching another man who was trying to duck out. He had a good reason, too. He was a heavy winner in the division poker game. He said his pack was stuffed with thousands of dollars in winnings and he offered me a small piece of his money to let him run to the rear. He wasn't worried about himself as much as he was about the money.

"What if I got hit?" he asked. "Some grave-robbing thief would clean my pack."

"I'll see that they bury it right with you," I promised. "Get those belts of machine-gun ammo around your neck and move out."

"I'm a sergeant," he told me.

"That's fine, Sergeant," I said. "I'm a private. Let's go."

We had easy going until we were in the high grass. There it was rough. The men with the belts of machine-gun ammunition couldn't run and they couldn't get down. The men carrying rifle ammunition in ponchos had a worse time. Nobody panicked until the first carrier was shot and killed instantly. His partner, carrying the other corner of the poncho, put down his load and howled like a dog, and that noise unnerved everyone in the party. Of the twenty, I got nine men to the lines. Probably no more than one other man had been hit. The rest either ran back or scattered to hide in holes in the grass. I had no time to flush them out of their cover.

After we got the ammunition out to the line, we couldn't find anybody to take it. Once more the companies were milling around, some men retreating and some attacking, but most of them were just lying there, hoping to get out alive. I dumped my ammunition in a company command post and went back to the bunker. It was like coming home to a house in the suburbs after a hot and hard day in the city.

I SPENT THAT LAST NIGHT on the line almost entirely out of the bunker. At dusk, as we were boiling coffee water at the entrance steps, a tremendous fall of artillery came down, and two old machine-gunners—who had transferred into the quartermaster section for safety—were hit and blown down the steps of the bunker. We never did make that coffee. We dragged the wounded men down into the darkened tomb and held matches while a corpsman tried to stop the bleeding. The floor of the bunker was soaked with blood. The salty smell of it was everywhere. When Mac came by looking for an escort out to the line, I was glad to go, and we went out of the company command post.

The remnants of our second battalion spent a terrible night up there. But, for the few men up on the higher ridge—mostly from C Company, First Battalion—it was far worse. All through the night we could hear them screaming for illumination or for corpsmen, as the Japs came at them from caves which were all around them on the hillside. Men were hit up there and we could hear them crying and pleading for help, but nobody could help them. The remains of the first and second battalions and the division scout section had been thrown in together, and most of the men were strangers to each other. Two or three men were killed by their own mates that night. Grenades slammed and the stinging sound of the shrapnel came down the hill. The cries of American and Japanese were all mixed together. It unstrung even Mac.

"I think we ought to get up there," he told the company commander.

"Stay put," the company commander snarled. "Those are some of my kids catching hell up there. How do you think I feel?" He listened to the whimpering calls from the hills, and his head was down between his knees and he cursed monotonously. But he was right. We would have done them no good. "This will be a long, long night," he said.

"A long night," Mac echoed. "I think I'll say a prayer for those kids. Naval gunfire can't help them, God knows."

Of the sixth and last day on Peleliu, I have no connected memory. Short sequences like bad dreams are all that I can recall.

There was a squat, black-bearded rifleman who spoke with a New Orleans accent. He carried nothing but a rifle and a bandolier of ammunition. His shirt was black with sweat and plastered to him, skin-tight, and he looked like a pirate. The colonel was talking to him as he got ready to lead his squad up the hill.

The rifleman said: "Colonel, we can go up there. We been up there before. And we'll go on up again until there's nobody left. But we can't hold that ridge, Colonel. We can't hold it unless there's more of us, sir. We can't hold it at all, sir. I mean——"

The colonel turned away without answering. He was on the verge of exhaustion himself.

I remember, too, an old sergeant with an ugly, Irish face. Perhaps he was only thirty or so but he looked like a hundred-year-old dwarf, red-faced, red beard, undershot jaw, bandy-legged—a wee and ugly gnome. The advance had been signaled, and the sergeant stood up on his twisted legs and waved the men forward toward the hill. A few men stumbled out of their holes. Some could not move. At least they didn't. They leaned on their weapons and looked sick with dread. The sergeant looked at the men. He turned away and his face twisted with sudden grief and tears came down his bearded cheeks. He waved his hand and rubbed his dirty face with his sleeve.

"Let's get killed up on that high ground there," he said. "It ain't no good to get it down here." As the men stumbled out for him, he said, "That's the good lads."

There were few platoon leaders and few sergeants. The young officers had been hit and the sergeants had been hit or they had folded, and the "duty" fell on those who would take it. Rank meant nothing. Privates who had something left led sergeants who didn't have it any more, but who would follow, even if they wouldn't order other men to. One big Italian man moved forward, dragging his blanket, unwilling to part with it, even though it tangled in his legs. Another man had his head covered with a poncho, so that only his eyes showed. The eyes were like those of a small burrowing animal driven to ground and cornered. A small Jewish man, who carried a company radio, moved around in a circle. He was determined to move, but he was too damaged by shock and fatigue to get his bearings. A scout, who walked near him, pointed him toward the hill and the two of them staggered out.

The whole motley lot—a fighting outfit only in the minds of a few officers in the First Regiment and in the First Division—started up the hill. I have never understood why. Not one of them refused. They were the hard core—the men who couldn't or wouldn't quit. They would go up a thousand blazing hills and through a hundred blasted valleys, as long as their legs would carry them. They were Marine riflemen.

A machine-gunner, a Lithuanian, sat calmly at his gun, alone and beyond the causeway. Fire threw rock dust and powder and shrapnel all around him, but he did not move and he did not even flinch. He made no effort to protect himself. His gun was neatly set and laid in to cover the break in the ridge through which any counterattack would come.

He said to me: "I can't go up that hill again. I got no legs now. But no Japs will come through that hole while I'm here." He was sharp-faced and clean, even in the middle of the barrage. I remember that.

In a swamp, an old sergeant crouched in his hole. He had been away from his outfit for two days and his were the motions of a hunted animal. "I got nothing more inside," he said. "Nothing. I don't even know anybody who is still alive. They're all gone, boy. Done, the whole lash-up."

I never found out what we were doing, tactically, on the sixth day. At first, I did what they told me to do, but no more. I ran around to the jumbled messes that were called companies and I tried to help our colonel keep some control of the scattered survivors of many outfits that made the last push up the ridges. Things started bad and got worse and, finally, hopeless. I quit.

I picked up the rifle of a dead Marine and I went up the hill. I remember no more than a few yards of scarred hillside, blasted white with shellfire and hot to touch. I didn't worry about death any more. I had resigned from the human race. I only wanted to be as far forward as any man when my turn came. My fingers were smashed and burned, but I felt no pain. I crawled and scrambled forward and lay still, without any feeling toward any human thing. In the next hole was a rifleman. He peered at me through red and painful eyes. Then we both looked away. I didn't care about him. He didn't care about me. I thought he was a fool and he probably thought I was the same. We had both resigned from the human club.

321

As a fighting outfit, the First Marine Regiment was finished. We were no longer even human beings. I fired at anything that moved in front of me. Friend or foe. I had no friends. I just wanted to kill.

The history of the First Division says that we were relieved late in the afternoon of the sixth day. I don't remember coming down the hill, but I remember sitting by a roadside, in tears. I don't know why. I hadn't cried at all up on the hill. I suppose I was becoming a human again, after some time away from being one. When you come off the hard places, you crawl on your stomach and then move on your hands and knees and then go forward crouching and, at last, you walk erect, and then you feel like a man and it feels awful. Ever since Peleliu I have wondered if animals in danger feel things keenly. I didn't, the one time I turned into an animal. I didn't even feel the pain in my hands until after I was off the line.

THE DIVISION HISTORY says that by nightfall on the seventh day the First Marine Regiment reported their casualties—1749 men. That was out of 3500. It seemed as though there were more. The line companies were decimated.

We camped back near the first ridge and ate hot food and read our accumulated mail. Then we moved across the island near Purple Beach and camped in a swamp, and the first night I was on guard a Japanese infiltrater got close in on me and I stood up just as he threw a hand grenade. We saw each other at the same time and I was quicker, or scareder. He knocked me down with the concussion of the grenade, but not before I knocked him flat with the direct burst of a Tommy gun. I took one small piece in the lower part of my back. I would have used it to get off the island, but we were going anyway.

On a dark and rainy day, eighteen days after we landed, we went out through heavy, oily swells and under lowering skies to load onto LSTs and eventually a hospital transport, the *Tryon*. We had had a few days' rest, but some of us had trouble getting up the cargo nets and over the rail with what equipment we still carried. My fingers bothered me still. The back was nothing. I remember the big, thick wrists of the sailor who helped me over the rail, who had looked into our faces and seen what was plainly there. He wanted to be com-

322

forting. He said: "You gave it to 'em real good, boys. Good on ya'."

An F Company rifleman heaved himself over onto the deck, and for a moment, he lay there helpless like an overturned bug or turtle. Then he got his legs under himself and stood up and pain showed in his face. He said to the sailor: "No—no, we didn't give it to 'em good. We didn't give it to 'em at all. We got beat." He looked back toward the low-lying island and shook his head, as though he still couldn't believe what had happened there. "We won before. We'll win the next one. But this time we got beat, swabbie.

"And that's the truth of it."

Generals Ushijima and Cho
Commit Hara-Kiri

by a Japanese Soldier

The end at Okinawa, the last battle of the Pacific
War against Japan, came on June 22, 1945. The day
before that, Lieutenant General Mitsuru Ushijima,
commander of the Japanese defense on Okinawa, and
his fiery chief of staff, Lieutenant General Isamu Cho,
having accepted the fact of their defeat, prepared
themselves for suicide. A large ceremonial banquet
was prepared inside the seaside cave which Ushijima
had made his headquarters. The generals and their
staffs sat down to eat. Then they drank numerous farewell toasts. Finally, they arose to make the final gesture to the Emperor, a scene vividly described by a
Japanese prisoner.

Alas! The Stars of the Generals have fallen with the setting of the waning moon over Mabuni. . . . The pale moon shimmers bluish white over the waters of the southern sea, but on Hill 89 which juts abruptly from the reefs, the rocks and boulders are dyed crimson by the blood of the penetration unit which, with burning patriotism, rush the American positions for the last stand. The surrounding area displays a picture of concentrated fireworks; bursts of naval gunfire, flashes of mortar and artillery fire, to which is added the occasional chatter of machine guns. . . .

Gathered around their section chiefs, members of each section bow in veneration towards the eastern sky and the cheer of "long live the Emperor" echoes among the boulders. . . . The faces of all are flushed with deep emotion and tears fall upon ragged uniforms, soiled with the dirt and grime of battle. . . . Four o'clock, the final hour of hara-kiri; the Commanding General, dressed in full field uniform, and the Chief of Staff in a white kimono appeared. . . . The Chief of Staff says as he leaves the cave first, "Well, Commanding General Ushijima, as the way may be dark, I, Cho, will lead the way." The Commanding General replies, "Please do so, and I'll take along my fan since it is getting warm." Saying this he picked up his Okinawa-made Kuba fan and walked out quietly fanning himself. . . . The moon, which had been shining until now, sinks below the waves of the western sea. Dawn has not yet arrived and, at 0410, the generals appeared at the mouth of the cave. The American forces were only three meters away. Four meters away from the mouth of the cave a sheet of white cloth is placed on a quilt; this is the ritual place for the two generals to commit hara-kiri. The Commanding General and the Chief of Staff sit down on the quilt, bow in reverence toward the eastern sky, and Adjutant J respectfully presents the sword. Finally, the time for the honored rites of hara-kiri arrives. At this time several grenades were hurled near this solemn scene by the enemy troops, who observed movements taking place beneath them. A simultaneous shout and a flash of a sword, then another repeated shout and a flash, and both Generals had nobly accomplished their last duty to their Emperor. . . .

All is quiet after the cessation of gunfire and smoke; and the full moon is once again gleaming over the waves of the southern sea. Hill 89 of Mabuni will live in memory forever.

The Day the Bomb Fell on Hiroshima

by Michichiko Hachiya

On August 6, 1945, the American B–29 bomber *Enola Gay* dropped the world's first combat atomic bomb on the Japanese city of Hiroshima. Dr. Michichiko Hachiya, director of the Hiroshima Communications Hospital—which served postal, telephone and telegraph workers in the Hiroshima area—tells of the agonies suffered by himself and thousands of others during that dreadful day and the one that followed.

327

6 August 1945:

The hour was early; the morning still, warm and beautiful. Shimmering leaves, reflecting sunlight from a cloudless sky, made a pleasant contrast with shadows in my garden as I gazed absently through wide-flung doors opening to the south.

Clad in drawers and undershirt, I was sprawled on the living-room floor exhausted because I had just spent a sleepless night on duty as an air warden in my hospital.

Suddenly, a strong flash of light startled me—and then another. So well does one recall little things that I remember vividly how a stone lantern in the garden became brilliantly lit and I debated whether this light was caused by a magnesium flare or sparks from a passing trolley.

Garden shadows disappeared. The view where a moment before all had been so bright and sunny was now dark and hazy. Through swirling dust I could barely discern a wooden column that had supported one corner of my house. It was leaning crazily and the roof sagged dangerously.

Moving instinctively, I tried to escape, but rubble and fallen timbers barred the way. By picking my way cautiously I managed to reach the *roka* and stepped down into my garden. A profound weakness overcame me, so I stopped to regain my strength. To my surprise I discovered that I was completely naked. How odd! Where were my drawers and undershirt?

What had happened?

All over the right side of my body I was cut and bleeding. A large splinter was protruding from a mangled wound in my thigh, and something warm trickled into my mouth. My cheek was torn, I discovered as I felt it gingerly, with the lower lip laid wide open. Embedded in my neck was a sizable fragment of glass which I matter-of-factly dislodged, and with the detachment of one stunned and shocked I studied it and my blood-stained hand.

328

Where was my wife?

Suddenly thoroughly alarmed, I began to yell for her: "*Yaeko-san! Yaeko-san!* Where are you?"

Blood began to spurt. Had my carotid artery been cut? Would I bleed to death? Frightened and irrational, I called out again: "It's a five-hundred-ton bomb! *Yaeko-san,* where are you? A five-hundred-ton bomb has fallen!"

Yaeko-san, pale and frightened, her clothes torn and bloodstained, emerged from the ruins of our house holding her elbow. Seeing her, I was reassured. My own panic assuaged, I tried to reassure her.

"We'll be all right," I exclaimed. "Only let's get out of here as fast as we can."

She nodded, and I motioned for her to follow me.

The shortest path to the street lay through the house next door, so through the house we went—running, stumbling, falling, and then running again until in headlong flight we tripped over something and fell sprawling into the street. Getting to my feet, I discovered that I had tripped over a man's head.

"Excuse me! Excuse me, please!" I cried hysterically.

There was no answer. The man was dead. The head had belonged to a young officer whose body was crushed beneath a massive gate.

We stood in the street, uncertain and afraid, until a house across from us began to sway and then with a rending motion fell almost at our feet. Our own house began to sway, and in a minute it, too, collapsed in a cloud of dust. Other buildings caved in or toppled. Fires sprang up and, whipped by a vicious wind, began to spread.

It finally dawned on us that we could not stay there in the street, so we turned our steps toward the hospital. Our home was gone; we were wounded and needed treatment; and after all, it was my duty to be with my staff. This latter was an irrational thought—what good could I be to anyone, hurt as I was?

We started out, but after twenty or thirty steps I had to stop. My breath became short, my heart pounded, and my legs gave way under me. An overpowering thirst seized me and I begged Yaeko-san to find me some water. But there was no water to be found. After a little my strength returned

329

and we were able to go on.

I was still naked, and although I did not feel the least bit of shame, I was disturbed to realize that modesty had deserted me. On rounding a corner we came upon a soldier standing idly in the street. He had a towel draped across his shoulder, and I asked if he would give it to me to cover my nakedness. The soldier surrendered the towel quite willingly but said not a word. A little later I lost the towel, and Yaeko-san took off her apron and tied it around my loins.

Our progress toward the hospital was interminably slow, until finally, my legs, stiff from drying blood, refused to carry me farther. The strength, even the will, to go on deserted me, so I told my wife, who was almost as badly hurt as I, to go on alone. This she objected to, but there was no choice. She had to go ahead and try to find someone to come back for me.

Yaeko-san looked into my face for a moment, and then, without saying a word, turned away and began running toward the hospital. Once, she looked back and waved and in a moment she was swallowed up in the gloom. It was quite dark now, and with my wife gone, a feeling of dreadful loneliness overcame me.

I must have gone out of my head lying there in the road because the next thing I recall was discovering that the clot on my thigh had been dislodged and blood was again spurting from the wound. I pressed my hand to the bleeding area and after a while the bleeding stopped and I felt better.

Could I go on?

I tried. It was all a nightmare—my wounds, the darkness, the road ahead. My movements were ever so slow; only my mind was running at top speed.

In time I came to an open space where the houses had been removed to make a fire lane. Through the dim light I could make out ahead of me the hazy outlines of the Communications Bureau's big concrete building, and beyond it the hospital. My spirits rose because I knew that now someone would find me; and if I should die, at least my body would be found.

I paused to rest. Gradually things around me came into focus. There were the shadowy forms of people, some of whom looked like walking ghosts. Others moved as though in pain, like scarecrows, their arms held out from their bodies with forearms and hands dangling. These people puzzled me until I suddenly realized that they had been burned and were holding their arms out to prevent the painful friction of raw surfaces rubbing together. A naked woman carrying a naked baby came into view. I averted my gaze. Perhaps they had been in the bath. But then I saw a naked man, and it occurred to me that, like myself, some strange thing had deprived them of their clothes. An old woman lay near me with an expression of suffering on her face; but she made no sound. Indeed, one thing was common to everyone I saw—complete silence.

All who could were moving in the direction of the hospital. I joined in the dismal parade when my strength was somewhat recovered, and at last reached the gates of the Communication Bureau.

Familiar surroundings, familiar faces. There was Mr. Iguchi and Mr. Yoshihiro and my old friend, Mr. Sera, the head of the business office. They hastened to give me a hand, their expressions of pleasure changing to alarm when they saw that I was hurt. I was too happy to see them to share their concern.

No time was lost over greetings. They eased me onto a stretcher and carried me into the Communications Building, ignoring my protests that I could walk. Later, I learned that the hospital was so overrun that the Communications Bureau had to be used as an emergency hospital. The rooms and corridors were crowded with people, many of whom I recognized as neighbors. To me it seemed that the whole community was there.

My friends passed me through an open window into a janitor's room recently converted to an emergency first-aid station. The room was a shambles; fallen plaster, broken furniture, and debris littered the floor; the walls were cracked; and a heavy steel window casement was twisted and almost wrenched from its seating. What a place to dress the wounds of the injured.

To my great surprise who should appear but my private nurse, Miss Kado, and Mr. Mizoguchi, and old Mrs. Saeki. Miss Kado set about examining my wounds without speaking a word. No one spoke. I asked for a shirt and pajamas. They got them for me, but still no one spoke. Why

331

was everyone so quiet?

Miss Kado finished the examination, and in a moment it felt as if my chest was on fire. She had begun to paint my wounds with iodine and no amount of entreaty would make her stop. With no alternative but to endure the iodine, I tried to divert myself by looking out the window.

The hospital lay directly opposite with part of the roof and the third floor sunroom in plain view, and as I looked up, I witnessed a sight which made me forget my smarting wounds. Smoke was pouring out of the sunroom windows. The hospital was afire!

"Fire!" I shouted. "Fire! Fire! The hospital is on fire!"

My friends looked up. It was true. The hospital *was* on fire.

The alarm was given and from all sides people took up the cry. The high-pitched voice of Mr. Sera, the business officer, rose above the others, and it seemed as if his was the first voice I had heard that day. The uncanny stillness was broken. Our little world was now in pandemonium.

I remember that Dr. Sasada, chief of the Pediatric Service, came in and tried to reassure me, but I could scarcely hear him above the din. I heard Dr. Hinoi's voice and then Dr. Koyama's. Both were shouting orders to evacuate the hospital and with such vigor that it sounded as though the sheer strength of their voices could hasten those who were slow to obey.

The sky became bright as flames from the hospital mounted. Soon the Bureau was threatened and Mr. Sera gave the order to evacuate. My stretcher was moved into a rear garden and placed beneath an old cherry tree. Other patients limped into the garden or were carried until soon the entire area became so crowded that only the very ill had room to lie down. No one talked, and the ominous silence was relieved only by a subdued rustle among so many people, restless, in pain, anxious, and afraid, waiting for something else to happen.

The sky filled with black smoke and glowing sparks. Flames rose and the heat set currents of air in motion. Updrafts became so violent that sheets of zinc roofing were hurled aloft and released, humming and twirling, in erratic flight. Pieces of flaming wood soared and fell like fiery swallows. While I was trying to beat out the flames, a hot ember seared my ankle. It was all I could do to keep from being burned alive.

The Bureau started to burn, and window after window became a square of flame until the whole structure was converted into a crackling, hissing inferno.

Scorching winds howled around us, whipping dust and ashes into our eyes and up our noses. Our mouths became dry, our throats raw and sore from the biting smoke pulled into our lungs. Coughing was uncontrollable. We would have moved back, but a group of wooden barracks behind us caught fire and began to burn like tinder.

The heat finally became too intense to endure, and we were left no choice but to abandon the garden. Those who could, fled; those who could not, perished. Had it not been for my devoted friends, I would have died, but again, they came to the rescue and carried my stretcher to the main gate on the other side of the Bureau.

Here, a small group of people were already clustered, and here I found my wife. Dr. Sasada and Miss Kado joined us.

Fires sprang up on every side as violent winds fanned flames from one building to another. Soon, we were surrounded. The ground we held in front of the Communications Bureau became an oasis in a desert of fire. As the flames came closer the heat became more intense, and if someone in our group had not had the presence of mind to drench us with water from a fire hose, I doubt if anyone could have survived.

Hot as it was, I began to shiver. The drenching was too much. My heart pounded; things began to whirl until all before me blurred.

"*Kurushii*," I murmured weakly. "I am done."

THE SOUND OF VOICES reached my ears as though from a great distance and finally became louder as if close at hand. I opened my eyes; Dr. Sasada was feeling my pulse. What had happened? Miss Kado gave me an injection. My strength gradually returned. I must have fainted.

Huge raindrops began to fall. Some thought a thunderstorm was beginning and would extinguish the fires. But these drops were capricious. A few fell and then a few more and that was all the rain we saw.

The first floor of the Bureau was now ablaze and flames were spreading rapidly towards our little oasis by the gate. Right then, I could hardly understand the situation, much less do anything about it.

An iron window frame, loosened by fire, crashed to the ground behind us. A ball of fire whizzed by me, setting my clothes ablaze. They drenched me with water again. From then on I am confused as to what happened.

I do remember Dr. Hinoi because of the pain, the pain I felt when he jerked me to my feet. I remember being moved or rather dragged, and my whole spirit rebelling against the torment I was made to endure.

My next memory is of an open area. The fires must have receded. I was alive. My friends had somehow managed to rescue me again.

A head popped out of an air-raid dugout, and I heard the unmistakable voice of old Mrs. Saeki: "Cheer up, doctor! Everything will be all right. The north side is burnt out. We have nothing further to fear from the fire."

I might have been her son, the way the old lady calmed and reassured me. And indeed, she was right. The entire northern side of the city was completely burned. The sky was still dark, but whether it was evening or midday I could not tell. It might even have been the next day. Time had no meaning. What I had experienced might have been crowded into a moment or been endured through the monotony of eternity.

Smoke was still rising from the second floor of the hospital, but the fire had stopped. There was nothing left to burn, I thought; but later I learned that the first floor of the hospital had escaped destruction largely through the courageous efforts of Dr. Koyama and Dr. Hinoi.

The streets were deserted except for the dead. Some looked as if they had been frozen by death while in the full action of flight; others lay sprawled as though some giant had flung them to their death from a great height.

Hiroshima was no longer a city, but a burnt-over prairie. To the east and to the west everything was flattened. The distant mountains seemed nearer than I could ever remember. The hills of Ushita and the woods of Nigitsu loomed out of the haze and smoke like the nose and eyes on a face. How small Hiroshima was with its houses gone.

The wind changed and the sky again darkened with smoke.

Suddenly, I heard someone shout: "Planes! Enemy planes!"

Could that be possible after what had already happened? What was there left to bomb? My thoughts were interrupted by the sound of a familiar name.

A nurse calling Dr. Katsube.

"It is Dr. Katsube! It's him!" shouted old Mrs. Saeki, a happy ring to her voice. "Dr. Katsube has come!"

It was Dr. Katsube, our head surgeon, but he seemed completely unaware of us as he hurried past, making a straight line for the hospital. Enemy planes were forgotten, so great was our happiness that Dr. Katsube had been spared to return to us.

Before I could protest, my friends were carrying me into the hospital. The distance was only a hundred meters, but it was enough to cause my heart to pound and make me sick and faint.

I recall the hard table and the pain when my face and lip were sutured, but I have no recollection of the forty or more other wounds Dr. Katsube closed before night.

They removed me to an adjoining room, and I remember feeling relaxed and sleepy. The sun had gone down, leaving a dark red sky. The red flames of the burning city had scorched the heavens. I gazed at the sky until sleep overtook me.

7 *August 1945*

I must have slept soundly because when I opened my eyes a piercing hot sun was shining in on me. There were no shutters or curtains to lessen the glare—and for that matter no windows. The groans of patients assaulted my ears. Everything was in a turmoil.

Instruments, window frames, and debris littered the floor. The walls and ceilings were scarred and picked as though someone had sprinkled sesame seeds over their surfaces. Most of the marks had been made by slivers of flying glass but the larger scars had been caused by hurtling instruments and pieces of window casements.

Near a window an instrument cabinet was overturned.

335

The head piece had been knocked off the ear, nose, and throat examining chair, and a broken sunlamp was overturned across the seat. I saw nothing that was not broken or in disorder.

Dr. Sasada, who had looked after me yesterday, lay on my left. I had thought he escaped injury, but now I could see that he was badly burned. His arms and hands were bandaged and his childish face so obscured by swelling that I would not have recognized him had it not been for his voice.

My wife lay to my right. Her face was covered with a white ointment, giving her a ghostly appearance. Her right arm was in a sling.

Miss Kado, only slightly wounded, was between me and my wife. She had nursed all of us throughout the night.

My wife, seeing that I was awake, turned and said: "Last night, you seemed to be suffering."

"Yes," said Miss Kado, chiming in. "I don't know how many times I examined your breathing."

I recognized Dr. Fujii's wife sitting motionless on a bench near the wall. Her face bore an expression of anguish and despair. Turning to Miss Kado, I asked what the matter was, and she replied: "Mrs. Fujii was not hurt very much, but her baby was. It died during the night."

"Where is Dr. Fujii?" I inquired.

"Their older daughter is lost," she answered. "He's been out all night looking for her and hasn't returned."

Dr. Koyama came in to inquire how we were. The sight of him, with his head bandaged and an arm in a sling, brought tears to my eyes. He had worked all night and was even now thinking of others before himself.

Dr. Katsube, our surgeon, and Miss Takao, a surgical nurse, were with Dr. Koyama, who was now deputy director. They all looked tired and haggard, and their white clothes were dirty and blood-stained. I learned that Mr. Iguchi, our driver, had contrived to rig up an emergency operating light from a car battery and headlight with which they had managed to operate until the light went out just before day.

Dr. Koyama, observing my concern, remarked: "Doctor, everything is all right."

Dr. Katsube looked me over and after feeling my pulse, said: "You received many wounds, but they all missed vital spots."

He then described them and told me how they had been treated. I was surprised to learn that my shoulder had been severely cut but relieved at his optimism for my recovery.

"How many patients are in the hospital?" I asked Dr. Koyama.

"About a hundred and fifty," he replied. "Quite a few have died, but there are still so many that there is no place to put one's foot down. They are packed in everywhere, even the toilets."

Nodding, Dr. Katsube added: "There are about a half dozen beneath the stairway, and about fifty in the front garden of the hospital."

They discussed methods for restoring order, at least to the extent of making the corridors passable.

In the space of one night patients had become packed, like the rice in *sushi*, into every nook and cranny of the hospital. The majority were badly burned, a few severely injured. All were critically ill. Many had been near the heart of the city and in their efforts to flee managed to get only as far as the Communications Hospital before their strength failed. Others, from nearer by, came deliberately to seek treatment or because this building, standing alone where all else was destroyed, represented shelter and a place of refuge. They came as an avalanche and overran the hospital.

There was no friend or relative to minister to their needs, no one to prepare their food. Everything was in disorder. And to make matters worse was the vomiting and diarrhea. Patients who could not walk urinated and defecated where they lay. Those who could walk would feel their way to the exits and relieve themselves there. Persons entering or leaving the hospital could not avoid stepping in the filth, so closely was it spread. The front entrance became covered with feces overnight, and nothing could be done for there were no bed pans and, even if there had been, no one to carry them to the patients.

Disposing of the dead was a minor problem, but to clean the rooms and corridors of urine, feces, and vomitus was impossible.

The people who were burned suffered most because as their skin peeled away, glistening raw wounds were exposed to the heat and filth. This was the environment patients had to live in. It made one's hair stand on end, but there was no way to help the situation.

This was the pattern conversation took as I lay there and listened. It was inconceivable.

"When can I get up?" I asked Dr. Katsube. "Perhaps I can do something to help."

"Not until your sutures are out," he answered. "And that won't be for at least a week."

With that to think about they left me.

I was not left long with my thoughts. One after another the staff came in to express their concern over my injuries and to wish me a speedy recovery. Some of my visitors embarrassed me, for they appeared to be as badly injured as myself. Had it been possible, I would have concealed my whereabouts.

Dr. Nishimura, President of the Okayama Medical Association, came all the way from my native city, ninety miles away, to see me. He had been crew captain of the boat team when we were classmates in Medical School. As soon as he saw me, tears welled up in his eyes. He looked at me a moment, and then exclaimed: "I say, old fellow, you are alive! What a pleasant surprise. How are you getting along?"

Without waiting for an answer, he continued: "Last night, we heard that Hiroshima had been attacked by a new weapon. The damage was slight, they told us, but in order to see for myself and to lend a hand if extra physicians were needed, I secured a truck and came on down. What a frightful mess greeted us when we arrived. Are you sure *you* are all right?"

And again, without stopping for me to reply, he went on to tell about the heartbreaking things he witnessed from the truck as he entered the city. These were the first details any of us had heard, so we listened intently.

While he talked, all I could think of was the fear and uncertainty that must be preying on my old mother who lived in the country near Okayama. When he had finished, I asked Dr. Nishimura if he would get word to my mother, and also to a sister who lived in Okayama, that Yaeko-san and I were safe. He assured me that he would, and before leaving he also promised to organize a team of doctors and nurses to come down and help as soon as he could get them together.

Dr. Tabuchi, an old friend from Ushita, came in. His face and hands had been burned, though not badly, and after an exchange of greetings, I asked if he knew what had happened.

"I was in the back yard pruning some trees when it exploded," he answered. "The first thing I knew, there was a blinding white flash of light, and a wave of intense heat struck my cheek. This was odd, I thought, when in the next instant there was a tremendous blast.

"The force of it knocked me clean over," he continued, "but fortunately, it didn't hurt me; and my wife wasn't hurt either. But you should have seen our house! It didn't topple over, it just inclined. I have never seen such a mess. Inside and out everything was simply ruined. Even so, we are happy to be alive, and what's more, Ryoji, our son, survived. I didn't tell you that he had gone into the city on business that morning. About midnight, after we had given up all hope that he could possibly survive in the dreadful fire that followed the blast, he came home. Listen!" he continued, "why don't you come on home with me? My house is certainly nothing to look at now, but it is better than here."

It was impossible for me to accept his kind offer, and I tried to decline in a way that would not hurt his feelings.

"Dr. Tabuchi," I replied, "we are all grateful for your kind offer, but Dr. Katsube has just warned me that I must lie perfectly still until my wounds are healed."

Dr. Tabuchi accepted my explanation with some reluctance, and after a pause he made ready to go.

"Don't go," I said. "Please tell us more of what occurred yesterday."

"It was a horrible sight," said Dr. Tabuchi. "Hundreds of injured people who were trying to escape to the hills passed our house. The sight of them was almost unbearable. Their faces and hands were burnt and swollen; and great sheets of skin had peeled away from their tissues to hang down like rags on a scarecrow. They moved like a line of ants. All through the night, they went past our house, but this morning they had stopped. I found them lying on both sides of the road so thick that it was impossible to pass without stepping on them."

I lay with my eyes shut while Dr. Tabuchi was talking,

339

picturing in my mind the horror he was describing. I neither saw nor heard Mr. Katsutani when he came in. It was not until I heard someone sobbing that my attention was attracted, and I recognized my old friend. I had known Mr. Katsutani for many years and knew him to be an emotional person, but even so, to see him break down made tears come to my eyes. He had come all the way from Jigozen to look for me, and now that he had found me, emotion overcame him.

He turned to Dr. Sasada and said brokenly: "Yesterday, it was impossible to enter Hiroshima, else I would have come. Even today fires are still burning in some places. You should see how the city has changed. When I reached the Misasa Bridge this morning, everything before me was gone, even the castle. These buildings here are the only ones left anywhere around. The Communications Bureau seemed to loom right in front of me long before I got anywhere near here."

Mr. Katsutani paused for a moment to catch his breath and went on: "I *really* walked along the railroad tracks to get here, but even they were littered with electric wires and broken railway cars, and the dead and wounded lay everywhere. When I reached the bridge, I saw a dreadful thing. It was unbelievable. There was a man, stone dead, sitting on his bicycle as it leaned against the bridge railing. It is hard to believe that such a thing could happen!"

He repeated himself two or three times as if to convince himself that what he said was true and then continued: "It seems that most of the dead people were either on the bridge or beneath it. You could tell that many had gone down to the river to get a drink of water and had died where they lay. I saw a few live people still in the water, knocking against the dead as they floated down the river. There must have been hundreds and thousands who fled to the river to escape the fire and then drowned.

"The sight of the soldiers, though, was more dreadful than the dead people floating down the river. I came onto I don't know how many, burned from the hips up; and where the skin had peeled, their flesh was wet and mushy. They must have been wearing their military caps because the black hair on top of their heads was not burned. It made them look like they were wearing black lacquer bowls.

"And they had no faces! Their eyes, noses and mouths had been burned away, and it looked like their ears had melted off. It was hard to tell front from back. One soldier, whose features had been destroyed and was left with his white teeth sticking out, asked me for some water, but I didn't have any. I clasped my hands and prayed for him. He didn't say anything more. His plea for water must have been his last words. The way they were burned, I wonder if they didn't have their coats off when the bomb exploded."

It seemed to give Mr. Katsutani some relief to pour out his terrifying experiences on us; and there was no one who would have stopped him, so fascinating was his tale of horror. While he was talking, several people came in and stayed to listen. Somebody asked him what he was doing when the explosion occurred.

"I had just finished breakfast," he replied, "and was getting ready to light a cigarette, when all of a sudden I saw a white flash. In a moment there was a tremendous blast. Not stopping to think, I let out a yell and jumped into an air-raid dugout. In a moment there was such a blast as I have never heard before. It was terrific! I jumped out of the dugout and pushed my wife into it. Realizing something terrible must have happened in Hiroshima, I climbed up onto the roof of my storehouse to have a look."

Mr. Katsutani became more intense and, gesticulating wildly, went on: "Towards Hiroshima, I saw a big black cloud go billowing up, like a puffy summer cloud. Knowing for sure then that something terrible had happened in the city, I jumped down from my storehouse and ran as fast as I could to the military post at Hatsukaichi. I ran up to the officer in charge and told him what I had seen and begged him to send somebody to help in Hiroshima. But he didn't even take me seriously. He looked at me for a moment with a threatening expression, and then do you know what he said? He said, 'There isn't much to worry about. One or two bombs won't hurt Hiroshima.' There was no use talking to that fool!

"I was the ranking officer in the local branch of the Ex-officer's Association, but even I didn't know what to do because that day the villagers under my command had been sent off to Miyajima for labor service. I looked all around to find someone to help me make a rescue squad, but I couldn't find anybody. While I was still looking for help, wounded people began to stream into the village. I asked them what had happened, but all they could tell me was that Hiroshima had been destroyed and everybody was leaving the city. With that I got on my bicycle and rode as fast as I could towards Itsukaichi. By the time I got there, the road was jammed with people, and so was every path and byway.

"Again I tried to find out what had happened, but nobody could give me a clear answer. When I asked these people where they had come from, they would point towards Hiroshima and say, 'This way.' And when I asked where they were going, they would point toward Miyajima and say, 'That way.' Everybody said the same thing.

"I saw no badly wounded or burned people around Itsukaichi, but when I reached Kusatsu, nearly everybody was badly hurt. The nearer I got to Hiroshima the more I saw until by the time I had reached Koi, they were all so badly injured, I could not bear to look into their faces. They smelled like burning hair."

Mr. Katsutani paused for a moment to take a deep breath and then continued: "The area around Koi station was not burned, but the station and the houses nearby were badly damaged. Every square inch of the station platform was packed with wounded people. Some were standing; others lying down. They were all pleading for water. Now and then you could hear a child calling for its mother. It was a living hell, I tell you. It was a living hell!

"Today it was the same way.

"Did Dr. Hanaoka come to the hospital yesterday? I saw him cross the streetcar trestle at Koi and head in this direction, but I can't believe that he could have made his way through that fire."

"No, we haven't seen him," someone answered.

Mr. Katsutani nodded reflectively and went on: "I left Koi station and went over to the Koi primary school. By then, the school had been turned into an emergency hospital and was already crowded with desperately injured people. Even the playground was packed with the dead and dying. They looked like so many codfish spread out for drying. What a pitiful sight it was to see them lying there in the hot sun. Even I could tell they were all going to die.

342

"Towards evening, I was making my way back to the highway when I ran into my sister. My sister, whose home had been in Tokaichi, must surely have been killed. But here she was—alive! She was so happy, she couldn't utter a word! All she could do was cry. If ever anyone shed tears of joy, she did. Some kind people lent me a hand in making a stretcher and helped carry her back to my home in Jigozen near Miyajima Guchi. Even my little village, as far removed as it was from Hiroshima, had become a living hell. Every shrine, every temple was packed and jammed with wounded people."

Mr. Katsutani had said all he had in him to say. He left our room, but instead of going home, he stayed to help with the wounded.

The stories of Dr. Nishimura, Dr. Tabuchi, and Mr. Katsutani left no doubt in my mind about the destruction of Hiroshima. I had seen enough to know that the damage was heavy, but what they had told me was unbelievable.

When I thought of the injured, lying in the sun begging for water, I felt as though I were committing a sin by being where I was. I no longer felt quite so sorry for those of our patients who were obliged to lie on the hard concrete floors in the toilets.

My thoughts turned to myself.

"If only I hadn't been hurt," I mused, "I could be doing something instead of lying here as a patient, requiring the attention of my comrades. Wounded and helpless. What a plight, when all about me there is so much to do!"

Fortunately, my dismal thoughts were interrupted. Who should make an appearance but Dr. Hanaoka, our internist, whom Mr. Katsutani had just told us was last seen at Hatsukaichi.

"Dr. Hachiya, you don't know how happy I am to see you!" exclaimed Dr. Hanaoka. "After seeing what has happened to Hiroshima, it's a miracle anyone survived."

"We have been worrying about you, Dr. Hanaoka," I replied, "because Mr. Katsutani told us only a few minutes ago that he saw you disappear in the direction of Hiroshima while he was at the Koi station yesterday. Where have you been, and how did you get here?"

"Now that I'm here, I wonder myself," said Dr. Hanaoka.

343

"Let me tell you, if I can, what happened. Somebody told me that a special, new bomb was dropped near the Gokoku Shrine. If what I was told is true, then that bomb must have had terrific power, for from the Gokoku Shrine clean out to the Red Cross Hospital everything is completely destroyed. The Red Cross Hospital, though badly damaged, was spared, and beyond, going towards Ujina the damage is slight.

"I stopped by the Red Cross Hospital on my way here. It is swamped with patients, and outside the dead and dying are lined up on either side of the street as far east as the Miyuki Bridge.

"Between the Red Cross Hospital and the center of the city I saw nothing that wasn't burned to a crisp. Streetcars were standing at Kawaya-cho and Kamiya-cho and inside were dozens of bodies, blackened beyond recognition. I saw fire reservoirs filled to the brim with dead people who looked as though they had been boiled alive. In one reservoir I saw a man, horribly burned, crouching beside another man who was dead. He was drinking blood-stained water out of the reservoir. Even if I had tried to stop him, it wouldn't have done any good; he was completely out of his head. In one reservoir there were so many dead people there wasn't enough room for them to fall over. They must have died sitting in the water.

"Even the swimming pool at the Prefectural First Middle School is filled with dead people. They must have suffocated while they sat in the water trying to escape the fire because they didn't appear to be burned."

Dr. Hanaoka cleared his throat, and after a moment continued: "Dr. Hachiya, that pool wasn't big enough to accommodate everybody who tried to get in it. You could tell that by looking around the sides. I don't know how many were caught by death with their heads hanging over the edge. In one pool I saw some people who were still alive, sitting in the water with dead all around them. They were too weak to get out. People were trying to help them, but I am sure they must have died. I apologize for telling you these things, but they are true. I don't see how anyone got out alive."

Dr. Hanaoka paused, and I could see he was anxious to get to work. With what there was to do, it would have been criminal to detain him.

Gradually, what these visitors were telling me began to fit into a pattern. A few comments from this one, a few remarks from another, were beginning to give me a picture of what Hiroshima was like.

Dr. Hanaoka had barely left when Dr. Akiyama, head of obstetrics and gynecology, came in. He was unhurt but looked tired and worn.

"Sit down and rest a few minutes," I said. "You must have been through a great deal. Where were you when the bombing occurred?"

"I was just leaving my home when it went off," said Dr. Akiyama in a tremulous voice. "A blinding flash, a tremendous explosion, and over I went on my back. And then a big black cloud, such as you see in the summer before a storm, began to rise above Hiroshima. '*Yarareta*,' I shouted; and that was it. What a hodgepodge was made of my house. The ceilings, the walls, the sliding doors—everything—ruined beyond repair.

"Almost at once, injured people began to line up before my gate, and from then until a little while ago, I stayed and treated them. But my supplies are all gone, and there is nothing left to treat them with. Twenty or thirty people are still lying in the house and there is nobody to take care of them. There is nothing anybody can do, unless I find some more supplies."

Dr. Akiyama, ordinarily easygoing and happy, had the look of a man distraught. Dr. Koyama came in while Dr. Akiyama was talking and so heard most of what he had been saying.

"Knowing you, I can imagine what you have gone through," said Dr. Koyama.

"I don't know," sighed Dr. Akiyama. "Today it's the same as it was yesterday. There is no end to that stream of miserable souls who stop at my house to ask for help. They are trying to reach Kobe, but they will never get there. And there is nothing I can do; nothing anybody can do."

Since Dr. Akiyama's home was in Nagatsuka, I got a general idea of what that suburb was like. The problem there was the same as in the Koi area. I could picture in my mind the wounded people walking in silence, like lost spirits, and answering, when questioned, that they had come "this way" and were going "that way." I could see them begging for water, hear their moaning, and see them dying. I might have been there myself, so vividly had my friends recounted to me what they had seen.

It was reported that none of the patients had any appetite and that one by one they were beginning to vomit and have diarrhea. Did the new weapon I had heard about throw off a poison gas or perhaps some deadly germ? I asked Dr. Hanaoka to confirm if he could the report of vomiting and diarrhea and to find out if any of the patients looked as if they might have an infectious disease. He inquired and brought word that there were many who not only had diarrhea but bloody stools and that some had had as many as forty to fifty stools during the previous night. This convinced me that we were dealing with bacillary dysentery and had no choice but to isolate those who were infected.

Dr. Koyama, as deputy director, was given the responsibility of setting up an isolation ward. He chose a site on the grounds beyond the south side of the hospital and with the help of some soldiers who happened along he managed to construct what amounted to a crude outdoor pavilion. What we were trying to do probably was not worth much, but it helped our morale to think we were doing something.

Dr. Katsube and his staff had an impossible task. There was scarcely a patient who was not in need of urgent surgical care. The doctors and nurses were all busy helping him. Even the clerical staff and janitors, and those among the patients who could so much as get about, were organized and instructed to help. If progress was made, it was hard to see. How Dr. Katsube did what he did was a miracle.

The corridors were cleared enough to be passable, but in a little while they were as crowded as before. One difficulty was the influx of people looking for friends and relatives.

Parents, half crazy with grief, searched for their children. Husbands looked for their wives, and children for their parents. One poor woman, insane with anxiety, walked aimlessly here and there through the hospital calling her child's name. It was dreadfully upsetting to the patients, but no one had the heart to stop her. Another woman stood at the entrance, shouting mournfully for someone she thought was inside. She, too, upset us.

Not a few came in from the country to look for friends

or relatives. They would wander among the patients and peer rudely into every face, until finally their behavior became so intolerable that we had to refuse them entrance to the hospital.

A new noise reached us from outside. On inquiry, I was told that Dr. Koyama had procured a company of soldiers to clean out the fire-damaged Communications Bureau, so that it could be put in use again as an annex to the hospital.

The pharmacy came to life. Our meager supply of drugs was sorted and prepared for use under the watchful supervision of Dr. Hinoi and Mr. Mizoguchi.

A little order was appearing; something positive was being done. Perhaps in time we could get control of the situation.

Mr. Sera, the business manager, reported. He told me that sixteen patients had died during the night and that he had shrouded their bodies in white blankets and deposited them at the side entrance to the hospital.

"Can we spare those blankets at a time like this?" I thought to myself.

I was reluctant to object openly to what Mr. Sera had done because his action had been prompted by his sense of propriety and respect for the dead. When I discovered, however, that the army detail, dispatched to remove the dead, had thrown the bodies, blankets and all, onto the platform of a truck without any ceremony whatsoever, I seized on this indignity to suggest that our blankets be saved. The living needed the blankets more than the dead.

Patients continued to come from all directions, and since we were not far removed from the center of the explosion, those who came were in a critical condition.

Their behavior was remarkable. Even though the ones in the hospital fared little better than those on the outside, they were grateful for a pallet in the most crowded ward. It seemed to satisfy them if they could get so much as a glimpse of a white-robed doctor or nurse. A kind word was enough to set them crying. For the most trivial service they would clasp their hands and pray for you. All were sufferers together and were confident that the doctors and nurses would do their best for them. Later, word came that this hospital was considered a good place to be in. The remark pleased us, but we were never able to feel that we had done as much as we should.

Earlier in the day Mr. Imachi and those who worked with him in the kitchen managed to prepare some rice gruel which they brought in by the bucketful and dished out with big wooden spoons. For me, this simple gruel made the one bright spot in the day. It was served again that afternoon, and the mouthful I had, and the grains of rice that remained on my tongue, made me feel that I was going to get well. But there were many who were too weak or too sick to eat. In time, the weakness of hunger added to their misery.

Night approached and still the only beds were straw mats laid over the concrete floor. Wounds were becoming more painful, and there were not enough drugs to make them easy. Fevers rose and the patients became thirsty, but there was no one to bring cool water to quench the thirst.

Dr. Harada, one of our pharmacists, was brought into the hospital severely burned, and right after him, old Mrs. Saeki's son in the same condition. Miss Hinada, one of our nurses, had to be confined because of a severe diarrhea that had begun earlier in the day. Since there was no one to nurse her, her mother, despite being seriously burned, was trying to do the job.

Mr. Mizoguchi came in: "Dr. Hachiya, I must tell you that Miss Hinada and her mother have become worse. It doesn't look like either of them will live through the night, and old Mrs. Saeki's son is losing consciousness."

All day I had listened to visitors telling me about the destruction of Hiroshima and the scenes of horror they had witnessed. I had seen my friends wounded, their families separated, their homes destroyed. I was aware of the problems our staff had to face, and I knew how bravely they struggled against superhuman odds. I knew what the patients had to endure and the trust they put in the doctors and nurses, who, could they know the truth, were as helpless as themselves.

By degrees my capacity to comprehend the magnitude of their sorrow, to share with them the pain, frustration, and horror became so dulled that I found myself accepting whatever was told me with equanimity and a detachment I would have never believed possible. In two days I had become at home in this environment of chaos and despair.

I felt lonely, but it was an animal loneliness. I became part of the darkness of the night. There were no radios, no electric lights, not even a candle. The only light that came to me was reflected in flickering shadows made by the burning city. The only sounds were the groans and sobs of the patients. Now and then a patient in delirium would call for his mother, or the voice of one in pain would breathe out the word *eraiyo*—"the pain is unbearable; I cannot endure it!"

What kind of a bomb was it that had destroyed Hiroshima? What had my visitors told me earlier? Whatever it was, it did not make sense.

There could not have been more than a few planes. Even *my* memory would agree to that. Before the air-raid alarm there was the metallic sound of one plane and no more. Otherwise why did the alarm stop? Why was there no further alarm during the five or six minutes before the explosion occurred?

Reason as I would, I could not make the ends meet when I considered the destruction that followed. Perhaps it *was* a new weapon! More than one of my visitors spoke vaguely of a "new bomb," a "secret weapon," a "special bomb," and someone even said that the bomb was suspended from two parachutes when it burst! Whatever it was, it was beyond my comprehension. Damage of this order could have no explanation! All we had were stories no more substantial than the clouds from which we had reached to snatch them.

One thing was certain—Hiroshima was destroyed; and with it the army that had been quartered in Hiroshima. Gone were headquarters, gone the command post of the Second General Army and the Military School for young people, the General Headquarters for the Western Command, the Corps of Engineers, and the Army Hospital. Gone was the hope of Japan! The war was lost! No more help would come from the gods!

American forces would soon be landing; and when they landed, there would be street fighting; and our hospital would become a place of attack and defense. Had I not heard earlier that soldiers were coming to set up headquarters in the Communications Bureau? Would we be turned out?

Were there no answers?

Dr. Sasada, Miss Kado, and my wife were asleep. That was good, but there was no sleep for me.

I heard footsteps, and a man appeared at the door, outlined in the flickering darkness. His elbows were out and his hands down, like the burned people I had seen on my way to the hospital. As he came nearer, I could see his face—or what had been his face because this face had been melted away by the fire. The man was blind and had lost his way.

"You are in the wrong room!" I shouted, suddenly stricken with terror.

The poor fellow turned and shuffled back into the night. I was ashamed for having behaved as I did, but I was frightened. Now more awake than ever, every nerve taut, I could find no sleep.

To the east there was a perceptible lightening of the sky.

My shouting must have wakened my wife because she got up and left the room, I suppose to find the toilet. Before long she was back.

"What is the matter, Yaeko-san?" I asked, sensing she was upset.

"*O-tōsan,* the hall was so full of patients that I could find nowhere to walk without disturbing someone," she answered, trying to suppress her agitation. "I had to excuse myself every step I took. Oh! it was terrible. Finally, I stepped on somebody's foot, and when I asked to be excused, there was no answer. I looked down; and do you know what I had done?"

"What?" I asked.

"I had stepped on a dead man's foot," she said, and with a shudder moved nearer.

happens to careful planning during a retreat.

Two soldiers already were carrying the wounded man. Another man staggered along beside them. At the first opportunity Clarke used his first-aid kit to bind the man's leg wounds, although his own shoulder still had not been treated.

This was sand soil, very loose, and it was difficult for two men to carry another between them. I said, "Hell, get this man up on my shoulders. I can carry him more easily that way by myself."

But Dean is always forgetting how old he is. That one-man carry didn't last long. The soldier was too heavy for me, and I was almost falling on my face. We went back to the two-man carry, and even then it seemed as if my turn came around every five minutes.

It was pitch-dark, and we were trying to move with as little noise as possible, to avoid stirring up North Korean patrols. The main group ahead kept moving too fast, away from us, simply because they had no way of telling that we weren't right behind them. The man we were carrying became more or less delirious; he drank all the available water and then called for more. We only hoped we knew where the party ahead was going; we kept struggling to catch up, but we had to stop for rest very often.

During one of the rest stops I thought I heard water running, just off the ridge to one side—I was sure I heard it. I started off in that direction, and the next thing I knew I was running down a slope so steep that I could not stop.

I plunged forward and fell.

A STATEMENT BY Lieutenant Clarke about these events declared, in part: "About twelve, midnight, the general told me he was going down [the hillside] for water. I wouldn't let him and told him that we had seen North Koreans (by presumption) tracking us to the base of the hill, and we could assume they were still there. Also told him that there probably was a stream on the other side of the hill.

"The next day—1:15 A.M.—while leading the patrol, I found no one was following me, and no noise to the rear. So I returned to find five men asleep on the ground. I called for the general, and one of the men answered that he had gone for water. As I figured the round trip could be made in an

The Ordeal of General Dean

by William F. Dean

On June 25, 1950, the armies of Communist North Korea crossed the 38th Parallel and invaded South Korea. Four days later they entered Seoul and began a lightning drive to conquer the entire peninsula before the United Nations, led by the United States, could intervene. In the following month the 24th Infantry Division under Major General William F. Dean was rushed to Korea from Japan and ordered to hold off the Communists while reinforcements and supplies were brought into Korea behind them. The last battle in that desperate delaying action was fought at Taejon, where Dean's men were defeated and scattered. The general himself ran a gantlet of fire leaving the burning city. And then, his jeep took a wrong turning . . .

Our jeeps tried to barrel through the snipers' fire, but it blocked us time after time. At one spot, a truck lay partially on its side in a ditch with the driver slumped in his seat. We stopped and I ran over. The driver was dead, but under the truck were a couple of men talking to each other about surrendering. One said, "We might as well surrender. There isn't any use in this."

There were some walking wounded here too, and I filled my jeep with them, then started talking to the men under the truck. A Communist showed himself in silhouette on top of a hill, so I grabbed an M–1 and fired. I used to be good with a Springfield, but I hate to admit that I'm no great shakes with an M–1. I don't know whether I hit this man, but he dropped and the sniper fire let up a little. I signaled to Clarke in my jeep and to the escort jeep—now filled with casuals or wounded men—to go on; and the two men who had been cowering under the truck came out to join me.

I had hoped that there would be no more vehicles on this wrong road, but an artillery half-track rumbled up. I think that was the most heavily loaded vehicle I ever saw. It was so crammed with men that we couldn't get in—we just got on, hanging by precarious toe- and hand-holds.

We rumbled ahead and presently caught up with my jeeps. They had been blocked and abandoned at a spot where the road made a slight S-bend as it approached a river and bridge. Here the Communists had set up a roadblock. Riflemen were along the S itself and at the left of the road, and apparently a machine gun was emplaced behind one of our wrecked vehicles at the bridge. Heavy fire swept the raised road, from in front of us and on the left side.

We tumbled off the road embankment into a ditch at the right for protection. Here I realized that I no longer had any weapon. I had left the M–1 on the half-track when I jumped for the ditch; my pistol had been lost somewhere, and the holster dangled empty at my hip.

Clarke was in the ditch with several other men. He h[ad] been an air officer, but now he showed infantry ability. Whe[n] I asked him to make an informal muster, he counted seventee[n] Americans and a terrified Korean civilian who spoke Englis[h] and later told me he had once worked for the U.S. Stat[e] Department in Seoul.

We started crawling away from the road the Communist[s] fire covered, around a small house, and through a bean or sweet-potato field. On the way the little Korean, something of a dandy from his appearance, fell up to his armpits in a honey [fertilizer] pit and was absolutely speechless thereafter. We reached the bank of the river, well away from the bridge, and lay there in a semicircle, waiting. I remember delivering a small lecture to the men about keeping off the ridge lines, about using their halizone tablets to purify the river water with which they were filling their canteens (neither Clarke nor I had one), and about patience. I said that we'd have to wait until full dark to go on, and that patience was very important. A couple of years later, I wondered a time or two just how patient a man was required to be.

The group had only a few arms of assorted kinds. Clarke, who had been hit in the shoulder, insisted that I take his pistol. "I can't use it anyhow," he said.

Our bank of the river was low, but a mountain rose directly from the other side. Our plan was to cross here where the Communist fire did not bar the river to us, then swing over the mountain and down to the highway again beyond the roadblock. In full dark we got across, wading, and started climbing the steep, unstable slope. It was rough going. I was leading, and presently Clarke worked his way up to me and said, "We have a badly wounded man behind us."

Clarke and I went back to help the wounded man, who was hit in both legs, and Captain Rowlands, the liaison officer who had been with us on the tank hunt earlier in the day, took the lead.

I had carefully planned the withdrawal from Taejon to include the blowing of bridges and tunnels at exactly the right time. Rowlands—and only Rowlands—was to have given the word to demolition squads, but he didn't reach any communications for three or four days, so as far as I know the demolition charges never were fired. That's the sort of thing that

hour, I set the goal of two hours as the maximum time that we could wait. The general didn't take a canteen or a helmet, so I assumed he was going to try to find some stragglers rather than to get water. At 3:15 A.M. I woke the men and we headed to the top of the hill, arriving just before dawn. . . . Just as it was beginning to get light, I had the men spread out and posted two as guards for one-hour shifts. I figured we'd at least be able to see what killed us, as we had no weapons. I no sooner posted the guards when I checked and found them asleep. I awoke them and asked them if they wanted to be killed. I don't remember their exact answers, but they were to the effect that they didn't care whether they were killed or not. So I stood guard until they woke up. At daylight I searched the area with my field glasses, saw that our vehicles (the ones abandoned on the road the night before) were gone, and three Koreans were sitting on top of a hill to the northeast of us. We spent the day where we were, on top of the hill. It was scorching hot. We had the shade of only a few bushes about a foot high. During the day the men almost turned against me because I wouldn't let them start off until it got dark. As it did begin to get dark we started south along the ridge until we reached a cliff at the southern end. At this point we walked around the top of a ledge, about six feet wide, and then slid down a slope. . . ."

The remainder of the statement details his party's further experiences in getting back to the U.S. lines, which they reached two days later, on July 23.

WHEN I AWOKE I had no idea how long I had been knocked out, and at first didn't realize that I had a gash on my head. But when I tried to rise on my hands and knees I found I had a broken shoulder. My abdomen where I'd had an operation a year before hurt fearfully. I was dazed and groggy. I looked at my watch, which read 12:30 A.M.—or that's what I thought it said, although now I believe it must have been later. I was down in a dry creek bed with very steep sides; and all I could think of was, "My God, what's happened to those people up there? I don't know where I am."

I don't think I had walked more than twenty yards or so from the rest of the party, but I couldn't tell how far my involuntary run had taken me, or how far I'd rolled in my fall.

I've tried dozens of times to reconstruct that run and fall in my mind, but I simply don't know how it happened. My present guess is that I was a hundred yards down the hill—not a cliff, but a very steep, sandy slope.

I heard water again, and I needed it badly. I crawled along the dry stream bottom and finally found a trickle oozing out of the rocks. I scooped out a hollow with my hands, and when it filled with water I stuck my face down in the dirty puddle and drank, not worrying at all about halizone tablets. I remember that I then started back up the barren hillside, perhaps on my hands and knees or just scrabbling, but I don't know what happened next.

I must have passed out again, because when I regained consciousness I was lying on my side—and an eight- or ten-man North Korean patrol was moving no more than ten yards from me. This was false dawn, just a faint glow over the eastern hills; but even in the improved light they failed to see me. I can't imagine why they missed me, but they kept right on going, scrambling up that steep incline like so many mountain goats, in the same direction that I had been headed.

I thought, "Oh-oh, this is the end for Clarke and the others. They're gone now." That was the lowest moment I've ever had in my life. I could see all those people on the hill being killed; and the realization that Clarke didn't even have a pistol—I had his—made me feel even worse. But there was absolutely nothing I could do about it.

I was also tortured by the thought, not new, that I should have done something about him earlier. Both Clarke and my other aide, Captain David Bissett, were married men with young children; and ever since we had come to Korea I had been trying to figure out some way to fire both of them without hurting their feelings. They were good aides and good officers, but my experience with aides and drivers for division commanders in wartime is that they are very likely to get killed. I felt I shouldn't have men with young children taking the risks they had to take. I had been able to keep Bissett at headquarters most of the time, although he was thoroughly angry with me and even told me, "General, I don't appreciate this. Why can't I have a company?"

But I had not done anything else about relieving either of them, and now I thought, "Well, Clarke's gone; and if I don't get back to headquarters myself, Bissett will ask for a line company for sure, and probably get killed too." They were both very fine men, and I'd never been so proud of Clarke as in the last few hours when he'd been organizing that column and keeping people together.

When the North Koreans were out of sight I crawled back to the trickle of water and drank again. I was dead tired, but I thought, "Oh-oh, I can't stay here. Other people may know about this waterhole." So I crawled up into some bushes fifteen or twenty feet away from it, just as daylight was coming on, and stayed there all day, only about half-conscious. I could hear trucks and people over on the highway we had left, a lot of noise, as if the Communists might be working on their vehicles, and some firing.

As soon as darkness came I started out again, first crawling back up the hillside, then along the top of the ridge, without seeing any sign of the party I'd lost the night before or of the Communist patrol of the morning. My shoulder was useless, so scrambling up the hill was difficult; on the top I was able to stagger along more easily. Then the ridge suddenly ended in a sheer cliff. A trail zigzagged down, but it was extremely steep, almost a hand-hold trail, and I had great difficulty with it. Walking itself seemed to do something to my insides; and it was especially hard for me to get to my feet after I had been sitting or lying down to rest.

Working at it a long time, I finally managed to get down about ten feet on the trail, where it flattened out in an escarpment, a sort of shelf on the side of the mountain. The trail went along it for a short distance, then dived another ten feet down to a second shelf. These ten-foot slopes were murder to get down. I barely managed to reach the foot of the second when rain started to pour down, as I think it can rain nowhere except in Korea. It came in torrents, and I was almost overcome by the desire for something to drink. There had been no water on top of the ridge. I found a big flat rock, perhaps six feet across, sticking up a foot about the ground level. I wanted to keep going but couldn't make it just then, so I lay down beside the rock and stretched my handkerchief out on top of it in the pouring rain. When it got soaked with water, I squeezed it out into my mouth, a few drops at a time. I think I spent most of the night doing that, instead of moving on toward our lines.

357

I was still lying there in the morning when I heard a noise, something scrambling down the same path I had used. I got around behind the rock and pulled my pistol, just in case it might be a North Korean.

But the man who lurched into view was a young American. He had not seen me yet—he was too busy making his way down that brutal path—when I called to him. "Who are you?" I said. "What outfit are you from?"

He jumped when he heard me but sighed with relief when he got a look and saw that I too was an American. He said, "I'm Lieutenant Tabor—Stanley Tabor—from the Nineteenth Infantry. Who are you?"

I tried to get up from behind my rock but had trouble. Then I said, "Well, I'm the S.O.B. who's the cause of all this trouble."

Tabor said he had been with Easy Company of the 2nd Battalion, which I had thrown into the river perimeter to bolster up the 34th's strength. In the retreat he'd been cut off and had started walking south by himself.

We started walking again that morning, Tabor carrying his carbine and I with Clarke's pistol banging against my leg. I've enjoyed walking all my life and usually can outwalk many young people. But not on this day. I had to keep stopping to rest because of the pain under my ribs and in my abdomen. I just wanted to sit down. After each rest Tabor would pull me to my feet, and we'd make a few more yards.

I said, "You go on ahead. One person can get through a lot quicker. I'm stove up, and there's no use pooping around here."

But he always would say, "No, two have a better chance," and would refuse to leave me.

About one o'clock that afternoon we found the highway again. But it was bordered by open fields, and every time we'd try to cross we would see vehicles or soldiers of the Inmun Gun [North Korean term for "People's Army"]. So we kept heading south through the brush, toward Kumsan, waiting for an opportunity to turn toward the east, in the direction of Yongdong, where I had left division headquarters.

That afternoon we stumbled into a family of refugees from Taejon, a mother and two teen-aged sons who had strung a rude tent—just a piece of canvas, really—beside a stream. None of them could speak English, but they gave us some of their rice and made us understand that we should stay out of sight under the canvas until dark. We got the idea that there were many North Koreans in the area, but none of them bothered us.

Both of us got some sleep. When we awakened we asked the family if they would guide us toward Yongdong that evening. They made us understand that this town—more than twenty miles east of Taejon—had also been captured by the Communists. The military situation, then, was in even worse shape than I had feared. We had to assume this news was true; and if it was, Tabor and I were in a bad spot. I knew it would be terribly hard to get all the way east to Kumchon, which would be the next logical place for division headquarters to move if Yongdong was lost. We would have to pass through a defile; and the hill country around Yongdong always had been full of Communists. Even in the occupation days hunters passed up this fine deer country because of the many guerrillas.

So I said, "We'll have to head south toward Kumsan, then try to get to Chinan, and east toward Taegu." In other words, I thought we'd make a big swing south, then cut to the east well below the main invasion route. This was to be my general plan for a long time.

That evening we started south again. There were no stars or other guideposts for holding our direction, and we didn't make much time. This was on the evening of July 22, and I guess my various injuries affected my mind, because the next days are more or less a blank. I know we had no food and that we did keep going, but the rest is just a haze of weariness, trying to get to my feet and failing without help, and everlastingly stumbling along one trail after another. Tabor must have kept us both going by will power, because I don't remember having any.

This may have gone on for one day or three. At last we reached a small town. I think we had turned around somehow and were heading west rather than south. This village may have been near Chinsan. At any rate we stumbled into it, and within a few minutes the whole population was around us. We asked for food, and someone brought us water with some kind of uncooked grain ground up in it. I've never seen or heard of it elsewhere. They also gave each of us two raw eggs. Two men in the crowd spoke some English, one of them well and one just a few words. The people seemed friendly, so we asked about where the Inmun Gun was, and whether they would guide us to Taegu. I offered them a million "won" (approximately $1100—the exchange then was about 860 to 1) if they would take us through. Even when Koreans speak English well, they often confuse figures, so I drew the figure in the dirt.

We should have noticed that the man who spoke better English had disappeared, but we didn't. The one who spoke less well said, "Okay, okay, come with me." He indicated that we should come to his house to get some rest, and that he would take us to Taegu in the morning. He led us to a house at the far edge of the village, where we took off our boots and entered an unfurnished room. The Korean sat on the floor with us and in his very broken English asked whom the village people should support. He diagrammed it: the Americans pushing one way, the North Koreans the other. It was all very confusing, he indicated, and I'm afraid we didn't help his confusion much. Instead we went to sleep on the floor.

Several hours later—it must have been early in the morning—we heard a rifle shot just outside the house. At the sound that little Korean never hesitated. He went out a door like a rabbit out of a box. He was gone, without any preliminaries.

Outside a voice called, "Come out, Americans! Come out! We will not kill you. We are members of the People's Army. Come out, Americans!" The English was the best that I'd heard a Korean speak.

Tabor said, "This is it," and reached for his carbine.

We didn't "come out." I said to Tabor, "Come on, get your boots on, in a hurry," and we both did. We left by another door—away from both the rifle shot and the door the Korean had used, and jumped into some high weeds right beside the house.

"I'll lead," I said as we started crawling up a little hill in the dark. "With the carbine, you can cover me better than I can cover you with a pistol. I'll be the point." I remember I also said, "I'm not going to surrender, Tabor. There won't be any surrender for me."

"That's the way I feel too," he said.

There were more shots. They heard us in the weeds and fired in that direction. We reversed our course and went right back through the village, which was in pandemonium, everybody in the street and everybody yelling. We went right through town, past those Korean civilians, but none of them did anything. Crossing back-lots and skirting around houses, we finally came out in a rice paddy at the other edge of town. These paddies are divided into small cells, perhaps thirty feet across, with high dikes between. The water was about four inches deep and the rice stuck up another four or five inches.

We dived into the rice and the water, crawling on our bellies, using our elbows to inch forward in the old infantry fashion. Two soldiers were across the paddy on a dike; they did not see us at first. I led out in the crawling, crossing one cell, then scooting over a dike and into the next, while the soldiers—wearing Inmun Gun uniforms, I think—continued to search from their vantage point on a parallel dike.

We crossed three of these cells, with the intervening dikes. Tabor was still with me. Then I went over another dike and crawled some more, but when I looked back, Tabor was not behind me—and I was not to see another American for three long years.

DURING THE THIRTY-FIVE DAYS I spent in the hills of South Korea several subjects cluttered my mind: food, inability to tell time of day or day of month, worry over my friends and aides, and the frantic necessity for getting back to United Nations lines with new information I had gathered about the enemy. These varied in importance from day to day, but all of them were there, all the time. So was an hour-to-hour, day-to-day concern about a pistol and just twelve rounds of .45 ammunition. Those twelve rounds were the most important in the world, because they were all I had.

While I lay in that rice paddy waiting for Tabor to catch up with me, I thought the time had come when I'd have to use that ammunition. I couldn't imagine what had happened to the lieutenant. We'd been doing very well, inching forward on our elbows and bellies, and there had been no sounds of firing or pursuit. Finally I crawled onto the edge of the paddy, where only a dike separated the rice land from a stream and a path beside it. Still he hadn't caught up.

I called, "Tabor! Tabor!" The only answer was from one of the Communist soldiers on a nearby dike. He fired at the sound of my voice. I clung to the ground and took out the pistol, getting ready to use it. I knew that I'd see the soldier's silhouette on the dike in the dim predawn light before he could see me. But he must also have realized this, because he never came closer. I waited quite a long time, then called, "Tabor! Tabor!" once more. Again, shots were my answer. After half an hour with nothing whatever happening, I crawled back to look over into the last paddy cell we had crossed together; but Tabor wasn't there either.

It was almost full daylight now, and my advantage over the Communists hunting me was gone. I felt like a sheep-stealing dog, but I had to go on. I crawled along the path beside the stream and finally found some foxholes, evidently dug by Communists for a roadside ambush. I was still within hearing distance of the village, but I figured that the last place pursuers would look for me would be in one of their own foxholes. I crawled down into one, past drying watermelon rinds the former owners had thrown out from some feast they had held while waiting for somebody to ambush.

I have never figured out what could have happened to Tabor that morning. It's difficult to keep going in a straight line when you're crawling with heads down, as we were, and the paddy cells were oddly shaped, never square. He may simply have become confused and changed direction, losing sight of me, then was unable to find me where I stopped beside the path. It's also possible that he dropped into one of the drainage or fertilizer holes which are in nearly every rice-paddy cell. For a day or so previous to this, we had been arguing a little about these. Tabor thought we should come down to the paddies, using the holes to hide in when necessary; but I had vetoed the idea, insisting that the only way to get anywhere in Korea is to keep to the high ground. It could be that he merely decided, once we were separated, to use his own judgment. However, I am convinced that he lost direction while crawling.

I learned in 1953 that Tabor had been brought into a

prisoner-of-war stockade at Taejon on August 4, 1950. Our flight from the village was in the early hours of July 25 or July 26, so I don't believe he was captured that day. The village people certainly would not have waited so long to turn him over to the nearest Communist headquarters for whatever reward was then being offered for lieutenants. I think he may have remained free several days after we lost each other, but no positive check is possible. He was in such bad shape when taken prisoner that he finally died, from malnutrition and pneumonia. Returning prisoners in 1953 told the story of his death to his wife, whom he had married three months before going to Korea, and also relayed his report of having been with me for two weeks in the hills. Actually our time together was two or three days, not weeks; but the story had passed through many hands before it came back to me.

I'm still heartsick about him. Perhaps I should have gone back even farther that morning in the paddies, but I don't think I could have found him. My recommendation that he be awarded a Silver Star for his disregard of his personal safety in staying with me was made after my return to this country.

No sooner had I dropped into that foxhole by the roadside than I saw a farmer carry in a little girl, about three years old, on his back. Thank God he was not coming from the direction of the village; presumably he did not know about the hue and cry for me. He definitely saw me, so there was no point in trying to hide. I tried for the first time what was to become a regular practice—when your hiding place in Korea is discovered, ask for food.

I got out of the hole and made signs. The word *pop*, made with a sharper sound than in English, means "rice" in Korean. I said, "Pop," and placed a hand on my stomach.

It worked. He made signs that I was to get back down in the hole and stay there, then went on. In about an hour he came back with a big bowl of rice, more than I could eat. After I had my fill I tore off the North Korean part of a map I had in my pocket (not being at all interested in North Korea just then) and wrapped what was left of the rice in it.

Then I crouched in the foxhole and took out the pistol again. When I tried to fire it, empty, nothing happened, which gave me special cold chills as I remembered my plan to use it against the soldier on the dike a couple of hours earlier. I spent the day stripping it all the way down, cleaning it as best I could of the mud and water it had picked up.

I had the twelve rounds of ammunition and the two clips. Then and later, I was torn by indecision: I'd burnish those shells every day, but I never could make up my mind permanently which was the better way to keep them. Should I have one shell always in the pistol chamber, and the other clip full—that is, carrying eight rounds—not worrying about the three remaining shells? Or should I put six shells in each clip and depend on having time to change clips in the midst of a fight? Neither system suited me, really, because neither could insure that I'd be able to use eleven for knocking out Communists and one for knocking out Dean. I figured this last was essential. Even if I could have stomached the idea personally, I knew that I couldn't afford to surrender, because of my rank. The Communists would be sure to capitalize on the surrender of a general, just as we had in Europe. They might even put out the information that I had gone over to their side, and there wouldn't be anything that I could do about it. I remembered that in Europe we had captured a German SS general who got lost in a retreat; and immediately our propaganda people had made capital out of him, telling the Germans in leaflets and broadcasts that he was just smart, he'd realized it was "a quarter to twelve" and had surrendered deliberately. That was not going to happen to Dean—not if bullet number twelve could prevent it.

I stayed in the foxhole all that day. Toward evening the farmer came back with more rice. When I showed him the rice I'd saved he grimaced and threw it away. When you want to keep cooked rice, you wrap it in a cloth so that it can "breathe." Wrapped in a tight paper, it sours within hours. I was to learn a lot about rice, and that was the first lesson.

After dark I left the foxhole and started walking again, still holding to my project of going south to get out of the way of the main troop movements, then east toward Taegu. I kicked myself for being without a compass. Traveling only at night, I could not use the sun effectively to check my direction; and the old Boy Scout system of getting a bearing from a watch was no good to me. My watch had stopped days before. Most nights the stars were obscured, and I had to go by guess-reckoning, which was often wrong. I think I made almost a complete circle during the next three nights, accomplishing nothing.

The only thing was, I did feel better. I could get up by myself now; and dysentery, which had bothered me during the first twenty days in Korea, was gone. In fact, my elimination came to a complete stop for thirty-two days. I thought I was a medical curiosity, but when I told my story years later in a Tokyo hospital nobody was impressed. Army doctors said anything under a hundred days was nothing to brag about. Nevertheless I'm still amazed.

On the night of what I think was August 1, I started walking early. I was up in the mountains by this time. I was making distance every night, and I thought, "All's well. I'll get through."

I was on a ridge, approaching what I think must have been Kumsan, although I wasn't coming from the proper direction. I seemed to be traveling east, from the direction of Chinsan, rather than from the south. That was what made me certain I must have been going in a circle. In the early evening I passed some women working in the fields. As I went by I noticed that a little boy of about nine left them and was following me. I went over a rise and slipped into some bushes, sure that I had eluded him. After some time I came out again and reached a hill overlooking the town. From my vantage point I picked out a house detached from the others and decided that when full dark came I would go there and ask for food. I had not eaten since the farmer gave me rice on July 25 or 26.

For some reason not clear now, I was quite certain the people in this particular house would feed me. But just as I got to my feet to go down and try my panhandling, a youth carrying a rifle came out and started running up the hill—running like mad. Pretty soon another came out and also ran up the hill. I thought it fortunate that I had waited as long as I had to case the town. Then at least three more youths ran out of other houses farther down the street. I couldn't tell whether they were armed, but none was in uniform. They all were heading more or less away from me. I hunched down in the bushes and was just about to congratulate myself on my hiding place when I heard a rustling behind me—and here was this nine-year-old, pointing down at me and trying to signal

365

to the men. He wasn't more than a couple of yards from me.

I lunged at him, and I'm afraid I wasn't very pleasant. I really cussed him out. He turned and ran; and I crawled out of there fast and went the other way. There was shooting all around me, and bullets clipped the bushes above my head. Somebody yelled as if he'd been hit, but Dean was on his way.

When I'd come to Korea I had hoped I soon would be a grandfather, but I didn't feel grandfatherly then. If I could, I'd have wrung that motheaten little buzzard's neck.

So I STILL HAD nothing to eat. I walked on through the night.

On the trail the next day I met a Korean man. Again there was no chance for concealment, so I walked up boldly and asked him for food. This time my system didn't work. He would have nothing to do with me, turning abruptly and walking away as if I didn't exist. I was worried for a while after that, but there were no sounds of pursuit. I decided he probably had told no one of meeting me. I think now this was a typical Korean act: to do nothing, to take no responsibility. If he had either fed me or reported me he would have been personally involved—and that's usually the last thing any Korean wants. I've been told that this fear of personal responsibility accounts for the fact that most Koreans will walk around a person dying in the street without making any attempt to give aid. So long as they act as if the dying person didn't exist, or the accident had not happened, they personally aren't responsible for it.

By that night hunger was beginning to be a vital problem. When I spotted some smoke rising I figured there must be a village near and I worked down toward it cautiously, remembering the small boy of the day before. It was a good thing I did. Just after I had scooted across a highway I saw at least ten big North Korean tanks rumbling through that village, heading south. This was obviously a main highway, and that village was no place for me.

I got better at sleeping by daylight and traveling by night, but I still wasn't making much progress. Those mountain trails wind around so in the ridges that you walk miles to make what is a short distance in a straight line. I was walking more easily now; although my abdomen still hurt and I couldn't raise my left arm. I wasn't suffering—except from hunger.

By this time I had changed my first objective to Chonju, even further south and slightly west of Kumsan. My reasoning was that some South Korean officials just might be left in that town, with some sort of transport. Perhaps I could get a ride to Taegu, or even along the extreme southern route all the way to Pusan.

The ridge trails were such slow going that I began to get down on the roads more often. When I'd approach a village in the early evening or late in the morning I'd leave the road and circle around the village through the hills, although this had to be done without trails in most instances. It was frustrating and took endless time.

About three nights after my experience with the small boy I started walking in the early evening and saw a village ahead. It was still light and I should have started another circle, but I was a little overconfident and stayed on the road.

Then I met another little boy. This one was five or six years old. As soon as he saw me he turned tail and ran back to the village screaming as if his end had come.

Well, I knew what that would mean. Instead of turning off the road, I hurried after him, almost running myself. Close by the first houses I jumped off the road into a ditch and a bunch of weeds.

Sure enough, here came all the males in town. I noticed only one rifle and one burp gun, but a number of the other men had bamboo spears. They all followed the little boy back along the road to the point where he had seen me—I could see the little devil pointing out the exact spot—then spread out and began the hunt.

Fortunately for me, this town was huddled between a hill on one side and some "kaffir" fields (maize) on the other. Beyond the kaffir was a stream. I crawled through the fields to the stream, walked along its bed in the same direction I had been going previously until I was well past the town, then came back up on the road. The last I saw of that place, the men were still beating through the weeds with their guns and spears, and all the women were standing out on the main street waiting for somebody to bring me in.

I still didn't like little boys, Korean variety.

Thereafter, whenever I came on a village in the middle

367

of the night, I just walked right through it, paying no attention to the dozens of dogs barking at me. Even when it was pitch-black I had no trouble knowing the villages were there. You always can smell a Korean town before you see it. You always can recognize the police stations too, because they're all built alike: a big stone wall, perhaps eight feet high, around a compound, double wooden gates at the front, and a twenty-foot round stone tower, like a silo, somewhere inside. Usually, I just ignored them. But one dark night when I was hiking along a rather good road, by Korean standards, someone challenged me from the shadows just as I passed the gates of the town jailhouse. He yelled one word, which might have meant "Halt!" from a spot no more than eight feet away.

I had no previous warning that he was there, and he startled me. He did more than that. He scared me half to death, and made me mad too—at myself for being careless and at him for being alive. I was so flustered that I did a foolish thing. I whirled and yanked out my pistol and walked right into him. He was just a youngster, I think, armed with a rifle that had a long thin Russian-type bayonet on it. I shoved my pistol right in his guts, hard, and he backed up. I backed him right into the gate. He was so surprised that he didn't do anything.

Just as he got inside the gate I turned and walked very fast in the same direction I had been going. It was only a few yards to the corner of this jailhouse compound. Here I turned to the left, ran along the wall all the way to the rear of the compound, turned left again along the back wall of the compound, made one more left turn, and came back to the road—on the side of the compound from which I had come originally. I waited there to see what would happen.

Inside the compound there was a lot of yelling as soon as the guard recovered enough to give the alarm, and a whole squad, some in uniform, some in civvies, poured out into the road and headed the way the guard had seen me go. As soon as I saw the direction they were taking, I walked back up the road on which I had entered the town. I'd noticed a Y-fork off the main highway a short distance before I hit the town. I went back to it and took the other arm of the Y—in the same general direction I wanted but not on the highway. I never did get back to that highway again.

The only explanation I have for the guard's failure to act

is that he was just rushed off his feet. If he'd ever lifted that damned rifle to his shoulder I would have had to kill him right there. But he didn't. When I thought about it later, I could see that what I'd done was a fine way to get killed for sure—but that one time the bluff worked.

I had one other close call, also in the middle of a black night. This time I stumbled into a town before I'd noticed, and again was in front of a police station. There had been a guard post in the road, I guess, and I walked right into a little charcoal fire they'd left burning. I don't know where the people were, and the only thing I could do was to keep on walking. I guess they never saw or heard me, because nothing happened.

None of the village dogs really bothered me. But up in the mountains, miles from anywhere, the big dogs kept by the charcoal burners around their huts sounded so ferocious, so bloodthirsty, that I stayed away from those huts even though I now needed food badly. Those dogs sounded as if they were quite capable of tearing me apart. I also wanted to avoid the charcoal people. Many of them had been Communist sympathizers and outcasts even in the old days, and I was afraid to trust them. I think now this was a mistake; but at the time I didn't feel that I could take the chance.

By this time my equipment was getting in very bad shape. I was wearing an oversized pair of coveralls—which I had got in exchange for my combat suit, too small for me, from a forward air observer at Okchon a few days before Taejon fell. These coveralls were quite cumbersome and bulky and had to be stripped off entirely when I forded a stream. My combat boots also were the worse for wear, and one was chafing the top of my foot badly. I had a watch that didn't work; a fountain pen that did; a pair of reading glasses; the remainder of my map of Korea; forty dollars in U.S. Korean-occupation scrip, which nobody wanted; and a pistol. I had no rain gear. When it rained I got wet. And it did rain, repeatedly and with fervor. When rain and dark combined I seldom knew where I was going for more than a few feet ahead. And when it rained during the day I lost sleep.

My hunger was becoming dangerous, but there was no-where to get food. Up here in the mountain area I seldom found a house standing—the result of the South Korean government's prewar campaign against the guerrillas, which had consisted largely of burning the house of anyone the constabulary or police even suspected of harboring or cooperating with guerrillas. And I was afraid to go down to the villages. During the day I could see that the Communists already had organized the whole area. Labor had been impressed all over the place. Men worked in big gangs, mostly on the roads; and old Japanese or Russian rifles and burp guns had been given to a few youths in each town. These kids were swelled up with the importance of their jobs as home guards and just itching for a chance to fire those weapons. I couldn't take any more risks.

I had found out some things about the Korean countryside too. It didn't pay me to start walking early in the evening or to walk very far into the dawn. In the evenings children and dogs were all around the villages; and in the early morning old men would come out, often with small youngsters trailing along, to look at the fields. They didn't work in those early hours but just walked out to look, as if planning the day's work. And like old men everywhere, they awoke very early. If I walked in the evening or after the first flush of dawn I was in danger of meeting somebody.

I also found that I had to pick my daylight hiding places well away from villages. During the day brush- and weed-gathering parties—old men, children, sometimes women—worked the untilled areas around the towns. Few Koreans can afford wood to burn in their homes, and they use the brambles and grass for cooking fuel and to make smudge fires against the mosquitoes in the evenings. Each village at nightfall looks as if it is on fire, each a sort of little Pittsburgh under its own pall of smoke.

These bramble-gathering parties cover a lot of ground. Village children also play away from the houses, so I had to find cover far out to be at all safe.

When I didn't, the results weren't good. One morning I stopped to take a bath in a stream as I was crossing it, and when I got started walking again—this was somewhere near Yongdam—women already were coming down to the river to wash clothes. I couldn't reach good cover and had to crawl into some bushes much too close to the community laundry spot. The women were not more than fifty yards from me, and I didn't dare to sleep, fearing that children wandering away from their mothers might find me. If they did, I wanted to be awake to know it.

Across the river and back from it about a quarter of a mile I could see a village, evidently the hub of the universe in this area. Soldiers came and went from the police station, and civilians constantly were reporting to the same head-quarters.

The women washing their clothes in the river had come from behind me, not across the stream, so I assumed there must be another village, out of my view but very close and on my side of the river. Three or four paths converged on the river bank where the women did their washing and exchanged continuous gossip.

I got through the day all right; but that evening one woman did not follow the paths the others had taken away from the river. Carrying a big pile of clean clothes on her head, she came up a path I had not seen before, not more than four feet from me. As she passed she looked right at me. If I had a face like hers, I could make a million dollars playing poker. There was no facial expression at all. Not a muscle twitched. She just looked and kept on walking.

I was still trying to decide whether that old girl with the washing on her head could possibly have failed to see me when my question was answered by the arrival of two young men who came from the direction in which she had gone. They walked right to my hiding spot. Again there was no use in trying to hide, so I asked for food, going through the *pop*-plus-stomach-gesture routine once more.

They answered "Okay, okay," and made signs for me to stay down, just as that first farmer carrying the baby girl had done days before.

I thought, "Boy, after a long time I'm in luck again." I could just taste that rice which would be along in a minute. Both youths went back up the path the way they had come.

The next thing I knew, I heard a terrific commotion, and rifle shots started coming over my head.

This place was an old orchard, all grown over with the weeds that sheltered me. When I raised up enough to look, I could see that in addition to the paths fanning out from the river bank, a wide path higher up paralleled the river some distance back. Beyond the path were houses, the village I had not been able to see while down in the weeds. Upstream from me was a ford across the river.

When the shooting started, so did a lot of yelling—and in the end that saved me. My two chums had brought out the home guard force in force. Men were already all around me in a big half-circle, and all the women and children in the world were standing up there on that raised path to watch the fun.

I could hear these men starting to close in toward me and the river, but it was a funny thing. I guess I was tired or something. I went to sleep between close-ins. I'd wake up with a start and think, "Dean, you damned fool, you can't sleep this way! They'll be on top of you in a minute." Then I'd drop off to sleep again.

But finally I did wake up enough to start crawling. I faded back up the stream, beside a fill. These people had known where I was when the show started, but they handed me one telling advantage, because every time a man in the half-circle would take a few steps forward to a new position, he'd yell like mad to let everybody know where he was. That helped. Once a man yelled just as I was about to crawl toward the very spot where he was. I waited, and presently he went on past me.

It was just dumbness on their part, but the fact is I slipped through the circle. They were still yelling and closing in, but I wasn't there any more. I just got out on the road and walked away, not stopping to say good-by.

I think this date was about August 15. I made good time that night, walking about twenty miles. When I didn't have anything else to think about, I'd go back to my worrying. I still was desperate to get back to our lines and the division, but I knew my information—that there were far more Communists on the south flank than anybody thought—would be too late to do any good. I just wanted to get back into the fight.

Then I'd worry about my aides and their families, being sure in my mind that both Clarke and Bissett were dead by this time, their young families fatherless because of me. I worried about those families and my own. By this time Mildred would know not only that I was missing but that chances for my return were dwindling. I hoped that some of her friends would have talked her into leaving Kokura, perhaps going to the States or to Puerto Rico to be with June. Much later I found this was just what our friends did do, although they were not able to convince her to leave Japan until August 15. She was in Puerto Rico when I was captured.

I also found that my hunch about Bissett had been partially correct. As soon as he was sure I would not return he tried to get himself assigned to a line company—he was an enlisted man and always believed that was where a fighting man belonged—but another headquarters grabbed him for G–1 work and never let him go. So he, like Clarke, survived the Korean war.

Sometimes I prayed for these people, as well as for the families of Bob Martin, whom I felt I certainly had sent to his death, Hatfield, and others I knew or thought were dead. These were actual prayers, repeated many times.

But when I dreamed it was mostly about food. I thought, "When I get back to headquarters and a lot of people are running around wanting to know what happened, I'll say, 'Now just a minute and I'll tell you all you want to know about it. But first bring me one of those fruit compotes from a ten-in-one ration. I want one of those cans of apricots or plums, in that thick sugary syrup. Then I'll tell you about it.' " I could just see that can of fruit and smell the juice.

One night I walked in the pouring rain, making wonderful time, and found a spot to sleep in some bushes on a hill across from a mill and a village. But when day dawned I realized that I'd been walking the wrong way all night. I was so disgusted that I took to the hills immediately and walked back practically all day. I think I made up most of the distance I'd lost during that blind night's walking.

The next night I decided to quit fooling around, trying to follow roads or trails. I'd go right over the mountains and ridges to the east. I decided at least to stick to one plan of action. I told myself, "Damn it, you're walking in circles, you're wasting time. You've got to get back to division. You should go straight east until you hit the railroad, then follow it south—and no matter how tough it is."

Well, that sounds good, but when you start crossing some of that country it's awfully rough. The mountains average only a couple of thousand feet in height, but they come right up off sea level, not by plateaus, so you have to climb every inch of every mountain.

That same night while I was lying down to rest on a very steep trail that went almost straight up the side of a ridge, I heard a clatter. Before I even could move a deer jumped right over me. If I had raised my head, his hoofs would have clipped me.

One problem up on the ridges was water. Very few have any water on them; and where there was a stream the Koreans had tapped it with an aqueduct to take the water down to the rice paddies in the flats. Once I wasted a whole day going down to the foot of a ridge to get a drink. At other times I'd head for patches of dark foliage, hoping that they would indicate a stream or pool, but often I found none when I got there. For food, I tried kaffir stalks and grass, both of which made me throw up. It was too early in the Korean summer for many of the crops to have ripened; and I had no weapons with which to catch game—in any case, I saw very little except some pheasants, and never got a standing shot at one of those. I did find one variety of wild berry several times. This was a sort of cane berry, somewhat like the salmon berry of the Pacific Northwest, without much taste. I suppose I ate a hundred of those, all told, while I was in the mountains. Once I also found a field from which potatoes had been dug—and located four, each about the size of a walnut, which the diggers had overlooked. I ate them raw.

As I grew weaker, my stomach regurgitated even water. I kept looking for corn, and could not understand why I couldn't find any. I knew it was grown in this part of Korea. Later I discovered that in South Korea the corn is almost always planted right in the dooryards of the houses, almost never in the fields. The same is true of melons and squash, so I had no chance to get any of these. Several times I saw the rude towers which growers of ginseng root (beloved of the Chinese as a tonic that will cure virtually anything from flat feet to unripe old age, and also the principal component for a 150- or 170-proof liquor which will blow the top off your head) build around their fields for the guards. But the guards are unfriendly to practically everybody during the seven years the ginseng requires to mature.

Although I continued to pass many burned houses in the mountains, it was not until August 19 that I finally found one lone house far up in the mountains and intact. I spotted this good-looking structure in the night; but I knew there seldom was any use asking for food at a Korean house between meals. With no refrigeration or other storage for cooked foods, they simply don't have anything to eat except when the family meal is being cooked.

I flopped down in a path about two hundred yards from this house and slept.

In the morning I was awakened by another man carrying a little girl on his back. These fathers carrying small daughters were my luck charms, I guess. I asked for food—and my luck was in. He led me back to the house and the whole family came out to greet me. The man turned out to be the eldest brother, about thirty-four. The family included another married brother, about thirty-two, their wives and children, and two younger single brothers, twenty-two and eighteen.

They brought food out to me right in the yard—rice and pork fat. I don't know what happens to the lean part of pigs in rural Korea, but the only part ever served by the country people is the fat. I ate this ravenously, although I never had cared for any kind of fat (much of my youth had been spent in arguments with my elders about the amount of it I left on my plate in Carlyle, Illinois).

With signs I then told the brothers that I wished to stay there four days. I'd lost weight and was terribly weak. I said to myself, "If I can just have four days I'll be all right. Just give me four days of rest, and I'll make it." I thought I had put over the idea and that they had agreed.

These people had an unusually nice house, and I was led to a lean-to, built against the back of it. But this lean-to was filled with flies, just infested with flies, thousands of them. Nevertheless I lay down on the mud floor—and fought flies. I stayed only five minutes. Then I had to crawl to the door and throw up everything I'd eaten. This was August 20 and the food was the first since July 25 or 26. I guess the pork fat was just too much for a stomach ignored so long.

At noon the family gave me more rice and some kimchee (fermented cabbage, with garlic). Again I threw it up. All of them were quite concerned about me. That afternoon I noticed some chickens in the yard, pointed to them, and tried to indicate by signs that I wanted some eggs. The family misunderstood (the most fortunate misunderstanding on record)

and instead killed one of the chickens. The result was some of
the best chicken soup I've ever eaten, full of potatoes and rich
with chicken fat. This I kept down. And the next day I kept
down all three meals, each of which consisted of rice, roasted
corn, and potatoes.

From the beginning I could tell that the second brother
wasn't enthusiastic about having me there. In a combination
of a few words of Korean and sign language he kept talking
about the Inmun Gun, and appeared very much surprised
when I indicated I had no desire to see any members of the
Communist Army. It's possible that up until that time he had
thought I was a Russian, but afterward he was increasingly
nervous. On the second day the two brothers brought up an
old man to look me over. He was a smiling old fellow, apparently friendly, but the Inmun Gun kept coming up entirely
too often in their conversation. I thought he was some old
harabachie (grandfather, literally) whom they'd brought from
a neighboring town to give them advice about me. I also
thought the signs were bad. I gave my watch (which wouldn't
work) to the younger brother, and my billfold (minus an
insert with my identification in it) and my fountain pen to
the elder brother, to buy the remainder of that four days of
food and rest.

That evening the bad news came. The elder brother, still
kindly, nevertheless told me I would have to go. Evidently he
was afraid that they'd all be shot if the Communists found me
there, and perhaps he was right. I didn't feel that any of these
people loved the Inmun Gun especially, but they undoubtedly
were afraid of it and wanted—like most Koreans—to keep out
of trouble at any cost. The elder brother had been in Muju
when our aircraft bombed that town, and he demonstrated
to me how terrible it had been: "Oo-umph, umph, umph!"

Previously I had asked directions to several different
towns, trying not to give out too much information about
where I actually was trying to go. So on this night the elder
brother gave me four ears of parched corn and some rice
wrapped in a cloth and led me out on a path about half a mile
from the house. There he left me.

It was a black night, I couldn't see; and perhaps in re-
action I was more tired than I'd been before. I'd taken only
a few steps before I stepped into a hole and fell on my face.

I managed to get about fifty yards farther, then just dropped down in the trail and went to sleep. I wasn't especially low in my mind, just tired.

I could tell when this man left me that he felt I wasn't going to make it. I could tell by his look that he thought, "You poor bastard, you're finished."

But I thought, "Well, you sad character, you just don't 'know.' I'm going to surprise you. I *am* going to make it."

The elder brother had showed me the direction toward the main road and had said *Taegu* often enough so I got the idea that this was the proper route to that town, seventy miles away as the crow flies. But I didn't worry about it the rest of the night.

In the morning a highly important event occurred. Dean's digestion began to work again, all the way. I've always thought of this day as the day of the great passage, although for a while I thought it also might be my last. I was still being happy about the whole thing when the second brother and one of the younger ones, out to gather wood, found me—and they weren't at all happy about the fact that I still was only half a mile from their house. They led me another half a mile along the trail to make absolutely sure I was headed right—and going away. We were far up in the mountains, and they took me to a spot from which we could look out and see in the distance a valley at least ten miles away, with a highway running down it. Very carefully the second brother showed me the routes—to Muju, to Chinan, to Taegu. He wanted me to get away, almost anywhere, but away. You might think this is difficult to convey when neither person speaks a word of the other's language, but he managed.

I went on alone again. Frankly I never did find the road he had pointed out. But long before I came even close to it I did find more food. As I was walking along the trail I heard a commotion ahead. I slipped up for a look and there was a whole gang of youngsters, twelve to sixteen years old, all beating peach trees in the orchard of a burned-out house. They were whaling the trees and of course knocked down and took away all the good peaches. After they left I managed to fill my pockets with the culls—wizened, half-ripe, and the size of walnuts, but food nonetheless. Then rain began again. I spent the night in the shelter of a piece of corrugated iron which

377

had not collapsed when the shack was burned.

After that I began to make time toward the east. I walked all through the daylight hours of August 23, ate my parched corn and felt so good that I walked all night too. I found another orchard and again filled my pockets with peaches, rested a while, then took off again, walking all the afternoon of August 24. That evening I hit a main highway. In the woods above it I rested until it was dark enough to start walking the road. I think I made twenty or twenty-five miles that night, and the only interruptions were when I had to hide out now and then to let groups of highway workers pass me on their way home. Fifty men were in one group, sixty-five in another. I just lay in a ditch and let them go by.

Early in the morning, following the hairpin turns of the highway, I saw a big village ahead. Evidently this was a particularly good farming area, because there were stables, barns and silos, in addition to the shacks common to most villages. I couldn't imagine what the people were raising, but I took no chances and made a big swing around the town.

But again I walked too long. Daylight caught me just opposite another village, on a brand-new, improved road, which I was sure must have been built with ECA money from the United States. I thought, "Well, these people should be as favorable to us as any Koreans, having had all this built for them." So I wasn't too much worried when daylight caught me. I just went off the road and up into some brush under chestnut trees, a spot from which I could see the village, less than half a mile away.

For quite a while previously I had been bothered by the decreasing number of our aircraft in the skies, and had long since abandoned my early dream that a plane would one day fly low enough to see me wave. For days none had been even close, although after my repatriation I learned from Lieutenant General Earle E. Partridge that he personally had spent long hours flying over the very area where I was wandering, searching for me from a light (AT-G) training plane. But he was doing most of that flying during the daylight hours when I was asleep.

While I rested under the chestnut trees my spirits were rising. I figured that I could walk the hundred and twenty miles to Pusan in ten days on the strength my two-day rest had given me. I was confident I'd be able to last through it. And there was one new wonderfully reassuring factor. Away over to the east I could hear the rumble of artillery—definitely guns, not bombing. I had not heard this since we'd left Taejon, so it was like hearing from an old friend.

"I'm on my way back," I thought. "I'm going to make it."

I slept fairly well during the morning. In the afternoon an old man and some boys came through the chestnut grove, carrying little pint-sized sickles with which to cut brush. They saw me. Once again I worked my system, asking for food. I thought, "Well, damn it, things are breaking my way now. I've been well fed and I'm on my way back. Everything favors me, so I'll just continue to ride my luck."

The old man smiled as if we were long-time friends and gestured toward the village. I rose and boldly marched down that new highway to the first house. The village was a one-street affair, with the street at right angles to the highway, and I stopped at the house that had the highway right beside it.

The man of the house was in the back yard, making straw shoes. His wife and children were watching. I made signs for food and got vigorous and friendly affirmative nods. The woman had no rice ready but put some on to boil. While I waited for it to cook the householder went right ahead making straw slippers. When he completed one he would put it on and dance around in the yard to show me how good it was. The children laughed, the shoemaker laughed, and so did I. This was my lucky day.

Then the woman brought out the rice, with garlic beads as a side dish. It was delicious. I ate all I was given and asked for more to wrap in my handkerchief.

I left there about five o'clock, and had gone only a short distance along the highway when a short little Korean passed me, hiking along as if he were going to a fire. He got about twenty feet ahead, then suddenly stopped, waited for me to catch up, and walked along beside me without saying a word. Just to break the silence I started asking him the route to Taegu and other towns in other directions. When we sat down to rest at a bridge he picked up some rocks and in the dust marked the routes to Taegu, Pusan, and Chonju. Although he spoke no English we managed to understand each other. I was still trying to cover up a little about where I intended to go, but I was beginning to be impressed with him. I made him the same offer I'd made back in the village before I lost Tabor—a million "won" to guide me to Taegu.

He sold me. I thought he understood everything. I asked him where the Inmun Gun was, and he told me they were at Chinan. He intimated that I shouldn't worry, everything would be okay—he would take me right past the Inmun Gun. I don't know how I got all that without any English, but I did, or so I thought. I was sure that's what he was trying to tell me.

We went farther down the road and came to a river where bombing had knocked out a bridge. He pointed that out, laughed as though he thought it exceptionally funny, and said, "Pi-yang-gi" [airplane]. He seemed pleased that the bombing had been so good.

To ford the stream I had to take off my coveralls. I undressed fully. He offered to carry my pistol for me, but I didn't let him.

When we reached the far bank and I had dressed again, we climbed up the bank—and there was trouble waiting for us. A village came right to the river at this point, and waiting for us was practically the full manpower of the village, ten or fifteen men in native clothes and all armed with clubs or spears. They'd seen us crossing and were waiting for us. The man in front, carrying a club, had an especially ferocious expression on his face and motioned to me to go back, that I couldn't even go through their village.

Well, I didn't want to undress again and cross that river a second time. I pulled my pistol from the holster and pointed it at them. As I walked toward them, making threatening motions with the pistol, the whole group backed away slowly.

Meanwhile the little Korean by my side kept jabbering to them, and I had the definite impression that his talk had more to do with their retreat than my pistol. I thought, "He's fast-talking them." Still with their clubs and spears but just standing there and not doing anything about it, the whole gang let us go through the town.

Before we had gone more than a fraction of a mile a second Korean caught up with us. I realize now that this was the same ferocious-looking character who had been at the head of the village mob, but at the time I failed to recognize him without his club. He seemed to be great pals with Han, the man who was guiding me; and Han made me understand that this new chum was "okay, okay." We three walked down the road together until we reached a bend.

Han said suddenly, "Inmun Gun!" and signalled to me to get down.

I thought, "Boy, this is bad. There's something around this corner." I jumped into some bushes beside the road, holding my pistol ready.

Han went on ahead but came back in a few minutes, saying, "Okay, okay."

"This boy is all right," I thought. "This is working out fine."

We went ahead, and around the bend found fifty or a hundred Korean civilians filling holes in the road. This was a project, really a major industry, and they all were working fast, although I saw nobody with guns keeping them at it. We walked right past, just as if we all had a perfect right to use the highway. Some of them looked up, but no one said anything or interfered with us.

When we came to another bend farther on we went through the same routine—the Inmun Gun! warning, Dean jumping into the bushes with his pistol, then an okay and another stroll right past a working party. This time I noticed two men with rifles, and there was an uncomfortable feeling along my spine when we turned our backs to them. But again nothing happened.

I thought, "This Han is a pretty good boy. He *is* going to take me through." But he did a couple of strange things, which should have warned me. One was walking so fast. He walked as if he were going to a fire, and I couldn't keep up with him. Finally I just sat down. I said, "All right, you people go ahead." But they both stopped with me, and Han tried to explain. He indicated that he was hungry and wanted to eat before we reached Chinan. It was getting late in the evening, and we had walked about eight miles, at full speed.

When we started again, however, we went only a short distance, then turned into a house beside the road. I understood that Han wanted to stop there for food. Once inside, they served us sake, but only a plate of garlic beads for food. I took one little glass of the liquor but ate all the garlic beads they brought. The people in the house wanted me to take more sake, and Han too urged it on me. I should have been warned by this. I did think, "What are these people trying to do? Get me drunk?" But my thinking didn't go any further than that.

While we were sitting in the house, and after a lot of conversation, a third man joined us. He walked along with us when we left. At the next bend we did the same routine a third time, with two men going ahead and one staying in the ditch with me. The stumbling block ahead was a small town, not a road crew. The two scouts finally came back and gave us the okay. We walked right through the town.

Just as we got on the other side of town there was some yelling behind us. I got out of sight while Han and his second friend went to talk, this time to our rear. Then Han called something to the fellow who had stayed with me (Little Ferocious, who had led the village gang), and he motioned me to come out. I did, once more putting my pistol back in the holster, then sitting down on the edge of the road. The road was on a cut above a stream, and we hung our feet over the edge. The night was warm and there was bright moonlight.

All of a sudden, around a corner from the village came about fifteen men, and somebody fired a rifle over our heads. I reached for my pistol and got my hand on it, but the little devil sitting beside me grabbed my wrist with both his hands.

I struggled to my feet, with him still hanging on, but I couldn't get the gun out. I fell in the dirt, he with me, and we rolled around in the road as I tried to get him over to the edge of the cut again, to kick him down toward the river. I thought the fall would break his hold, even if we both went over, and I'd have a chance.

But the gang had only about twenty-five feet to rush us, and before I could get this character to the edge they were on top of us. About three rifle barrels were on my head, and as we wrestled around, they kept bumping me. It was very annoying.

They were all yelling, and I suppose they were telling me to surrender, but I kept on fighting with this fellow who had a hold on my arm, and trying to kick somebody where he'd never forget it. But he never let go. I yelled, "Shoot! Shoot, you sons of bitches! Shoot!"

I remember thinking, "This is an ignominious way to have your lights put out, but this is it."

Then they were twisting at my arms. There were several